AROUND
THE MOUNTAINS

King George III and Queen Charlotta.
From mezzotints dated May, 1762,
one month before Charlotte was chartered and given the name of the queen.
Courtesy of an area resident

AROUND THE MOUNTAINS

—

HISTORICAL ESSAYS

ABOUT

CHARLOTTE, FERRISBURGH

AND

MONKTON

BY

WILLIAM WALLACE HIGBEE

—

EDITORIAL COMMITTEE
Kathleen McKinley Harris
Kathleen Manchester
Harriet Patrick
Hazel W. Prindle
Phoebe Siemer
Katherine Teetor
Mary G. Lighthall, Editor-in-Chief

THE CHARLOTTE HISTORICAL SOCIETY
CHARLOTTE, VERMONT

To Harold M. Carr
1911-1987

The Charlotte Historical Society, Charlotte, Vermont

Copyright 1991 The Charlotte Historical Society
All Rights Reserved

Printed by Academy Books, Rutland, Vermont
Second printing, 1991

Library of Congress Catalog Card Number: 91-70434
ISBN 0-914960-88-1

Front endleaf, back endleaf and back page: Maps from the Beers Atlas of Chittenden County, 1869, and of Addison County, 1871.

Contents

Appendixes:

Acknowledgements

Major financial support for this book came from the citizens of Charlotte when they unanimously voted funds for it at town meeting in March of 1990. Without that monetary and moral support from fellow citizens, the project might have been discontinued. Previous to that the IBM Corporation and the Chittenden County Historical Society had given grants for the project. Anonymous donors have helped finance some of the costs of production. Their donations have made this book a more comprehensive and longer-lasting record.

Photographs have been acknowledged in the captions. Those without any source listed were originals from the Lighthall Darkroom in Charlotte. Many of the copies of antique photos were made there, too. To the following go thanks for use of their photographs and other illustrations: Doris Agan, the American Morgan Horse Association Archive, Rod Baldwin, Carolyn Bates, Eleanor (Prindle) Benning, the Bixby Free Memorial Library, Edith Byington, William and Laura Carroll, Inez Willard Chioffi, Dorothy and Allen Cole, Phyllis Deming, Karl Devine, Mary Field, William Mott Hall, the Horsford family, Warren Lawrence, Peg MacDonough, Paul Marcotte, the Martin/Frost family, Marion Melby, the National Geographic, the New York Historical Society, Arthur T. Prime, Hazel Prindle, Rokeby staff members Karen Peterson and Joseph Watson, the Root family, Nancy Preston Sabin, the Sheldon Museum, Eugene Shortsleeves, Special Collections of the UVM Libraries, Margaret Sunderland, Paul R. Teetor, Jennie Thomas, Susie Tremblay, the Vermont Division of Historic Preservation, the Vermont Historical Society and the owner of the Wheeler/Kingsland Collection. Many of these owners loaned their originals thus giving better reproductions in this book.

Maps are from the state Department of Transportation, the Beers Atlases of Chittenden and Addison Counties, Vermont, 1869; the Walling maps of Chittenden and Addison Countries, 1857. Avery Palmer, the Bixby Free Memorial Library, Franklin A. Cole, Gerald and Barbara Fitzgerald, Mary King and Harriet Patrick each owned one or more of these maps and allowed them to be used herein. Frank Thornton made the maps of the original grants and the so-called second division.

The paintings used in illustrating Higbee's homeland came from Mrs. and Mrs. William G. Crawshaw, the Shelburne Museum and anonymous owners. Sketches were done by Charlotte artists Jennie Cole, Shirley Thompson and Charlie Lotz.

Many people know a lot of local history. For this book they verified facts, located sites and furnished artifacts. "Where was the ferry across the Little Otter?" was a typical question. Answers were unfailingly given by those asked, if they knew. If they didn't know they usually gave a reference to one who did. Such people were: Harley and Shirley Allen, Fred Anderson, Don Armell, Ethel Atkins, Rod Baldwin, Carl Braun, Clair Broughton, Buff Clark, Kevin Dann, Karl Devine, Morris Glenn, Mary Granger, Georgina Hurd, Marty Illick, Fred LaBarre, Marjorie Beach Mahoney, Isabel Munett, Lois Noonan and Kathleen Stearns of the Bixby Library, Avery Palmer, Karen Peterson, Marylee Russell Rose, Nadia Smith of Special Collections, UVM Libraries, Sylvia Sprigg, Charlotte Tatro, Roy Thorp, The Vermont Historical Society staff, Titia VanderNoordaa and Truman Webster. The sources of the material used in the "Introduction to William Wallace Higbee" also helped in research on the manuscript.

The staffs of the Ferrisburgh and Charlotte town clerks' offices were always patient and helpful with searches for, and the photocopying of, the records in their care.

Jack and Susan Williamson of Williamson Publications and staff members, Peg, Melisa and Denise never lost their patience even when the copy machine gave out under the burden of work on this book. They also answered many questions about the details of publishing.

Roy Thorp furnished the Daisy Williams scrapbook for photocopying.

Without technical support for computer hardware and software the project would have failed. Carl Dow, Richard Haskell and Anna Lighthall analyzed problems, provided solutions, untangled software glitches, saved lost files and for all that receive only genuine thanks for their professional expertise.

Thanks must be given to those who over the years have donated to the Charlotte Memorial Museum. The amount of material from that source used in this book shows what a fine collection it has. Just as we recognize Higbee's effort, so we acknowledge the work of the Museum's founders and those who kept it going. We have benefited from their efforts and are pleased to give the results of their work a wider audience.

The Byington girls, Anna and Ethel, who tried unsuccessfully to go around a mountain using Higbee's directions. Courtesy of Edith Byington.

An Introduction to

William Wallace Higbee

by

Kathleen McKinley Harris

One day in the 1930s, so the story goes, Wallace McNeil, the grandson of W. W. Higbee, and two Charlotte women set out in a Packard to retrace one of the trips described in the manuscript of *Around the Mountains*. Anna and Ethel, known as the Byington girls, and Wallace followed the manscript carefully but got hopelessly lost in Monkton. They ended up in Starksboro. The book they were following was written by W. W. Higbee.

William Wallace Higbee, author of *Around the Mountains*, was born in Charlotte on January 13, 1842 the second son of Peter Van Vliet Higbee and Miranda Harding. His parents moved from Ferrisburgh in 1837.

His father was born in 1811 in a house located across the road from the Dean House--now the 1810 Farm House and Restaurant--in Ferrisburgh. His paternal grandparents, William and Olive (VanVliet) Higbee settled in Charlotte in 1816. His grandfather, William, like many other early Charlotte settlers, was born in Dutchess County, New York.

His mother, Miranda, was the daughter of Caleb and Judith (Bart-lett) Harding who settled in Chittenden County in 1790. Miranda was born in Shelburne in 1814.

Peter and Miranda, who married in 1838, had three children: Edgar W., William W. and Caroline E.

William Wallace grew up in a farmhouse located near the intersection of Guinea and One Mile Roads in Charlotte. His Harding grandparents lived across the road.

What is known of his childhood is only what can be inferred from passages in *Around the Mountains* where he writes of a wild-Indian youth he shared with most American boys of his day, the outdoor life Rowland E. Robinson writes about in his stories.

"The Boy," a transparent name he uses in these autobiographical passages, spends idyllic hours in Charlotte's fields and woods. A portrait emerges, too, of the Boy in his one-room school, of his respected school marm, and of the community's adults working at home industries, not all of them farming, for during his boyhood every stream seemed to support a mill or factory.

Although Vermont may be an Eden

in the summer, six months of winter always follow. Likewise, Vermont's economy has always gone through periods of boom and bust. The year his Higbee grandparents moved to Charlotte, 1816, or "Eighteen Hundred and Froze to Death," was the year it snowed every month in Vermont and there were no crops.

By 1830 much of Vermont's game was gone; most of its primeval forest was cleared, for an early house burned as many as forty cords of firewood annually in its fireplaces. Also lumber and potash from wood ashes fueled two of Vermont's early economic booms. After the trees were cut, stream flow was reduced causing many mills to be useless and in parts of the state the thin soil of the hill towns was wearing out.

People were caught up with Western Fevers and began leaving the state, often selling their small farms to big sheep farmers. First they were drawn to the Holland Land Company Purchase in western New York. Later they caught Ohio Fever and Michigan Fever as the boundary of the West kept moving onward.

By the year of William Wallace's birth, 1842, Vermont had experienced more than one Sheep Mania. In 1840 there were six sheep per capita in Vermont with Addison County supporting 373 sheep per square mile. At the height of the sheep craze, Vermont had 100 woolen factories. A Merino sheep farm of over a thousand acres was as near as Rokeby, the Robinsons' holding in Ferrisburgh.

In 1842 there was a decline in wool prices. It coincided with the Vermont farmers' achievement of a fifty percent increase in wool per sheep due to their careful breeding practices and husbandry. As the bottom fell out of wool prices, Vermont sheep farmers increasingly emphasized the breeding of fine Merinos. Henry Thorp was a breeder of Atwood Merinos in Charlotte. His advertisement is shown on page 170.

More farmers turned to dairying; first, favoring the cattle breeds of Durham, Devon and later, Aryshire. The West Charlotte Cheese Factory established in 1867, received milk from 300 to 400 cows. The Charlotte Cheese Factory, also founded in 1867, received milk from 175 cows.

Refrigerated railroad cars developed in 1851 made it possible to ship butter in quantity to the Boston market. In the 1890s Charlotte dairymen organized the cooperative Lakeview Creamery company. Their butter prints are illustrated on page 129. In May 1897 the Lake View Creamery received 17,000 pounds of milk daily.

Only the lake towns were gaining in population by the middle of the century, in part because of steamships, but also because of the limestone-rich land and a growing season a month longer than in some Vermont counties. Charlotte was so suited for agriculture that its population remained stable "for over sixty years" and "wealth flowed in upon them," as the Rann *History* reported in 1886.

One asset most of Vermont's youth had, both those who left and those who stayed, was an education. During the decade of 1840 to 1850, 300 new schools were built in Vermont, the number of academies (at least equivalent to present day high schools) doubled, as did college enrollment.

Aside from what William Wallace writes about his "common school" days in the guise of The Boy and the Vermont Legislative Directory of 1888 statment that he "was educated at the common schools and academies," there is no paper trail about his Charlotte education. In the manner of many Vermont families who have scrimped so their children could get an education, William Wallace's mother and father saw to it that their son, William, had an academy education.

Where he went is not known. Perhaps he was sent to the Vergennes Classical School which had an excellent reputation with a respected headmaster, "Uncle Ben" Allen, a Middlebury graduate whom Higbee writes about. Higbee also mentions Hinesburg, Williston and Bakersfield academies as choices for Charlotte students to attend for two or three years. His brother, Edwin W., also was educated, eventually becoming a medical doctor in Northampton, Massachusetts. Edwin married a Smith College graduate, Netta E. Wetherbee, class of 1880. What kind of schooling was provided for their sister, Caroline, is not known.

Another important educational influence on William Wallace, as it was on most nineteenth century Vermont children, was the church.

Which church his parents were affiliated with during his childhood has not been discovered, although his respectful treatment of the Ferrisburgh-Charlotte Quaker community indicates there were Friends in the Higbee family. Higbee implies that his grandfather was a Quaker buried in the cemetery near Rokeby. Records of the Charlotte Congregational Church show his parents Peter V. and Miranda Higbee were admitted to membership by letter in 1863 although another record book lists them as members as early as 1857.

The Sabbath day, as might be expected in a Protestant denomination which was the direct descendent of the Puritan church, was strictly observed with a morning service at ten-thirty, Sabbath school at noon, and a sermon in the afternoon. The building was unheated, and there was no hot lunch.

But it was not the interminable hours spent sitting on hard church pews that left the most lasting impression on other Charlotte children his age. "I have to confess that my memory of Sunday was chiefly centered on the beautiful drive to and from church," wrote Caroline A. Yale, a Charlotte girl six years younger than William. Miss Yale went on to become principal of the Northampton School for the Deaf, the school where Grace Goodhue taught before her marriage to Calvin Coolidge.

William Wallace Higbee maintained his ties with the Congregational Church throughout his life. He might rightly be called a pillar of the church. He was Sunday School Superintendent from 1871 to 1874 and he was "chorister of the choir."

Since one meaning of *chorister* is leader of the choir, he may have been choir master.

In 1861 when William Wallace was nineteen, his father, Peter V., a general farmer who held many town offices, represented Charlotte in Montpelier. That same year his father acted as moderator of Charlotte's first Civil War meeting, a special town meeting held May 14 "to see if the town will raise money to defray the expenses of the families from said town who may enlist in the service of the United States." (Chapter XLII)

Although 102 Charlotte men served in the Union forces and the rich Champlain Valley town bore its financial share of the cost of the war, William Wallace did not do military duty. He therefore missed the central experience of most Vermont men of his generation. During the Civil War Vermont had 34,328 men under arms and proportionately more men killed in battle than any other state in the union. There is no way of knowing how many men who served from other states were originally from Vermont.

Perhaps William Wallace's father paid another to take his place during the war as Cyrus Pringle's uncle, Pitt Hewitt, offered to do for him. Why he did not serve is unknown.

Lee surrendered to Grant at Appomattox Court House April 3, 1865. On April 14, 1865, Lincoln was shot at Ford's Theater. That same year William Wallace Higbee, 23, graduated from Albany Law School in New York State, a school rated as a famous legal institution. The year after Higbee graduated, another young man, a war veteran from Ohio, Major William McKinley, studied for a term at the same school.

Less than half the Vermonters who served in the Civil War returned to the Green Mountain State to live. Many veterans took homesteads in the West. A man was credited with the amount of time he served in the Union Army against the time required to prove up a homestead. Young Vermonters, equipped with a good education or a trade and practical skills, often rose to prominence in the West.

Whatever motivated him, William Wallace joined the flood of Vermonters and emigrated to Michigan where he taught school for about two years.

Although there were Vermonters in the nineteenth century and also in the twentieth who only made the trip to town once a year for a barrel of flour, it is a misconception to think all Vermonters were confined to their mountainous state. Many were widely travelled.

Contact with the broader world began long before the Civil War soldiers saw what fertile, stone-free fields lay beyond the Green Mountains. By 1814 there was stagecoach service--Higbee writes of the stagecoach days--and the trip from Burlington to Troy, New York took 24 hours. After 1825 and the opening of the Erie Canal, a traveller could make the trip West almost entirely by water. He could catch a steamer on Lake Champlain to Whitehall, New York, continue on canal boats to Troy or Buffalo or farther at 1.5 cents per mile. One departure point was as close as Vergennes.

The J. SHERMAN ran a regular schedule from Vergennes to Buffalo in 1840. The company advised, "To Passengers, particularly from Vermont, those moving or visiting their friends...will almost always find someone going into their immediate neighborhood - thereby making the trip more agreeable."

By the time William Wallace was a grown man, there was the railroad. The Rutland and Burlington Railroad through Charlotte, was built in 1848-1849. The coming of the railroad changed life in Vermont forever, causing towns to wither when it bypassed them, making it possible to get Vermont cattle to the Boston meat market without old time cattle drives.

Whatever means he chose to go West, he was in Owatonna, Minnesota, on August 17, 1867, when he married Julia A. Phillips and recorded the event in his Bible. Julia, born in Scott, New York, was the daughter of Horace and Julia A. Phillips. The Higbees' daughter, Carrie Augusta, was born in Owatonna May 30, 1868. However, the young Higbee couple did not settle permanently in the West and he brought his family to Charlotte. By 1871, William Wallace was Sunday School Superintendent and was elected town clerk in 1873.

Their home was on Route 7 in the old homestead, originally the Jeremiah Barton tavern, sited close to the road, directly across from the sprawling house of S. A. Williams' which also may have been a tavern.

An unsubstantiated story has it that both houses were stops on the Underground Railroad and that there once was a tunnel connecting the two houses beneath the highway.

There is no record of why the Higbees left the West. Judging from his spirited promotion of the Champlain Valley in *Around the Mountains*, he may have decided that opportunity was as great in his beloved home town as in the raw West. Perhaps he tired of teaching school. Perhaps he came home because his mother was sick. Miranda Higbee died Sept. 8, 1874 of consumption at age 60. Perhaps, like many a Vermonter, he was homesick for the green hills of home.

Any plans for the future William and Julia had were wiped out when Julia died May 23, 1878. The Town Record states she died of consumption, but the family remembers she died of milk fever (undulant fever). She was 31. It is likely she died of tuberculosis, especially if the young Higbees were living in the same household with his parents. Tuberculosis often claimed a whole family, and cattle were carriers of the disease.

Ten-year-old Carrie was sent West to be raised by an aunt in Minnesota. Carrie always called her dead mother Julia, "my angel mother" and kept Julia's white china with gold trim for Doris, her first daughter. Years later, Doris served a ladies' group from this china and the gold came off when she washed it.

Carrie grew up to be a "pompous Methodist," probably learning these attitudes where she was raised. She wouldn't have rubbing alcohol in the house. Her father did not share her restrictive opinions. In contrast with his Methodist daughter whose religion would have prohibited it, he was always very much an actor. He was often involved with "vaudeville" and performed in area shows as well as singing in the church choir. His namesake and grandson, Wallace McNeil, who put on the first movie show in Charlotte, had the same tendency, a characteristic the McNeils say was the influence of the Higbee family.

W. W. did not wear mourning long. On Oct. 1, 1879, he and Ada S. Booth of Ferrisburgh were married in Ferrisburgh by the Rev. H. B. Putnam of the Charlotte Congregational Church. Ada was the daughter of Ezra and Sophia (Whalley) Booth.

By 1882 he was listed as a farmer with 184 acres and a dairy of 25 cows. Although he was unusual for his time--a law school graduate when most Vermont lawyers qualified by reading law--he did not practice law formally. His name was not in lists of lawyers in Chittenden County. There were no lawyers listed in Charlotte in 1886.

But W. W.'s legal training assisted him in his duties as town clerk. His townsmen elected him to the position 39 times and he served 38 years. According to Hazel Prindle, a recent town clerk, his records indicate he was very competent.

His great granddaughter, Nancy Preston Sabin, asked her mother why, if Grandpa Higbee was so intelligent, was he town clerk? Doris McNeil Preston, Carrie's daughter answered that it was a position of respect and it permitted him to know everybody's business.

"He was always ready to help somebody. He was a busy man. When you went there, he did it all by hand," said Eugene Shortsleeves. "No typewriter. He did it all with his pen and pencil. And you'd go there and say, 'Well, Mr. Higbee, I wish you would look up so and so, see how long they'd been here'. ...He was a man for knowledge and to help somebody. He wasn't a man who all he thought of was money. He was such a nice man. My father thought the world of him."

Della (Bacon) Minor Rule, who also knew Higbee, said the Higbees were "wonderful people."

Men and women with higher education were more in the minority in past generations. Doctors, ministers, teachers, lawyers and librarians were accorded respect in Vermont towns. "Everybody in town if they got into any kind of trouble, 'Well I'm going down to Mr. Higbee,'" said Eugene Shortsleeves. "[I] could tell, even when I was a kid, he had a lot of knowledge. Not very many went to law school in those days."

By 1882 his father, Peter V., had moved permanently to Cassopolis, Michigan. A daughter, Mabel Ada, was born to William Wallace and Ada, May 15, 1882 when Higbee was 40 years old. In the prime of his life, he was probably five feet eight inches tall, bearded and nice looking.

All his life he was an active worker for the Republican party which was the party of choice for Vermonters following the Civil War, with the recent veterans forming a cohesive group within the party. On Saturday, Aug. 2, 1884, according to the *Burlington Free*

Press, "the Republicans of Charlotte met at the town hall and formed a Blaine and Logan campaign club." W. W. Higbee was president of this club. That year the Democratic candidate, Grover Cleveland, won the election.

Higbee's abilities did not go unnoticed. In 1886 Charlotte sent him to Montpelier as their representative, and he served on the committee on education. His appointment to that committee was appropriate for among his other services to the town, he was school director. He also sent his daughter, Carrie, to a two year seminary at a time when it was unusual to send a girl away to school, to waste money on a woman. Although W. W. was thrifty to the point of being miserly--"I can't express the importance of frugality," said Nancy Sabin about her great-grandfather's character--yet education and family values were most important to him.

The county elected him to the legislature again in 1888 as a senator. That same year his father, Peter V. Higbee, died in Cassopolis, Michigan. W. W. recorded the event in the Bible below his entry of Julia's death. He was not elected to the legislature again.

W. W.'s daughter, Carrie, married Lyman Brooks McNeil on Sept. 4, 1895. With this marriage the Higbees were allied with a family prominent in Charlotte's history as the owners of the Charlotte-Essex ferry since the eighteenth century. Carrie's father-in-law was known as "Squire McNeil" according to his grandson, Wallace McNeil.

To illustrate the weighty influence of the McNeils on town attitudes, Wallace McNeil told the story of "beloved" Dr. F. A. Falby, who came to Charlotte in the 1890s. It was difficult to establish his practice because there was already a doctor in town. Falby said he gained acceptance after Squire McNeil summoned him by letter to attend him.

After her marriage Carrie moved to the McNeil home on Greenbush Road. The McNeil house with its outbuildings, including four carriage houses, covered a large area. In 1946 when the barns caught fire, it took three days for them to burn and Burlington sent a fire engine. The present craft shop, *The Needleworks*, is on the site of the eggery.

Carrie Higbee made it a condition for her marriage to Lyman McNeil that the McNeil house be divided in half so Carrie and her mother-in-law could maintain separate households under one roof, an indication of the power this young woman had.

In his later years Higbee became an insurance agent for Vermont Mutual and Union Mutual, selling fire insurance, and for Hickok (now Hickok and Boardman), selling life insurance. He covered his territory with horse and buggy at a pace which gave him ample time and opportunity to learn the byways and visit with their residents. Not only did the insurance business supply Higbee with source material for his series of newspaper articles, but it probably provided him with the financial resources to get out of dairy farming and move from the Jeremiah Barton tavern. He built a new house on a lot of about an acre on Greenbush

Road, almost across the road from the McNeil house where his daughter, Carrie, lived. The year the Higbee house was constructed is unknown, but on Jan 5, 1901 W. W. and his daughter, Mabel, deeded the Route 7 home place and 171 acres more or less to S. A. Williams. The sale price was $6,200.

A member of the Miller family of Ferrisburgh, several of whom were renowned as carpenters, built Higbee's Greenbush house and also the Frank Root house on Ferry Road which is now a childcare center. The same Miller built the Byington/Varney house on Route 7 and the Smith/Burleigh/Carpenter house on Lake Road. A similar house, also thought to be a Miller house, is the Willard house on Route 7 in Ferrisburgh. Higbee writes about the Miller family in Chapter XVI.

Higbee also kept the town clerk's office there in a shed--since torn down-- attached to the house. The present owners of the house found one wall took an unusual amount of blown-in insulation, far more than estimated, and discovered they were filling the site of the town vault.

In addition to his duties as town clerk and insurance agent, W. W. and his wife carried on some real estate transactions. He often, as the respected man he was, acted as an executor of wills.

Probably W. W. Higbee always wanted to write but did not have the time to do so until he left farming. He did write one article--Chapter I--which was published in 1874 in the *Burlington Free Press*, but the majority of his articles was published in the *Vergennes Vermonter* between 1896 and 1904. Most of his articles ran in 1897. Besides the 1874 article, only the articles on the Civil War, McNeil's Cove, Mt. Philo, and the Breezy Point Library were in the *Free Press*.

H. P. Smith in his 1886 *History of Addison County* touted the *Vergennes Vermonter* as being "among the best country papers of New England." Admittedly, it is necessary to allow for Smith's local bias. By the 1890s Vergennes already had a long history of supporting newspapers. Its first weekly, *The Vergennes Gazette,* was published in 1798.

Higbee wrote the series of articles with newspaper publication his only goal as he explained modestly in *A Communication* in the *Vermonter and Citizen,* Dec. 20, 1897, "Several have kindly asked if these papers are likely to appear in any other form than through the column of the *Vermonter.* Probably this is about the limit of their career and the writer thanks the public right heartily for its patience in this much of an affliction." (App. IV)

But it is clear from his comment that both he and his readers thought about making a book from the collected columns. From the beginning he uses the roads around the mountains as a loose unifying device, an idea he perhaps borrowed from Rowland E. Robinson who published a history of early Ferrisburgh in the *Vergennes Vermonter* in 1894 entitled *Along Three Rivers.* Not only would Higbee have read Robinson's history in the paper, but since the Robinson family maintained the Ferrisburgh town clerk's office at Rokeby, Higbee would have had frequent contact with his counterpart in the neighboring town.

He apparently wrote the articles for the newspaper deadline, spurred on by favorable reader response. There is a break in the series lasting from Jan. 14, 1898 to July 7, 1899. Higbee's silent period may be explained by the death of his second wife. The newspaper editor would have continued to print *Around the Mountains* and not left a gap if he was working from a finished manuscript.

Ada S. (Booth) died on Jan. 6, 1898. She was 42. The cause of death was "consumption of the lungs." Their daughter Mabel Ada was then 16.

William Wallace now had lost his mother, his first wife and his second wife to the white plague. He shared his tragic loss of loved ones to consumption with many others. It has been stated that early in Vermont's history tuberculosis was the cause of a quarter to a third of the annual deaths. Effective medication was not available until the late 1940s. Until then, the only treatment was fresh air, good food and rest: the so-called Saranac Lake approach. The only prevention was isolation. Vermont had so many consumptive patients that it ran sanatoria for them in Pittsford and Barre.

Higbee did not retire after Ada's death. He carried on his extensive insurance business and was reelected town clerk year after year. He soon took an interest in a much younger woman, Mary Cook, who came from a successful sheep-raising family whose home was at the intersection of Ferry and Lake Roads and is now owned by Francis and Theresa Knowles. Mary was one of the ladies who started the Breezy Point Library. He eventually devoted a column to the library's history. That column was taken from a public address given when the library opened in the old church and was published in the *Free Press*. It is his last published work yet found. (Chapter XLV)

On March 12, 1902 Higbee's second daughter, Mabel Ada, 20, married Henry Prindle Hill, a 28-year-old farmer bearing the names of two old Charlotte families. A few months later on May 21 Higbee followed his daughter's example and married Mary (May) Callendar Cook, 37. May was president of the Breezy Point Library. It was her first marriage. The bridegroom was 60.

An undated newspaper clipping states that the "nuptial ceremony" took place at the home of Mary's brother with the Rev. Hervey Gulick of the Charlotte Congregational church presiding. Miss Emma Leavenworth played the bridal march from *Lohengrin* on the organ. About one hundred guests attended the wedding of Miss Mary Cook to the Hon. William Wallace Higbee "who has held all the important offices" at his townsmen's disposal. The writer of the article rejoiced that Higbee had selected his bride from among Charlotte's fair daughters. The bride wore white chiffon over white taffeta and carried white roses. "Notable among the tokens of esteem was a silver chafing-dish presented by members of the Breezy Point Library association."

Wedding guests included Higbee's brother and sister-in-law, Dr. E. W. and Mrs. Higbee of Northampton, Massachusetts, Lieut. Gov. Allen, John Wheeler and sisters Carrie and Fannie, Walker Fields and others of Ferrisburgh; Mr. and Mrs. C. P. VanVliet of Shelburne; Attorney A. L. Sherman and mother; Mrs. George H. Root and Mrs. John Yale of Burlington.

The presence of Lieut. Gov. Allen indicated Higbee continued his participation in state politics. The apex of his political career came when he was prominently mentioned as a candidate for lieutenant governor in the Charles J. Bell campaign. Bell was Vermont's governor in 1904-06.

After 1902 Higbee wrote only three more published articles. In 1910 he gave up his insurance business. Carrie Clarke Prindle, one of the first female insurance agents in Vermont, took it over, but he did not retire as town clerk.

His grandchildren, Wallace and Doris McNeil, remembered Grandpa Higbee as being very stern. When Grandpa Higbee laughed, little Doris was afraid because a laugh wasn't a normal sound to come out of him. She remembered him as having a very dry sense of humor. Doris never acknowledged Higbee's third wife, Mary.

From Grandfather Higbee and the McNeils, too, the children learned to take a stoical attitude toward personal problems and that private difficulties were not discussed outside the home.

Higbee had need of stoicism at the end of his life. By town meeting, Feb. 17, 1911, Higbee was suffering from the kidney ailments, then called Bright's disease, that would take his life. In the minutes of that town meeting the citizens recorded their " sincere sympathy to W. W. Higbee in his illness and our thanks for the able manner in which he has performed his official duties for the town of Charlotte for over 38 years as town Representative, County Senator, and as Town Clerk and Treasurer." A copy of the resolutions, presented by Dr. W. H. H. Varney, was sent to Higbee. The Hon. W. W. Higbee was also unanimously re-elected as town clerk.

On March 8, 1911, the official record states that W. W. Higbee appointed his wife, M. C. Higbee, as assistant town clerk. William Wallace Higbee attested to the appointment in the shaky handwriting of a mortally sick man. Dr. F. R. Falby attended W. W. from Dec. 2, 1910, until his death March 13, 1911, just five days after he relinquished his official duties to May. He was 69 years old.

The *Burlington Free Press* reported March 21, 1911, that Netta Higbee, William Wallace's sister-in-law, attended his funeral. He was buried in Grandview Cemetery next to his parents. Two wives are on one side. His third wife's grave is on the other.

May Higbee served as town clerk from 1911 until she died in 1920.

Higbee's will shows he left everything to his widow, May Cook, except for $1000 to each of his daughters and his gold watch and chain to his grandson, Wallace McNeil. He also gave Wallace the bottom half of his roll-top desk. Receiving only half a desk made

Wallace angry. The family saw this gift as an example of his almost miserly thriftiness.

To his daughter Carrie Higbee McNeil he gave his manuscript of *Around the Mountains*, inscribing it to her. Neither the desk nor the manuscript are mentioned as gifts in the will.

His obituary did not allude to his writing, but his efforts as a writer and historian did not go unnoticed. His writings circulated in manuscript form in Ferrisburgh. And on the envelope containing his will dated June 16, 1909, in the Chittenden County Probate Court, some anonymous person has pencilled in without comment: "Charlotte Chronicle."

Like most Vermonters, Higbee knew how difficult it is to make a financial go of it. A farmer with a dairy of 25 cows when the milking was done by hand, Higbee was no stranger to hard, physical work. He, like many practical Vermonters past and present, found it imperative to have several means of making a living. When he wrote of the ways his neighbors earned their livings, it was from a participant's point-of-view.

He was immersed in the cultural life of his community and state as churchman, town clerk and local politician. Filtered through his mind are the major movements and ideas current during his lifetime: Vermont's economic and political history, what was happening in the churches and schools in the Champlain Valley, western migration, Manifest Destiny, the anti-slavery movement, the Civil War, Social Darwinism, a belief in progress.

He was qualified by his experience of the broader world to draw valid comparisons between his Champlain Valley towns and other places. Besides his law student days in Albany and his two-year stay in the mid-West, his references to Mt. Tom indicate he visited his brother and sister-in-law in Massachusetts.

Perhaps he should be seen first, as Harold Carr pointed out, as a local promoter. Vermont from 1850 to 1880 suffered from a declining rural population, the result of out-migration and a shift in population from rural to city areas within Vermont. Influential Vermonters shared his anxiety over the shrinking, shifting population. From 1890 to 1910, 101 rural Vermont towns lost population and a large number were at a standstill. Old Home Week was one of New England's responses to the alarming population loss, an effort to attract its native-born and their dollars back into the home state. Higbee's promotion of the Champlain Valley is a similar reaction.

He read what a well-read American of the nineteenth century would read. He quotes from or makes reference to Washington Irving, James Fennimore Cooper, Nathaniel Hawthorne, Oliver Wendell Holmes, Harriet Beecher Stowe, Shakespeare and Tennyson. He apparently subscribed to a New York newspaper, for he writes about the pervasive influence on Vermonters of the *New York Herald Tribune*.

The sources he mentions for Vermont history include Zadock Thompson, a history of the Champlain Valley by Winslow C. Watson of Port Kent, New York, and Rowland E. Robinson. He had access to a collection of the early journals of Vermont governors and councils placed in the town clerks' offices by legislative act in 1872.

As a trained lawyer he was schooled to do accurate research. Clearly, accuracy was an important goal for him as indicated by his letter to the editor dated December 20, 1897 which was published in the *Vermonter and Citizen*, to correct an error in the list of Monkton representatives in his December 3, 1897 article. (See App. IV, A Communication)

He is refreshingly free of prejudice. He likes women and respects their achievements. He believes wholeheartedly in American democracy, Vermont-style. He is sympathetic to the rights of blacks but he views the American Indian as a noble savage, a romantic figure as in James Fennimore Cooper's novels. Like most of his contemporaries, Higbee believes in the inevitable triumph of the white man over the red man. There is little mention of either Roman Catholics or French Canadians in his writing, but when he does touch on these subjects he is free of the intolerance his more famous neighbor, Rowland E.

Robinson, displays. He also records very little about some geographical areas of the three towns.

A Higbee sentence is typically nineteenth century and shows the influence of his training in rhetoric. He links clauses together elaborately and sometimes seemingly endlessly. He often makes use of the orator's favorite, the periodic sentence. Coupled with long complicated sentences is the fact these articles were printed originally in a newspaper. To save space, the typesetter ran Higbee's articles in great blocks of print with few paragraph breaks.

The reader of this book will find shorter sentences, more paragraphs and less repetition than in the original newspaper articles. But Higbee's rural, nineteenth century Vermont imagery, wry Yankee humor, leisurely pace and occasional passages of Victorian sentimentality have not been edited out.

Higbee lacks Rowland E. Robinson's artist's eye. Like Abby Hemenway, he loves facts and details. But the flaw of including everything is also both writers' chief virtue. *Around the Mountains* is a treasure trove of how life was lived in a special time and place.

Sources

This biographical sketch is based in part upon the author's interviews with Elinor Prindle Benning, Marion Folsom, Barbara Horsford, Della Bacon Rule, Nancy Preston Sabin, Eugene Shortsleeves and a 1977 interview with the late Wallace McNeil by Lee Barlow.

Standard public records were consulted as were the issues of *Walton's Vermont Register* for the years of Higbee's life; the archives of the Charlotte Congregational Church; the 1896 *Burlington Free Press* index for Charlotte; a scrapbook and the vertical files of the Bixby Free Memorial Library; the Albany Law School Alumni Association records; also correspondence with the Beacon, New York Historical Society, Historic Northampton, Northampton, Massachusetts and the Steele County Historical Society, Owatonna, Minnesota.

In addition the following works were used:

Bassett, T. D. "500 Miles of Trouble and Excitement: Vermont Railroads, 1848-1861," from *In a State of Nature: Readings in Vermont History,* ed. by Samuel B. Hand and H. Nicholas Muller, III. Montpelier: Vermont Historical Society, 1982.

Benedict, G. G. *Vermont in the Civil War,* Vol. II. Burlington: Free Press Association, 1888.

Child, Hamilton, *The Gazetteer and Business Directory of Chittenden County, Vt. for 1882-83.* Syracuse: Child, 1882.

Curtis, Jane and Will and Frank Lieberman. *The World of George Perkins Marsh.* Woodstock: Countryman Press, 1982.

Doyle, William, *Vermont Political Tradition And Those Who Helped Make It.* Barre: Northlight Studio Press, 1984.

Hemenway, Abby Maria. *The Vermont Historical Gazetteer,* Vol 1. Burlington: Hemenway, 1868.

Meeks, Harold A. *Time and Change in Vermont.* Chester, Connecticut: Globe Pequot Press, 1986.

Morgan, H. Wayne. *William McKinley and His America.* Syracuse Univ. Press, 1963.

Rann, William S., ed. *History of Chittenden County Vermont.* Syracuse: D. Mason & Co, 1886.

Robinson, Rowland E. *Uncle Lisha's Outing, The Buttles Gals,* and *Along Three Rivers,* Centennial Edition with foreward by Edward D. Collins. Rutland: The Tuttle Co., 1933.

Smith, H. P., ed. *History of Addison County Vermont.* Syracuse: D. Mason & Co. 1886.

Stilwell, Lewis D. *Migration from Vermont.* Vermont Historical Society: Montpelier, 1948.

Swift, Samuel. *History of the Town of Middlebury.* Middlebury: A. H. Copeland, 1859.

Titus, Honey. "Old Home Sunday" in the *Charlotte Congregational Courier,* Sept., 1988.

Wells, George F. "The Status of Rural Vermont" in the *Twenty-Third Vermont Agricultural Report.* St Albans: Cummings Printing Co., 1903.

Wilson, Harold Fisher. *The Hill Country of Northern New England.* New York: Columbia University Press, 1936.

Yale, Caroline A. *Years of Building: Memories of a Pioneer in a Special Field of Education.* New York: Dial Press, 1931.

Marker for the Higbee lot in Grandview Cemetery, Charlotte. Photo taken in 1990.

The Higbee house on North Greenbush Rd. From the time it was built he kept the town clerk's office here, a practice continued later by his widow, May Cook Higbee. Photo taken in 1990.

Julia Phillips, the first wife of W. W. Higbee and mother of Carrie Higbee McNeil.

Carrie Higbee McNeil, only daughter of William Wallace and Julia Phillips Higbee. All family photos courtesy of Nancy Sabin.

William Wallace Higbee.

I

The Town of Charlotte a Century Ago

17 October 1874

History becomes interesting as time passes and one generation reads the doings of a former. This is my only excuse for this sketch of a quiet and rural people and their surroundings.

About a century ago, though to be accurate about the matter twelve years must be added to this, the political history of Charlotte commences on June 24th, 1762. George the Third, "For the due encouragement of settling a new plantation within our said province, by and with the aid of our trusty and well beloved Benning Wentworth, our Governor and commander-in-chief of our said province of New Hampshire" granted an amount of territory containing 23,060 acres, to be divided among seventy-one grantees, share and share alike, "and that the same be and is hereby incorporated into a township by the name of Charlotta." Thus, in the second year of King George's reign, as is stated in the grant, Charlotta wheeled into line, though as a part of his "said province of New Hampshire."

Among other things, the grant contained certain "conditions precedent," as legal men say. The first of these was that every grantee should plant or cultivate five acres for every fifty acres of his granted share, otherwise the share became forfeited.

The second provision provides "That all white and other pine trees within the said township, fit for masting our royal navy be carefully preserved to that use, and none to be cut or felled without our special license for so doing, upon penalty of the forfeiture of the right of such grantee." It is evident that King George had a very limited idea of the resources of his provinces, or he was disposed to cover all the known waters with "royal navies." At all events, some of the "white and other pine trees" would not be called for as decreed.

The third provision set aside seventy acres to be laid out into town lots, one of which was to belong to each grantee. These were laid out on the pasture lot now owned by H. C. Leavenworth and Alonzo H. Barker, and on the piece opposite, owned by John Quinlan. Each grantee was to pay on the 25th of December, annually for ten years from the date of grant, one ear of Indian corn; after 1770 each settler or inhabitant was to pay "one shilling proclamation money" for every one hundred acres owned.

The first town meeting, according

Benjamin Ferris, Jr.'s 1763 survey map of the "Township of Charlotta in New Hampshire." Drawn from the original in the town clerk's office.

B W

111 Pa trips Thos ar	112 Nathaniel Porter Jun	113 George Frost Esq	114 Isaac Cole	115 Benjamin Ferriss Jun	116 Josiah Bull	117 Samuel Coe	118 Robert Southgate
	103 Jedediah Dan of H falls	104 Daniel Chase	105 Benjamin Ferriss	106 Joseph Ferriss	107 Dobson Wheeler	108 Josiah Akin	109 Wing Kelley	110 Anthony Tripp

Top irregular lots:
- 122 Joseph Fenner Jun
- 121 Nehemiah Merritt Jun
- 91 Josiah Bull Jun
- 120 John Brownson
- 119 Zebulon Ferriss
- 111 Thomas
- 118 Robert Southgate

91 Josiah Bull Jun	92 Reed Ferriss	93 Jonathan Akin	94 John Hoag 2d	95 Thomas Darling	96 Elijah West	97 Elihu Wing	98 David Palmer	99 John Wing	100 Elias Palmer
81 Glebe for the Church of Eng	82 John Burling	83 Nehemiah Merritt	84 John Lawrence	85 Daniel Merritt	86 Theodore Atkinson Esq	87 Jonathan Dow of H falls	88 Joshua Delaplaine	89 John Cromwell	90 Mark Hd. Wentworth Esq
71 Steward Southgate	72 Daniel Wing	73 James Franklin	74 Free School	75 Undivided	76 Undivided	77 Lott Tripp	78 George Soule	79 David Akin Jun	80 Isaac Martin
61 Timothy Dakin	62 Elijah Doughty	63 John Nelson Esq	64 Undivided	65 Undivided	66 Undivided	67 William Field	68 John Franklin	69 Samuel Bound	70 Samuel Franklin
51 Settled Minister	52 Enoch Hoag	53 Peter Palmer	54 Town Plot	55 Undivided	56 Undivided	57 Undivided	58 Undivided	59 Undivided	60 Undivided
41 David Ferriss	42 John Hitchcock	43 Thomas Franklin Jun	44 Undivided	45 Undivided	46 Undivided	47 Undivided	48 Undivided	49 Undivided	50 Undivided
31 John Temple	32 Incorporated Society	33 John Hoag Marsh	34 Undivided	35 Undivided	36 Undivided	37 Undivided	38 Undivided	39 Undivided	40 Undivided
21 Undivided	22 Abraham Thomas	23 Robert Caswell	24 Undivided	25 Undivided	26 Undivided	27 Undivided	28 Undivided	29 Undivided	30 Undivided
11 Undivided	12 John Southgate	13 Stephen Noble	14 Undivided	15 Undivided	16 Undivided	17 Undivided	18 Undivided	19 Undivided	20 Undivided
1 Undivided	2 Walter Franklin	3 Undivided	4 Undivided	5 Undivided	6 Undivided	7 Undivided	8 Undivided	9 Undivided	10 Undivided

3

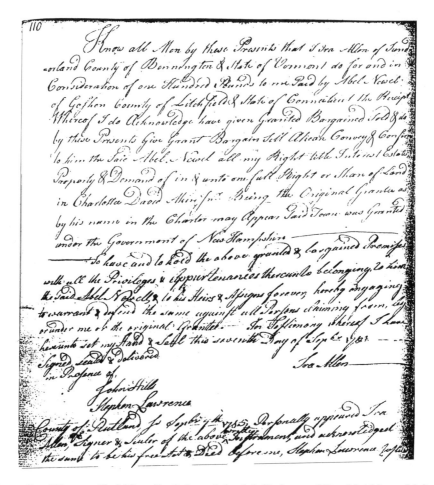

Deed from Ira Allen to Abel Newell of the original full share of David Akin, which was lot #79. For more about the Newells see Chapter X.

to the provision of the grant, was held on the last Thursday of July 1762, "which said meeting shall be notified by Benjamin Ferris, who is hereby appointed moderator of the said first meeting which he is to notify," and "that the annual meeting forever hereafter for the choice of such officers for the said town shall be on the second Tuesday of March, annually."[1] At this meeting in July, 1762, Benjamin Ferris, Jr., was elected "Proprie-

tor's Clerk and Register"; also "Voted that John Wing, George Soule, and Josiah Bull, shall be a committee to agree with the committee of the other townships how to settle the lines between said Charlotta and the townships of Ferrisburgh, Monkton, and Hinesburgh and also to see what part of the costs the proprietors of Charlotta shall pay."

It was also voted "that the clerk shall record the patent for said Char-

4

Ira Allen from a miniature painted between 1793 and 1798 by an unknown artist. The original is owned by the University of Vermont. Courtesy of Special Collections, University of Vermont Libraries.

lotte and have four shillings, York money,[2] for the same," and "that the clerk shall record all deeds brought to him, and have one shilling and four-pence for the same." The above embraced all the business of importance transacted by the town of Charlotte, July 29, 1762.[3]

The names of Ethan and Ira Allen figure more or less prominently among the real estate transfers of that and a latter day. Ethan Allen deeded property to David Ferris, David Breakenridge, and Charles McNeil; Ira Allen to Abel Newell. The general survey was made by David Ferris and Benjamin Ferris, Jr. in 1763.

During the earliest days of the town of Charlotte the Ferris family

were prominent. David Ferris, Zebulon Ferris, Joseph Ferris, Jr., Benjamin Ferris, Read Ferris, and Benjamin Ferris, Jr., were among the original grantees in the first division of two hundred acres to each proprietor. The first division was made of lands lying west of the center of town, but David Ferris had a tract of two hundred acres--lot No. 41--on the south line of Charlotte. Joseph Ferris, Jr. took lot 122, embracing the end of Thompson's Point. Benjamin Ferris, Jr., was at one time proprietors' clerk. His lot was near the lake, No. 115. He was the surveyor who laid out and plotted the first division in 1763, and his sheepskin or parchment survey is fastened with white tape in book "A"

5

or the "Proprietors' Record" of Charlotte. In this survey Benjamin Ferris, Jr., was associated with David Ferris.[4]

There were a large number of transfers made by the Ferris family during the first thirty-five or forty years of the town's history, but the family must have removed later on for these transfers grew less and less, the last being a quit claim deed from Mehitable Peck to Walter M. Ferris of New York City and described as "the old Walter Ferris farm in Charlotte." This farm is understood to be the one now owned by John J. Stapleton.[5] At this time, 1899, no one by the name of Ferris lives in Charlotte.

The foregoing, though possessing no great attractions for many, will be read with some interest by the citizens of Charlotte, giving some of the facts of our early history; and many are not so far removed from the stirring times of a century past, but that a reference to them seems like a echo of a voice heard long ago. These fertile fields have, under their age, emerged from the gloom of the damp woods; and prosperity, for which we should be very thankful, has been in good part the result of the early settlers toil and anxious care.

Such a horse and carriage would be fine for a Higbee trip. Nancy, a family favorite, was photographed on the Charles Root farm around 1900. Courtesy of the Root family.

II

Charlotte to West Ferrisburgh

6 September 1895

The three counties, Addison, Chittenden, and Franklin, comprise the Vermont front of Lake Champlain, and more varied and beautiful scenery would be hard to find. Commencing in Addison County, the frontage varies from a few feet of bright greensward above high water mark to the bold and rocky shores of Basin Harbor and extending to the Big Otter. North of this, in the towns of Ferrisburgh, Charlotte, Shelburne, Colchester and Alburg, beautiful and lordly bays, jutting points with rugged, rocky faces and numerous islands, present a grand or beautiful variety, according to the point of view.

An inland drive from Charlotte to West Ferrisburgh, with fair September skies and over fine roads, is a luxury pure and simple. Driving along the old stage road, over which the four-in-hands used to rush in stagecoach days, to the "Center," and then westward through "Chicago" and the Potter woods, through gateways and other ways one comes to the banks of this same "Big Otter." There, a quarter of a mile downstream, on sward green as the Emerald Isles, you strike the "Ferry" where a resonant halloa brings out the captain of the ferry. A few pulls on the submerged iron cable brings the flat bottomed craft to the hither bank. A short pull and fifteen cents if you go one way, but a "quarter over and back the same day." A sharp pull up a deuced steep clay bank, and you stand in West Ferrisburgh ready for a drive in an unknown land, but among a most hospitable people.

From the ferry to Basin Harbor country the road winds over creek and meadow, through pine woods and hickory groves, past the home of the late Allen Beach, and then southward in many an abrupt turn and curve that keep the imagination alive. The traveler in the carriage seat gathers magnificent views of the Green Mountains and the foothills on one side and the nearby Adirondacks on the other.

About a mile north of the "Harbor" a friendly hand and a plainly printed sign inform the passerby that the "Booth and Hickok cottages" are not far away. And so, in sooth, a little drive among cedars innumerable, and past the beautiful home of Mr. and Mrs. Carlos Kimball, one finds these summer dwellers among the sweet-scented pines and cedars packing up

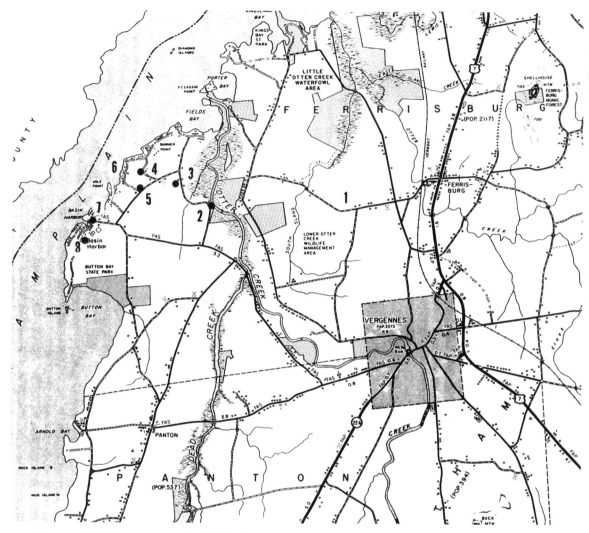

Route of Higbee's trip to Basin Harbor in 1895 shown on a current Dept. of Transportation map. One section of road has been abandonded since Higbee's time. Location of the ferry and some other sites are approximate. The ferry operated for only about two years at "Rock Landing".

1. Little Chicago Rd.
2. Ferry across the Big Otter.
3. The "late Allen Beach" House. This A. P. Beach was the grandfather of Allen Penfield Beach, who took over the Basin Harbor Club from Ardelia Beach in 1909.
4. The Carlos Kimball cottage.
5. Basin Harbor School, not mentioned by Higbee but a site to help locate other places.
6. "Booth and Hickok" cottages.
7. Winan's, a boarding house and predecessor of the present Basin Harbor Club.
8. William Newton's house.

SUMMER RESIDENCE OF **F.M. STRONG.** ONE MILE SOUTH OF FORT CASSIN ON LAKE CHAMPLAIN.

A summer home on Lake Champlain in the area where Higbee travelled to Basin Harbor. From the "Illustrated Combined Atlas of Vermont," published by H. W. Burgett & Co. New York. 1876. Charlotte Memorial Museum Collection.

and "away for home", after a two month stay in a summer home so delightful for situation and so improved by care and artistic taste that one could wish to abide here a lifetime. A pleasant visit, though short, with Mrs. Kimball, who was an old schoolmate in the days long gone, rounds out a trip to this lakeshore not soon to be forgotten.

On the road south to the "Harbor" a party of young men from the University at Burlington were practicing their skill at angles and levels and chains. Probably several future famous civil engineers will remember with great satisfaction their struggles with facts and figures while boarding in 1895 at "Winans'."

An old resident, William Newton,

in the vicinity of the eightieth mile-stone of life, pointed out the changes that had occurred since boyhood, and there were many. The old farms remained, but the feet that trod them and the hands that tilled them walked and toiled no more. And this it seems will be our lot to the end of time.

The view from West Ferrisburgh is superb. One gets a sweep of fifty to seventy-five miles of the mountains, Camel's Hump, and Mansfield, and the intervening landscape of plain and hill fills out the picture. It seems but a stone's throw to the wonderfully rugged New York side. This part of Vermont was among the earliest in settlement, and there are many traditions of hardship in the "Indian days." But those days have long gone, and the steamboat and electric light and the ever-present "wheel" man jog us along in a modern way.

But we bid our kind host and his hospitable family good-bye and once more brave the dangers of the "Ferry" to return to the more broken but equally fertile Charlotte.

Arrival at a tavern such as Martin's in North Ferrisburgh around 1825. Adapted from "Perley's Reminiscences" by Perley Poore. A. W. Mills. 1886.

III

Looking Backward on a Quiet Rural People
and Their Surroundings

18 December 1896

The sayings and doings of one generation, either written or handed down as tradition, constitute history. The unlettered red men sat around their campfires and repeated to sons and sons' sons the wild doing of their tribe until an unbroken chain composed of the links of memory stretched from the distant past.

The places where our forefathers lived, the houses they erected, the roads they built, the fields they tilled, are dear to us, and our interest increases as the passing years remove them further from us. The future is a book unread, and only the hand of Time can cut its leaves for the perusal of men. The past is ours for pleasure or pain, and happy is he who recalls it with more joy than sorrow.

The silent cities of the dead surpass the busy haunts of men in populations; but the bustle of a hurrying world disturbs not the serenity of their repose. On the hillsides, in the valley, former generations speak to us as only the dead can speak, and a saddened memory "recalls their virtues and chastens their vices."

To revive these recollections is a pleasure, not a task, and if they who read these lines gain profit, or at least do not begrudge the time spent in their perusal, this sketch of a quiet and rural people may have its modest and humble uses.

Some 1500[6] feet above the level of Lake Champlain, the summit of Mount Philo is an outlook well repaying the labor of the sightseeker. North and south, an unbroken range of lake for forty or fifty miles narrows as it goes south and stretches into quite a sea towards Burlington and the north. The rugged and towering outlines of the Adirondacks add majesty to the beauty of lake and bays, dotted with islands. Some twenty miles southward Snake Mountain reaches well up into the sky, while between lies a choice portion of the Champlain Valley, if not the finest. The eye ranges over lesser hills and delightful valleys, beautiful farms, here and there a village and church spires. To the east, the Green Mountains, with their foothills reaching this way many miles are decked with the colored foliage of pine, beech, maple, poplar, and birch that crown and beautify our Vermont hills.

Further south, but separated by a half mile of valley, Fuller and Shellhouse mountains reach on into

11

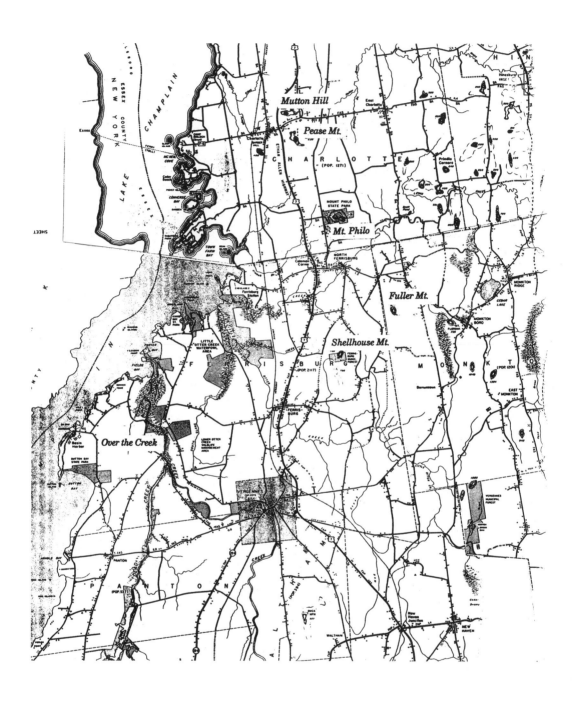

Higbee Country with favorite mountains. Adapted from Vermont Department of Transportation 1984 map.

Monkton and Ferrisburgh. They lack the rugged sides of Philo, but are steep enough for dangerous wood roads; and it is no unusual thing for the teamster and wood-chopper to outdo each other in the narration of hairbreadth escapes.

About midway in Ferrisburgh Shellhouse Mountain[7] presents a bald, red rock, westward front where a well informed hunter posts himself for the unsuspecting fox. And while waiting for his foxship, the sportsman satisfies his poetic soul with an outlook charming and complete. The whole of West Ferrisburgh, stretching miles away to Lake Champlain, embracing that land known as "Over the Creek" and south to the venerable city of Vergennes, is taken in a single glance.

Almost at the north end of Fuller mountain lies the "Center" with its score of houses, a blacksmith shop, store and post office--a typical country hamlet. It can almost be called a hamlet of churches for no fewer than three church edifices testify to the staid and substantial qualities of its rural people.

"Over the Creek" lies a territory five or six miles north and south, reaching westward to the lake, some of the finest meadow and grazing land in the valley. However, Indian incursions were here more frequent as they stole along Lake Champlain in their boats that floated on the water "silent as a feather."

These people "over the creek" must be animated with patriotic impulses to travel so many miles for "lection" and Town Meetings. Unless

The Old Congregational Church
Ferrisburgh Vermont

The Congregational church on the west side of Route 7 in North Ferrisburgh as sketched by Rachel Robinson. The last minister served there in 1918. The building is now the Grange Hall and also serves as the meeting place of the Ferrisburgh Historical Society. Courtesy of Karl Devine.

they come over the ferry, it is a long road around through the ancient City;[8] and anxious candidates have, doubtless, looked many times longingly southward for the banners of the advancing host. And quite a host indeed, for they muster about eighty voters over there, and when the battle is nearly a drawn fight between the "Center" and "Northburg" like Blucher at Waterloo, they arrive in the nick of time. The busy politician knows full

View from Shellhouse Mountain looking west, showing Otter Creek and some of the "over the creek" area of Ferrisburgh. Courtesy of Bixby Free Memorial Library, Vergennes.

well the value of their alliance, and so it happens that "business" calls him frequently to the west side, and he fails not to set up a few pins here and there; perhaps to be knocked down the very next day by the "other fellow."[9]

The adjoining town of Panton, with discriminating worldly wisdom, has sought on various occasions to engraft this territory onto their own--and a royal addition it would be to them. But the people are loyal to their old town and old traditions, and prefer that "over the creek," territory remain in the grand list of Ferrisburgh.

The Little Otter, so pleasantly made famous by Rowland E. Robinson, winds through the town. His quaint conceits are fresh and invigorating as the breezy woodlands he delights in picturing. His blindness has shut out the glorious sunlight--but the beautiful dreamlands through which his blindness leads him and the people who walk and talk, and the birds who sing, might perhaps have seemed less real had the shadows never fallen.

A winding picturesque road follows along the eastern and northerly base of Shellhouse mountain until it brings the traveller to Northburg.

To the west of Mount Philo, and about a mile distant, is the old stage road that used to be the thoroughfare to Whitehall and so on to New York. Here the old stagecoach with four and often six horses took its regular trips, and jolly days they were too. It was great fun to the young folks, and the old folks as well, to watch the rattling equipage as it went down a sharp hill on the keen run to get half way up the other side with the impetus of the great rush.

Tavern stands were numerous and all of them well patronized. At Martin's was kept a relay of stage horses for the "change," and this was a busy place in the old days before railroads turned things topsy-turvy. "Martinville" was quite as important in the way of location and business as many of the Western "cities" whose bonds for water works, etc., numerous frugal Vermonters now sadly number among their doubtful assets.

"Squire Martin"[10] was the trial justice in those days, and it was doubtless his good fortune to have joined in wedlock many of the lads and lassies whose bridal journey then did not include a trip to Europe. He built the house now owned by a grandson, Carlos S. Martin.

It was after the Rutland and Bur-

Martin's Tavern, corner of Route 7 and the Hollow Road, North Ferrisburgh. The left (north) end is the older building. In later years the south end became a store. The building burned in 1923 or 1924. Mr. Seguin and then Mr. Deshaw had overnight cabins there, followed by the present Jimmo's Motel. Courtesy of The Wheeler/Kingsland Collection.

lington Railroad came into operation about 1848 that the road leading westward from Martin's was opened, and a heavy growth of hemlock timber occupied the present highway. Greenbush afforded most of the gravel used in ballasting the railroad. Several acres were drawn off by trains of dump cars, and the grass-grown depression near the Stephen Ball homestead marks the spot.

Further north, out near where the Thorp brook enters the Cove, was a large barn-like concern where the shovelers boarded. These railroad employees came from all points of the compass, and payday was apt to be followed by a whoop and holloa of battle, for clannish pride and something stronger than Cove water frequently started many an animated discussion.

There is a peculiar charm about the old coach days that lingers in the memory like some strain of a half forgotten song. Morning and night, summer and winter, with something like the regularity of railroad trains, the stage went by. The driver, who knew everybody, was a hero to the boys as he cracked the long lash that lay snugly coiled up behind him or hung in loosely gathered loops in his hands. And the way he circled with his four-in-hand in front of the awaiting travelers was marvelous to the young and sometimes a little dangerous to the elders. But the driver was engineer, brakeman, fireman, and conductor, all in one, and no wonder he put on a few airs when occasion arose. He deserved it.

Sometimes the horses came prancing in, gay as peacocks, when the roads were good. But when the clay was soaked with rain and the stage happened to be unusually full, the horses arrived all mud from head to heels, such a looking lot.

Then came the work for the stableman, and it would do you good to hear the veteran George Yott, who was head stableman and crack stage

16

driver in those days, tell about the rattling times to get those horses ready for the next "change."

And it had to be done, too. Horses then were like engines now. When their "run" came things must be clean and steam up, or woe to the luckless chap in charge. So into the night it went and often all night, the washing and rubbing down, and the innumerable attentions that the first-class horseman George Yott then was, knew how to give.

One driver, I think his name was Meigs, was a great whistler, and many a free concert he gave--and it was good music too.

Just north of Martin's was the "pine woods," a cluster of beautiful pines on a knoll since cut down for a barn--and here the stage driver invariably blew his bugle blast.

After the railroad came, there was a short lived rivalry between steam power and horse flesh as to which should carry the mail, and a light express with picked horses dashed over the dusty roads. But whatever the outcome, steam is king, perhaps to be dethroned in turn by heaven's lightning imprisoned in the electric wire.

Old people will recall a day in May, some fifty years ago, when the stages were stalled in the snow. Cherry trees were in bloom, sheep had been turned out to pasture, when a blinding snowstorm came and continued until highways were blockaded all around. A southbound stage was stalled in the woods north of Solomon A. Williams's house who recalls, as a boy, going with the rest with shovels and oxen to haul them out and open the road.

"A large barn-like concern" for housing railroad workers. Two of these buildings -- portable by railroad flat cars -- are in use now at the Shelburne Craft School. Their location is near where they were left when the railroad was completed in 1849. Local historians have many details of their 140-year history. Sketch by Jennie Cole.

Know all men by these presents that I Norman J. Allen of Ferrisburgh Addison County and State of Vermont am held and firmly bound unto Absolom L. Wheeler of Ferrisburgh afs. in the Sum of fifteen thousand Dollars to be paid to Said Absolom L. Wheeler or his certain Attorney executors Administrators or assigns for which payment well and truly to be made I bind myself my heirs executors and Administrators firmly by these presents.

Dated the 26th day of April AD 1853

The Condition of the above Obligation is Such that if the above named Norman J Allen, Shall Well and truly pay, or cause to be paid all the liabilities, debts, and obligations of whatever name or nature, which now are or may hereafter come against the late firm of Allen & Wheeler and fully indemnify and absolve the above named A. L. Wheeler from all cost, charges damage or expence in consequence of Said liabilities then this bond or obligation to be null & void otherwise to remain in full force & effect

In Witness Whereof I have hereunto Set my hand and Seal this 26th day of April AD 1853

In Presence of
M. W. Carpenter

N. J. Allen

Ferrisburgh April 27th 1853   Personally appeared
Norman J Allen the Signor & Sealer of the above instrument and acknowledged the Same to be his free act & deed

Stoddard Martin   Justin Race

The bond of Norman J. Allen to Absolom L. Wheeler signed in 1853 when they formed the partnership which operated a store in the Hollow for many years. Courtesy of the Wheeler/Kingsland Collection.

IV

The "Hollow" and Ball Games

25 December 1896

At the base of Philo another north-south road, that was largely used in an earlier day, intersects the stage road at Shelburne Village. Out of this run other ways that encircle the mountain, making one of the finest of scenic drives.

To gain a view of the valley that one will not soon forget, go southward on this road and a little beyond the Smith Jones farm, now owned by Frank A. Lewis. Here looking west, south, and north, the viewer enjoys an uninterrupted sweep of farm land, wood land, lake, and distant mountain chains. The outlook is unsurpassingly beautiful, restful in its calm repose. A tired brain worker from the city of Washington spent hours here laying at full length on the greensward, feasting his soul on these great bounties of nature.

It is not definitely known who or what gave the name Philo to the mountain, but tradition has it that an old Indian fighter and famous hunter of that name camped on its side.[11] And it is said that its bold western front was visited many a time by this brave pioneer as an outlook for outlying savage foes.

On the west side is a cavern of unknown dimensions that is well known to foxes, and probably many a wolf or bear who have made it a summer residence or a secure sleeping apartment for a winter's doze.

A little below the cave and on the southern side, a huge stone, like a chair, is imbedded in the ground, and for want of a better name, it has been called the "Devil's Chair." Here the climber of the mountainside invariably rests and gets an outlook far off to the south; but why so beautiful a seat

The Devil's Chair on Mount Philo. Photo taken in 1984 when the view was obscured by woods which have covered most of the mountain since Higbee's time.

19

A bark mill powered by a horse on a sweep from an 1805 U.S. patent .

should be connected with such an ugly personage will always remain a mystery, as is the name "Philo".

Between here and Fuller Mountain in Ferrisburgh is Lewis Creek, a winding stream of much more consequence in the early days than now, since its volume of water has diminished so as to afford scanty dependence to the mill men. Years ago it was well stocked with salmon, and many a fine string was caught in an eddy at the foot of a rapid while waiting for a grist at the "Hollow" mill.

This "Hollow" is a busy and prosperous hamlet, nestled down in one of the coziest little valleys imaginable, and the traveler comes upon it as suddenly and unexpectedly as one stirs up a bevy of partridges.

But its busiest days were the old days when Lyman's woolen factory

used to whir and rattle all day and far into the night, and the old English miller came to wait on his customers dressed in the old-style long stockings and short breeches that were somewhat of a novelty to the younger eyes at least.

A tannery furnished a market for a limited quantity of homegrown hemlock bark, and the boys used to help break it up for the fun of seeing it devoured by the groaning and squeaking old mill in the floor below. Once one of the boys by sad mishap came near being ground up with the bark, but the hopper was unusually full and the old horse on the sweep heard the "whoa" in the nick of time. After that, the boys were missing from the bark loft.

The valley here is very narrow and spring freshets with the grinding ice have disturbed the quiet of the hamlet many a time. But some special good fortune must be hanging over them, for little or no damage has been done for years, and the "Creek" comes down in the friendliest of ways. Perhaps, after all, the old times were no busier than now, but it seems so, looking backward.

At the west end of the valley street stands the Methodist church and the mellow tone of its bell awakens many pleasant woodland echoes.

One by one the men who were active then have gone. Some sought other homes, but most of them have passed into the silent land. Of the

The Methodist church in the Hollow from a photo owned by Rokeby Museum.

remaining, perhaps Edward A Keeler and Moses L. Robinson are the only ones whose activities date to half a century ago. Mr. Keeler came to the "Hollow" in 1845, and for a long time carried on the wheelwright and cabinet business in the shop where John Besette now is. An active and hearty man now in his eighty-second year, Mr. Keeler has followed in their funeral processions the caskets of nearly all his contemporaries. Indeed, his hands have fashioned many of the narrow houses in which they sleep.

Samuel Coughlin used to run a whiskey still where Charles L. Palmer's house stands and the "thirst" line in those days ran pretty near its front door according to history.

An old-time and successful merchant, Cyrus W. Wicker commenced trade in 1836 in a building that stood on the green in front of Martin R. Allen's house. It was Wicker and Haskell then. Afterwards Mr. Wicker continued the business alone, in the building where C. H. Mallory now trades, and later on Wicker located west of the creek, on the site of the present J. L. St. Peter's brick store.

Rowland T. Robinson owned and repaired the grist mill in 1824, but later on sold it to Henry Miles,[12] and Miles sold to Mr. Hagan, the English miller. Norman J. Allen traded in the old Wicker store west of the bridge about 1839[13] and after that went into company with Absalom L. Wheeler. The firm of Allen & Wheeler continued a successful business for years in the store that was transformed into the spacious building now used by Stoddard N. and Martin F. Allen.

21

Clarkson G. Webb.

Carpenter & Showles were in trade for a while, and afterward Orris Showles carried on the tin business just back of the St. Peter store. Aaron Webb made boots and shoes in the building now occupied by his grandson, Clarkson G. In those days cowhide made none too good boots for a boy to "kick out." When first put on they were about as pliable as a length of stove pipe and grew more and more conservative with increasing age.

John Sedgwick had a tailor shop nearly across the street from Webb's. A. W. Billings commenced harness making over C. W. Wicker's store east of the bridge, but afterwards bought the building occupied by him when he died. Frank Yandow had a blacksmith

The saw mill and the covered bridge in the Hollow, view looking west. The bridge is now preserved at the 1810 Farmhouse Inn and Restaurant on Rt. 7. Photos taken around 1900. Courtesy of the Wheeler/Kingsland Collection.

22

Like many other towns, Charlotte had a cornet band to provide local entertainment. The musicians are assembled here in uniform and with their instruments, although there is no name identification or date. The Charlotte Memorial Museum has one of the silver cornets and this photo.

shop west of Esther Newell's and just north of this shop were the clay pits where the brick was made for the "Mud Church." These bricks were not baked, thus the name of the church.

In those days there were no dwelling houses between the home of the late Norman. J. Allen and the house now occupied by Mr. Dow, but at that time by Franklin White.

The present cornet band at the Hollow is a worthy successor of a similar organization existing about forty years ago, and many a summer evening was enlivened by the musicians, whose names cannot be now recalled. Fast-day[14] used to possess great attractions for the youngsters, for there was generally a rare game of baseball on deck. It was quite a different affair from the game of today. Two of the best players would "choose sides," and it was an honor to come next to the captain. It meant that you came next in ability to throw a ball, "fugle"[15] all over the street trying to hit it--but above all you could yell. Every one made about as much noise as he consistently could, and each individual player was umpire. So, between taking general charge, as well as his turn at the bat, and dodging the ball sent after him between bases, every one was chuck full of fun.

It was not so deadly as the modern game, either. Instead of being a round stone sewed into a piece of leather, the ball was yarn, wound onto a wad of rubber to make it bound well, and the catcher was not constrained to fasten a monkey cage over his face to keep from having his brains knocked out. But this has come to be a very scientific age, and an old-time ball player would find himself as much out-of-date as Rip Van Winkle after waking from his comfortable snooze of twenty years or so on the Hudson.

A stump fence near the blacksmith shop in the Shelburne Museum. Photo taken July 1990

V

Stump Fences, the Erie Canal
Cattle Drives and Fox Hunting

1 January 1897

Hardly an acre of land on the southern side of Philo is now in the name that held it then. Louisa Lacoy lives where her husband Jacob built his little home about forty years ago. The Jeremiah Fonda place is owned by Dr. George Collins. Where Stephen Jones built his home, Henry Germain now lives. Where George James lives, Peter Van Vliet brought up his fifteen vigorous boys and girls. The Seth Langdon farm was owned by Peter V. Higbee and Amos Cogswell owned the farm next east of there, now held by Carleton Eno and J. G. Barton.

"Uncle Amos" Cogswell had a particular antipathy to skunks, and it was good as a circus to hear him tell about "hitting them right over the sampment." Where this particular spot was situated in a skunk's anatomy, history has not pointed out; but it seemed the safest and best place of attack, and the consequences were generally fatal to the hunted.

The Allen, George Sherman and S. B. Prindle farms were included in the estate of the late John Quinlan, but now owned by Joseph J. Quinlan. Several will recall the burning of Michael Quinlan's house, where the John Quinlan house now stands, when

Mr. Quinlan and some of his family perished in the flames. Farther east, Sherman's mill used to be of lively interest in early days, only a vestige of the old dam now remaining. Uncle George Sherman, as everybody called him, lived to a good old age and dearly loved to drive a good team persisting

The Quinlan family cemetery located west of the Quinlan (Sherman) covered bridge and north of Spear St. Ext.

in the use of high-lived horseflesh long after a wise regard for everyone's personal safety demanded the most sedate of plugs.

North of the creek and nearly on opposite sides of the road, Edward Daniels' wheelwright and William J. Scott's cooper shops kept the people running on wheels and pork barrels. James Washburn came next and William Hyde, whose descendant, Heman, now living in Monkton, is an encyclopedia of past events. Uncle "Billy" Tucker used to live around a little hill some distance from this highway and residents along the way to the Hollow never needed a clock of a Sunday morning for Uncle Billy always started for church at just such an hour and jogged just so fast after his bob-tailed old mare. Levi Cogswell, a brother of Amos, lived to a good old age a little north of Mr. Tucker's.

The old road running north and west around the mountain, used to go through the woods near the Prindle place, but it was deemed best to shun the hill, and so a romantic woodland drive was discontinued. Near the "rocks" on this road the old school house used to stand where it was no uncommon thing to count forty rollicking girls and boys as steady attendants, especially in the winter. And why not, for children were in order then and district schools patronized.

Near the school house lived Caleb Harding with thirteen children;[16] across the road William Higbee with twelve;[17] John and James Palmer gave no small assistance in increasing the roll; a fun-loving delegation from Peter Van Vliet's; William Barton's family, anywhere from one to a lot full from "Guinea" (so called on account of the numerous colored folks who answered to the name of Morocco) until the old school house was packed and jammed and had to burn down to get a little rest and quiet.

Then came the inevitable wrangle about where the new house should be built, ending in dividing the district, and consequent decline of the glorious old days. After the new house in No. 7 [The Quinlan School], the small one was erected near Otto C. Palmer's and became No. 14. [at the northwest corner of the intersection of One Mile Rd. and Guinea Rd.]

Among the first teachers, and one of the best in No. 7, was Miss Maria Rich who with her sister Katharine taught a number of successful terms before the war in the South where there was a large demand for educated Northern girls.

William Higbee was coming from the Sherman neighborhood one dark night and when, in the woods on the top of the hill where the Prindle house afterwards stood, he heard the scream of a panther south of him. It was as near to go home as to turn back. So he armed himself with a stout club and went down the hill and through the still more dismal brook-run at a charging step. He was thirty rods or so towards home from this brook when the animal gave another scream in the road he had just passed over. It was rather a nervous if not a dangerous time, but no harm came of it and a large panther was killed in Jericho a couple days after, probably the same one.

A panther such as William Higbee heard on his walk home from Sherman's. Sketch by Jennie Cole.

What is now fine meadow and pasture was then an unbroken stretch of heavy pine and hemlock. Nearly the whole of this fine tract was at one time owned by the Palmers, and indeed some eight or nine hundred acres still remain in the name, about the only instance in the whole round of the mountain.[18]

Many of the farms in this vicinity have miles of stump fence and it used to be as good as a circus to witness the approach of the old-fashioned stump machine with its frame like a barn, an immense wheel, great dangling iron hooks, the locomotive power being four to six yoke of oxen sustained and animated by half a dozen yelling men.

Peter Stebbins owns the Cram farm and Timothy Stebbins' and Francis Barker's place. The highway past

Abel C. Palmer's skirting the north side of the mountain used to connect with what was then an open road running to the stage road, then just north of S. A. Williams' house, westerly to the dwelling of the late George L. Root, and from there by the present route to the ferry.

Before the advent of railroads, McNeil's Ferry was the principal shipping point for a large territory and the above highway was one of the most traveled in town, portions of Monkton, Hinesburg, and Starksboro coming this way to the lake.

Distance has not been annihilated so very long, after all. It is only some forty-five years ago that a company of neighbors assembled at the David Van Vliet place, a little east of George James' to say goodbye to friends going

The Solomon A. Williams house on the west side of Rt. 7 south of the Wildwood West development. Daisy (Mrs. John) Williams lived here and for a time operated a guest house. The scrapbook containing many of the Higbee essays was found here. Just north of the house a laneway going west toward the lake is what remains of the road that ran from the Stage Road (Rt. 7) to Greenbush Rd., passing south of the Root (now Lawrence) house and thence to Lake Road.   Courtesy of Special Collections, UVM Libraries.

A stump machine, sketched from U. S. Patents by Jennie Cole.

The George L. Root (now James Lawrence) house on Greenbush Rd. viewed from Lake Rd. The discontinued east/west road crossed the field and bridged the railroad tracks near the large tree (arrow) and continued east to Route 7 near the Solomon A. Williams house (p. 28). Higbee Road then extended to Mt. Philo Rd. The white house on the ridge is near where Higbee Road intersected with Mt. Philo Road. Photo taken April, 1990.

to far-away Ohio. Covered wagons were to be their homes for months, and it seemed they were never to be heard from again. Letter writing was more of an expensive luxury, it is true, for it took twenty-five cents for postage to Ohio then, instead of two cents now for carrying a letter nearly around the world. If one was in a wonderful hurry in those days, he took the Erie Canal at Albany and slammed along at a rate of five miles an hour to Buffalo. What a wonder that any of them ever survived such a breathless journey.

A trip to New York City was quite an affair, taking about two weeks to go and come, and "going to market" twice a year for the spring and winter trade meant considerable to the oldtime "store keepers" in the "Hollow." Instead of telegraphing for goods to come by express the next day, as occasion required, or filing an order with the omnipresent, unduly modest "drummer,"[19] the tradesman had to depend upon his memoranda and his wits for a proper six months' supply. And if he bought right, he just needs take with him a good supply of ready cash. So about going-to-market time, the "books" were closely scanned, and all customers were expected to balance up with hard dollars the deficiency left after the crediting of butter, pork, eggs, paper rags, dried apples and chickens.

South from the Solomon A. Williams' place on the old stage road to Martin's, the changes since 1848 are as distinctly marked as on the other sides of Mount Philo. Commencing north were William R. Williams, Caleb E. Barton, John Hazard, D. C. Palmer, Ebenezar Ward, Midas Prindle, Hinman Beers, Abner Squires, Nathan and Albert Marble, John Dakin, Medad Martin, John Charter. The Williams, Palmer, Prindle, and Martin farms remain in the name; and of the above enumeration, Ebenezar Ward alone is living.

Thus time "makes havoc with us all." One generation passes, leaving room for another. Older settlers came and disappeared before the memory of the present writer, and this sketch does not claim a full enumeration. But even in these days of long journeys by sea and land, this unadventurous trip around Mount Philo may not have been in vain.

Pease Mountain lies about a mile north with perhaps a little less elevation. Its western and steepest side presents a less bold and rocky front than Mount Philo; but together they lend distinguishing character to the landscape. The traveler up and down Champlain never fails to mark the peculiar formation of these twin hills, covered with verdure to the top. A feature in common is their gradual sloping to the eastward, up whose incline fairly good carriage roads can be easily made when the mountain summits come to be inhabited by summer sojourners, as will most certainly happen at no distant day, for no more charming sunsets or cooling breezes are to be found along the whole Champlain. Pease Mountain is

The Higbee Mountains of Charlotte. From left: Mutton Hill (elev. 660), Pease Mountain, (elev. 800) Mount Philo (elev.980), as seen from the town recreation area on Lake Rd. Photo taken April, 1990.

elevated enough for a bird's-eye view east, west, north and south; Mt Philo and Pease Mountain are not too high for distinctness of vision.

Whether the glacial or some other age is responsible for these formations, the reader is at liberty to determine for himself; but some gigantic forces must have evolved these rocky piles and planed down the fruitful valley between.

Along the elevated table land running south from Pease Mountain are found, a few feet below the surface, regular shell beaches that show the wash of water as plainly as the beach of the lake shore. The stones and gravel are identical with that washed up by the lake. Whether the water of Champlain ever climbed so far out of the present bounds is another thing left with the reader to decide. Or was this whole country submerged then drained by the Hudson and Saint-Lawrence? The rock fronts with an incline to the eastward and a bold west-

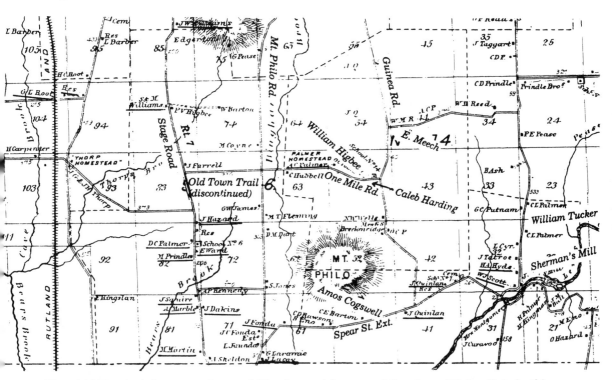

The 1869 Beer's Atlas map of part of Charlotte with some of the places Higbee lists in this trip around Mount Philo. He started on the southwest side, at the intersection of Mt. Philo Rd. and Spear St. Ext. Names from the text are underlined, added information is in larger type. The Child "Chittenden County Gazetteer of 1882-83" lists William Higbee (grandfather of the author) as living on road 53, the present One Mile Rd, on the farm that later belonged to O. C. Palmer. He later lived with his son Peter V. Higbee (father of the author) on road 61 which is the part of Spear St. Ext. south of Mt. Philo. The Gazetteer also states that William and Miranda (Harding) Higbee had eight children.

ern projection continue through this part of the Champlain Valley.

To the southeast a level tract of the first greening land stretches away to Lewis Creek. In an earlier day, the late Judge Ezra Meech of Shelburne owned over a thousand acres in this tract and here pastured some of the finest steers that went into market.

"Jack" Simonds of Bridport, Addison County, was a famous drover and butcher, and it was no unusual thing for him to go south over the "main road" with two to three hundred cattle in a drove. He would commence buying in Canada, collecting his drove as he came south, and the youngsters were filled with awe and delight when the bellowing herd came in sight.

They were generally preceded by a man on horseback, and followed by several barefooted boys. Somewhere amongst all this was the ever-present cattle dog with bright eyes and his ears as erect as the quills of a porcupine and so evidencing his feeling of canine responsibility.

South and southwest of the Meech tract were several hundred acres of heavy timber, mostly pine and hemlock, and this was a veritable hunters' paradise. In the great hollow trees innumerable coons domiciled by day and attended husking bees at night; and the jaunty fox took many a cozy noonday nap on the moss-grown logs or aroused himself to drive off an intruding partridge who insisted on "drum-

Copyright 1885

THE DRUMMER'S LATEST YARN.

ming" his foxship out of camp. But when the cold weather came and skins were "prime," the fox often had other business on hand and had to scurry many a mile between meal times, with a half-dozen eager hounds filling the echoing hollows and hillsides with their music.

One old Irishman in particular was an enthusiastic hunter. He was never known to have killed anything with his ancient musket, but he kept a hound just the same, and whenever the dog came into hearing, his old master would invariably say, "Whist there now; will ye mind the yowl of 'im?" And no matter what the order of the day, business was suspended so long as the "yowl" was in hearing. There were several great hunters then, and it was the usual thing for them to congregate on Thanksgiving Day and let loose fifteen to twenty dogs. Tillie Burritt of Hinesburg, William R. Williams, and John G. Thorp

of Charlotte were all keen and untiring sportsmen and it was a sharp fox that escaped them all. Bounties were paid for fox skins in those days, and the town clerk's books show numerous entries wherein business was thus happily combined with the huntsman's pleasure.

One of the hunters, William R. Williams, is said to have killed eighty foxes in sixty consecutive days. Out of these somber hemlocks over and around Pease Hill and Mount Philo to Ferris Creek[20] and back, their yelling pack hustled the quarry, and it was not unusual to hear the dogs far into the night. A favorite runway off the mountain was a few rods east of S. B. Langdon's down the length of his meadow to the wooded banks of the creek. Sometimes the dogs and fox were pretty close apart, and the meadow run of about a hundred rods seemed sufficiently exciting for both the hunters and the hunted.

The Quinlan school in 1979 when it was used as a storage shed on the Dike farm. It is on the south side of Spear St. Ext. west of the Quinlan (Sherman) covered bridge.
Left: Donated by Dorothy Rutter Engberg. Charlotte Mem. Museum Collection

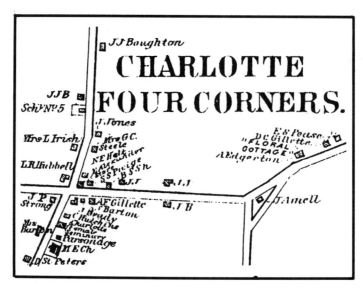

The Beers 1869 Insert Map of Charlotte 4-Corners: the intersection of Ferry Rd. (E-W) and Greenbush Rd. (N-S). In this century, the store on the NE corner belonged to Stanton Williams, later to his son Wilson (Bill). It continues as The Old Brick Store operated by Gary Therrien. The whipping post might have been where the WWI monument is now. The Barton Tavern ("L. R. Hubbell") on the NW corner is now a private home.

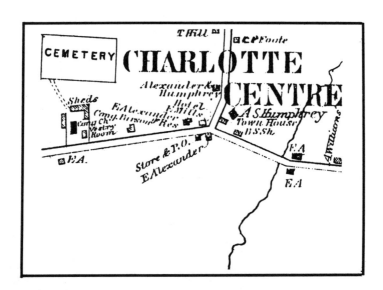

The Beers Insert Map of Charlotte Center: the intersection of current Church Hill (E-W) and Museum Rd. (N-S). The "Town House" is now the Charlotte Memorial Museum. The "E. Alexander Res" is now the Pinney Antique Shop and home. The Barnes tavern ("Hotel") steps can still be found at the edge of the road. The spring that supported early development of this area is between the site of the tavern and the Pinney house.

VI

The Naming of Mutton Hill, the Whipping Post, Potash and Taverns

8 January 1897

The larger part, if not the whole of Pease Mountain[21], is lease land, the rental being used for school purposes. In the early days, a certain tract of land was set aside for the "first settled minister," and it seems the minister either selected the top of Pease Mountain or it was selected for him. Perhaps an undefined fear of another Deluge led to this choice, as a kind of Ararat in case of necessity. Possibly the thrifty early settlers thought the land at the bottom of the mountain better than that at the top and acted accordingly. On these points history has been silent.

It is known that the Reverend Mr. Yale occupied these lands and built a stone house on a level tract towards the southeast side of the mountain. As time passed it became the home of wood choppers, and after the wood was cut, woodchucks and squirrels were tenants in common. Finally the old walls were drawn away to become new ones somewhere else, and a fine old mountain mansion dwindled away to a hole in the ground, where there was once a cellar.

Twice within a century the mountain has been pretty generally denuded of its forestry.[22] But with un-diminished vigor the soil has renewed its verdant crown, until no more gorgeous combinations of crimson and brown and green and gold creep into the artist's dreams than greet the delighted eye when the hazy Indian summer enchants us.

George Pease, father of Edward S. Pease, leased this mountain and, in the earlier days of the Rutland and Burlington Railroad, furnished large

The Pease house on Mt. Philo Rd. from a painting done about 1930. It has been restored and now, more that one hundred years after the George Pease estate was settled (see previous page), it is the Green Mountain Bed and Breakfast. Artist unknown. Charlotte Memorial Museum Collection.

quantities of wood for their engines whose fuel was not then made up so largely of coal. He built a plank sluice on the west side of the mountain, down which hundreds of cords of wood came rushing with the velocity of thunderbolts. Mr. Pease was a man of boundless energy, and to clear off this mountain and hustle wood and logs to the bottom was merely a pastime.

A narrow valley, some half a mile long, separates Pease Mountain from "Mutton Hill," whose name so suggestive of rich living, was acquired more than a hundred years ago.[23] One Sunday, when the good people had betaken themselves to church, probably not far from where the meeting-house now stands, their logical conclusions on theology were interrupted by a breathless messenger announcing that a bear was hid in the bushes a little to the north.

In those days, as now, it was deemed good politics to "kill bears when they are around" and so the meeting suddenly adjourned, and everybody joined in the "surround." The circle of armed yeomanry grew smaller and the prospect for bear meat larger and larger, until a big black ram that had somehow escaped from the tender shepherd's care stalked out of a thicket ready to bunt the whole concern into the middle of next week.

Whether the thread of the discourse, thus suddenly snapped, was resumed, history saith not, but one thing is certain: the territory in question came immediately to be known as Mutton Hill and will probably so remain to the end of time.

One thing is certain: we were always a law-abiding people, and it is not so very many generations ago that a whipping post graced the Four Corners. It stood on the green, near the house of Mrs. Celinda Hazard and Ezra Holt was the legally constituted guardian thereof. There is no recorded evidence of who or how many were entertained in this way. But

The tenant house for the George Lowry Root farm. It stood west of the main house which is on Greenbush Rd. and was near the railroad on the now-abandonded road. Courtesy of the Root family.

there are traditions of some, over-glib of tongue, being thus prevailed upon to overcome their weakness and become models of society.

Near the foot of the meeting-house hill and where Edgerton's cider mill now stands, was a distillery, and the plot of land surrounding it is designated in Charlotte land records as the "old still lot."[24]

West of S. A. Williams on the discontinued highway leading to George L. Root's can be seen the foundations of an old potash, and it is only recently that an immense pine trough for catching lye has succumbed to the ravages of time. In the early days, pearlash came pretty near being legal tender, but whether admitted on the basis of 16 to 1 will have to be referred to financial experts. West of the potash, and on the corner south of the George L. Root house, was a store that used to be conducted by George Newell. The building was moved across the road and is now used as a horse barn by Charles L. Root.

The corner where are now the store and other buildings owned by George A. Foote was one of the busiest locations in an early day and so continued until the establishment of a post office at East Charlotte[25] and fluctuation in the tide of trade wrought the inevitable changes of time. In the hands of first one and then another of the family it was known as "Barnes" for miles around, and no resort was more popular. Gen. Hezekiah Barnes built the first store on this spot, being part of the present one of Mr. Foote's. On the north side

The George A. Foote store and associated buildings at the intersection of Church Hill Rd. (or Old Rt. 7) and Hinesburgh Rd. It remained a store for many years and is still in active use as a dwelling and studio. The original photo shows a bit of the Barnes tavern's porch floor, indicating the photographer stood there on that snowy day around 1905. Courtesy of Elinor (Prindle) Benning.

of the road and just above the spring he built a large log tavern where old-time hospitality was dispensed in such a royal way that he was soon lacking of room and erected the building now occupied by Wilbur Field. It has been estimated this house has been standing about one hundred and forty years, and it is today firm and square as a brick.

The road leading to Burlington went a little west of its present loca-tion and up a sharp pitch, and Mr. Barnes kept a pair of oxen in yoke night and day to help teamsters up this hill. The consideration was small, but so much business was done that the ox team paid abundantly for all their keep.

The stone house, where Ezra and H. D. Alexander live, was built for a cider mill, and doubtless contributed, in a mild way, to the popularity of the location. Here congregated the grim

A Travelling Tavern Story. The Hezekiah Barnes tavern as it appeared in 1949 just before it was moved to the Shelburne Museum. Old Route 7 is visible on the left. Photo was taken by L. L. McAllister of Burlington. Courtesy of the Shelburne Museum.

warriors who made "June trainings" a "thing of joy;" and tradition has it that at close of day the field was often strewn with the temporarily disabled but still enthusiastic firemen.

The first merchant was Hezekiah Barnes, Jr. then Noble Lovely, after him Horace Cook and after Cook, Samuel H. Barnes. A man by the name of Staples succeeded S. H. Barnes; and later on, it became Staples and Lyon. The latter firm dissolved, and Ezra Alexander was then associated with Abial Lyon as Lyon & Alexander. The firm was in trade five years, after which Ezra Alexander did business alone from 1848 to 1872. For years Alexander did a large business, buying country produce in connection with a Boston commission house. Trade came here from a number of Eastern towns and goods were sold by the wagonload.

There used to be a store on Mutton Hill a little south of James P. Kehoe's, kept by Nathaniel and George Newell. Nathaniel Newell built the brick house owned by the late Edgar

AUCTION SALE.

Will be sold at Auction on Saturday the **16th** day of September inst., at the Barne's place, in Charlotte, the following valuable property,

About 11 acres of land with a valuable Stone House and Store in the same building.

9 Feather beds, nearly new,
5 French bedsteads,
Sundry articles of bedding,

2 Gold watches,	2 Matched tables.
2 Good Waggons,	2 Bureaus,
2 Double sleighs	3 Doz. chairs,
1 Single do.	3 Looking glasses,
1 Harness,	3 Stands, 2 clocks,
2 Buffalo robes,	1 Hair matrass,
A lot of stone ware	25 lbs. Woolen rolls,
4 Draft chains,	Lot of crockery,
1 Cow and calf,	2 Britannia tea-pots,
6 Stoves and pipe,	1 Carpet,
1 Good new safe,	6 Table cloths,
26 Silver spoons,	3 Rocking chairs,

Sundry articles for House-Keeping and Dry Goods, too numerous to mention. The whole of said property to be sold without reserve to close the estate of *Mrs. Samuel H. Barnes.*

E. HOLT, *Administrator.*

Sale to commence at 10 O'clock am

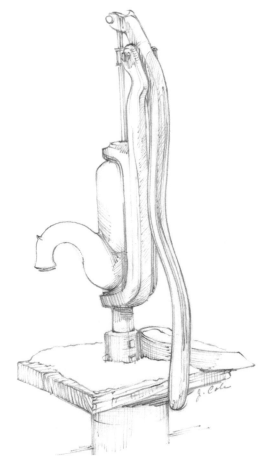

Above: The Barnes property was sold at auction by the agent/entrepreneur, Ezra Holt. The likely date is 1854. Copy of a broadside in the town clerk's office.

Right: The village pump which, though now unused, presumably is connected to the Barnes spring. Sketch by Charlotte artist, Jennie Cole.

Two unidentified children pose in front of a barn just west of the George A. Foote store at the intersection of Church Hill Rd. and Hinesburgh Rd. The barn's design matched that of the Foote store. It burned later and the present one was built. Photo around 1905. Courtesy of the Root family.

The George Lowry Root house on Greenbush Rd. around 1905. It was built between 1810 and 1815 by Francis Breakenridge. When the east-west road made a four corners here it was the center of some commercial activity including a store on the east side of Green-bush Rd. Courtesy of the Root family.

Edgerton, and it was used as a tavern.

In those days "taverns" were found anywhere along main highways. It was the custom for everybody to take a drink; travel was done by horse conveyance or boats, and most of the old-time inn keepers were prosperous.

Sheldon Wheeler, father of the late E. H. Wheeler, had a tannery and shoe shop on the "Hill" and did a flourishing business in his day. The late Aaron Webb of North Ferrisburgh learned his trade of Mr. Wheeler.

Across the road from Wheeler's on the farm now owned by Mrs. Charles Wooster, William Pease conducted a flourishing business as blacksmith, wheelwright, and manufacturer of harness hames[26]. This was run for many years by his sons, W. R. & Loren Pease. Our townsman, Marcus B. Reynolds, used to work at blacksmithing and hame making for the Pease brothers. Not a vestige of any of these enterprises remains.

The old house formerly occupied by the late Charles P. Foote on the "Hill" is one of the oldest in town. Across from the Foote house, Truman Hill kept a tailor shop where wedding outfits for former generations were made to order. A little south, the old town "pound" kept open doors for stray cattle and swine. It cost you nothing to get in, but often a nice little sum to get out.

41

The Wooster house, southeast corner of Old Rt. 7 and Mutton Hill Rd. On the back of the original photo: "The house that William Pease built probably about 1806. After his death a daughter Minerva Pease Sherman and her husband John Sherman bought it. She was great aunt to Charles Wooster, brought him up from a young child after his mother died. Standing are John Sherman and his wife Minerva. In carriage is Charles Wooster. The above by Carlene Wooster Carpenter daughter of Charles Wooster and born and reared in this house. 1971." Warren Lawrence owned the house for many years and sold it in the late nineteen eighties. Photo courtesy of Warren Lawrence.

The 1812 (Newell) tavern on Old Rt. 7 circa 1910 after it had become the home of the Edgerton family. The building was restored in 1981 and serves as office and residential space. Courtesy of the Charlotte Mem. Museum.

VII

All Roads Lead to the Ferry

15 January 1897

There was a store at the Four Corners, run with varying fortune by Bradshaw & Co., then by a man by the name of Perkins. Noble Lovely was in trade here when the store burned down, about 1840. It was rebuilt by Dr. Luther and Annie Stone and William Wright formed a co-partnership in the business until superseded by William Sherman and Eugene Bisonnette. After them came George C. Steel, who continued in trade until his failure, about 1868.

The "Corners" had its tavern, of course, kept by Joseph Barton, father of the late Sheriff Barton; Charles Kasson; Calvin C. Martin; and latterly by Luther R. Hubbell. Joseph Barton used to keep a public house where Hiram H. Jones lives, but, later on, in the house now owned and occupied by L. R. Hubbell. Hon. John A. Kasson of Iowa was born in this house, and was quite a lad when his parents removed from town.[27]

Ezra Holt, grandfather of John H. Thorp, lived in the house now occupied by Mr. Thorp. He carried on the business of harness and saddle maker in a shop that extended south to the store. This shop was burned with the store, but the house was saved. Mr. Holt was acting justice, did most of the conveyancing, etc., and was for years the financial agent of Harmon and Belden Nobles of Essex, New York, who made large loans here. The town records show that the "Nobleses" were extensive holders of Charlotte real estate mortgages.

Ammi Gillette kept a shoe shop where Mrs. N. C. Bush lives. Mr. Gillette was remarkably well informed in matters of local history, as was the late Nelson F. Holt. It has often been remarked that "neither of them ever forgot anything," and it is to be regretted that extensive notes were not taken from the personal recollections of these two men. Mr. Holt kept a diary of daily happenings for years. It now is in the possession of John H. Thorp, his grandson.

There are in existence several long sleighs built probably fifty to seventy-five years ago by Carlton Hutchins, an old-time mechanic of the Corners. Aaron L. Beach had a blacksmith shop on the corner, south of the Charles B. Cook place.

It is said almost the first, if not the first, store between Vergennes and Burlington was built and run by George Thorp, and stood just north of

The former Barton tavern building on the northwest corner of Greenbush and Ferry Roads, now a private home. It was the birthplace of the Honorable John A. Kasson. A 1979 photo.

the driveway at the old Thorp homestead. It seems the east and west highway ran where the present one now does at an early date, but the one leading south was opened and recorded by the surveyor at a considerably later day. Probably the former was used getting to the lake.

In ancient days it is said "all roads lead to Rome," and from frequent reference in town records, it seems that many if not all roads led to "The Ferry." The road to the wharf was somewhat south of the right-of-way now used to the beach, until the upland is reached, when the old route was identical with the present one.

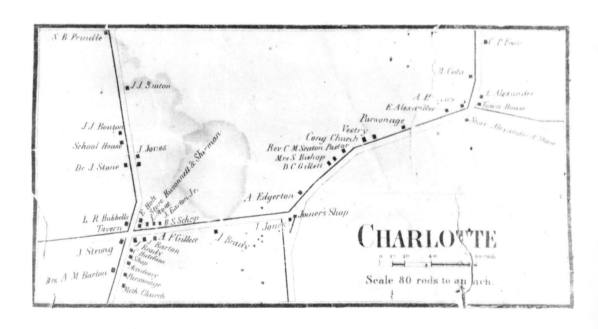

Walling 1857 Insert Map of Charlotte Four Corners. Several of these names appear in this chapter. West of this map and on Ferry Rd. were A. Beach's blacksmith shop on the south side and the C. B. Cook farm on the north side at the intersection with Lake Rd. Courtesy of Avery Palmer.

44

The Thorp house where George Thorp ran a store. The house is now the Laberge farm at the corner of Thompson's Point and Greenbush Roads. From the Walling 1857 map of Chittenden county. Courtesy of Avery Palmer.

Some idea can be formed of the wash of the lake when we are told that to follow directly eastward, where the old-time highway ran, would carry us a long way out into the bay. It is predicted that some day the two bays will come together, and by and by the "heirs, executors, administrators" of Cedar Beach property may be the owners of island homes unsurpassed in beauty.

For many years ferrying was done by sailboats, but at a later period business came to where the old wharf now is, and about 1830 McNeil & Ross put on a horse boat.[28] The horse boat made large money for its owners some

twenty years and one day when nearing this side, with a heavy load of cattle, it collapsed, like the parson's one-horse chaise.[29] Cattle and horses had to swim for it, and the worn out old boat was towed to the south side of the bay and beached on the sand.

The advent of steam cars made all these changes -- revolutions, one may call them. The line boats stopped at McNeil's both ways. Nearly all the produce going to market from this and the towns east and south of us, and the goods supplying dealers in these towns, was loaded and unloaded at the ferry. Northern New York was then being developed, and a large amount

"A Lake Ferry-boat" from "A Family Canoe Trip", by Florence Watters Snedeker, Harper & Brothers, New York. 1892. Courtesy of The Village Bookshop, Shelburne.

of travel on that account followed. No inconsiderable profit resulted from the "Society of Friends," who came this side for their "yearly meeting."

On the wharf stood a store run by Sylvester I. Lovely, who married Mary McNeil, a daughter of Captain Charles McNeil. This store and storehouse was some eighty feet long and had an immense trade, as goods could be sold cheaply on account of no expense in hauling after leaving the boats.

This old store always did a rushing business, and to keep up its reputations, finally went down with a rush. About 1840, Abail Lyon bought an immense quantity of oats in Canada to be shipped in barges through the lake

to New York. When they got as far as here, it was found the grain was heating, so the barges were moored alongside the dock and great quantities of oats transferred to the floors of the store and storehouse to cool off, resulting in a mixed pile of oats, lath, plaster and timber. It is said a number of barrels of eggs were buried in the oats on the barges, and the first intimation they had of the grain heating was the peeping of a lot of newly-hatched chickens. It was probably one of the first incubators in use here.

According to the records, a road led to Thompson's Point in a very early day, and a man by the name of Michael Bull was among the first to

46

The Old Brick Store at the Four Corners. The Bell System blue bell logo on the porch post was adopted by the company in 1889. Undated photograph. Courtesy of the Root family.

live on what is now a part of the town farm. It is not plain why this name was given to the point composed of lots No. 121 and 122 of the original survey. Lot No 121 was set to Nehemiah Merritt, Jr.; No. 122 to Joseph Ferris, Jr.; in grants made in 1763.

There are ten transfers made by Ethan Allen, in this order: to David Ferris, David Breakenridge, Charles McNeil, Justin Wheeler, Jonathan Sawyer, Asa Barnes, Charles McNeil, Thomas Chittenden, Thomas Chittenden again, Charles McNeil. Most of these Allen lands are along the lakeshore, according to the numbering of the lots. The early settlers seemed loath to get far from the lake, and this is understood when we re-

View west down Depot hill from the Four Corners. Charlotte Memorial Museum Collection.

Greenbush Rd. looking south to the Four Corners as on a postcard mailed in 1911. The street was narrow and unpaved, but this and another scene show sidewalks on both sides. Charlotte Memorial Museum Collection.

Greenbush Rd. looking north circa 1885. The wall of the Old Brick Store is on the right, the picket fence of Barton's (Hubbell's) tavern on the left. Scales are in the green beside the store. The house behind the store later belonged to the Deyette family and Tina (rhymes with Dinah) Deyette was the telephone operator there for many years. Charlotte Memorial Museum Collection.

member that their only way of carrying bulky articles was by water. Their nearest mill or market for a long time was Skenesboro, now Whitehall. Possibly the fashion of hats, sleeves, and things did not change four times a year then, and it did not matter so much if milliners and dress makers lived a little off the trolley line.

There has been considerable change in some of the main roads. It is said the road near Edgerton's, instead of going east as now, went around the westerly side of the Jones hill coming out of Mutton Hill about where Joseph Besette's house is.[30] It was changed to its present line when Hezekiah Barnes built his log tavern and established his store near the spring. The old stage road used to bear to the right and, near the John Hazard place, went about half way between W. W. Higbee's and John Parkin's, coming into the present course a little north of the James B. Williams' place. The change in this highway was brought about by Jeremiah Barton, who built the house now owned by W. W. Higbee. Mr. Barton had kept a very popular tavern here for many years.

It is singular that after the taverns were built the highways immediately changed and pointed in their direction. It would be exceedingly unseemly to insinuate that there was anything more than a coincidence in this. South of Mr. Higbee's[31] and on the east side near the brook, "Nat" Martin had a tannery where he advertised to make the best of leather as he always kept it in the proper vats "a year and eighteen months." Mr. Martin built a large stone house on the west side of the road on land now owned by S. A. Williams and this house was once a tavern. Some people may have gone hungry in those days, but it is doubtful if any suffered of thirst.

According to the records of land transfers, the Newell, Hosford, Yale, Thorp, McNeil, Leavenworth, Hill, Barnes, Meech, Rich, Allen, Palmer, Wheeler, Wooster, and Williams families came into town not many years apart. Daniel Hosford, as this name was largely spelled then,[32] was a surveyor, and many surveys of lands and highways were made by him. Benjamin Ferris, Jr., surveyed and made the original chart of the town in 1763, and he was proprietors' clerk.

Looking east on Ferry Rd. by the Old Brick Store. Charlotte Memorial Museum Collection.

The other Barton tavern which later was the home of Peter V. Higbee and his son, W. W. Higbee. It is on the east side of Rt. 7, on the south corner of Higbee Rd. and opposite the Solomon A. Williams house.

The meadow behind Higbee's house on Rt. 7. where Indian artifacts were found. His favorite mountain (Philo) is in the background. Photos taken in July, 1990.

VIII

Early Church/Town Affairs

22 January 1897

Church and State were more mixed in management in the early day, and the records are well filled with proceedings of town meetings held to settle questions of theological import. An early law released from certain taxes those who differed with the "majority" in religious belief, and page after page of the early records are filled with certificates like the following:

This is to certify that I do not agree with the majority of the people in religious sentiment in this town.

Such a certificate, duly recorded by the town clerk, exempted the maker from being taxed to support the established church. There have been instances in which men suffered for conscience sake, but here, it seems, conscientious scruples kept a man from suffering in the way of taxes.

Mention has already been made of the Congregational Church in Charlotte in connection with town records, but an historical sketch, taken from a manual of the church, printed in 1879, and prepared by the present clerk, Deacon Henry W. Prindle, may be of interest. The church organized January 3, 1792, and then consisted of four members--John Hill, Moses Yale, Daniel Hosford, Jr. and Joseph Simonds. The members assembled at the home of Daniel Hosford, Jr., and passed the following resolutions:

1st. That John Hill serve as moderator.

2nd. That D. Hosford, Jr., serve as clerk.

3rd. That the church will give Daniel O. Gillette an invitation to both the pastoral oversight and care of the church.

Mr. Gillette accepted the call and remained pastor until 1799.

At a town meeting held July 3, 1791, it was voted "to settle Rev. Daniel O. Gillette at 90 pounds a year, to be paid in beef, wheat, and pork, and the payments to be made Christmas Day." A Merry Christmas for the Rev. Mr. Gillette.

It seems strange, looking back, but in 1798 Asabel Strong, town clerk, on "application made by a sufficient number of the inhabitants as required by law," called a town meeting for the "first Monday in March next at the school house near Major Hezekiah Barnes' at nine o'clock in the forenoon, to see if the town will vote a

120

Chittenden fs. Charlotte December 7th 1804

I do not agree with a Major part of this Town
in religious opinion
Wait Martin

Rec'd for record and recorded the original this
10th December 1804. — Jeremiah Barton Town Cl

This is to Certify I Moses Allen do not agree
in Religious Sentiment with the Majority in
this Town. — Moses Allen
Dated Charlotte 10th December 1804.

Rec'd for record and recorded the original this
10th Day December 1804. Jeremiah Barton Town Clk

Charlotte December 8th 1804. —
I declair myself not to belong to the Society
now formed in this Town. — Moses Godwin

Rec'd for record and recorded the original this
10th December 1804. — Jeremiah Barton Town Clerk

Chittenden fs. Charlotte 8th December 1804.
This is to Certify that I do not agree with
a Major part of the Inhabitants in religious
opinion in this Town. — Hill Chandler

Rec'd for record and recorded the original the
10th December 1804. — Jeremiah Barton Town

State of Vermont Chittenden County fs. Be it remembered that at
Charlotte in the County aforesaid on this 9th day of May A.D. 1813
Jonathan Breakenridge Jun'r of Charlotte afores'd and Mary Willson
of the same place were duly joined in marriage. By me
Zadock Wheeler Jus. Peace

Recorded March 1814 —
Attest Zadock Wheeler Town Clk

---

*Some of the certificates from those who disagreed with the religious beliefs of the town.
Higbee is right: there are many in the early town records. Charlotte has its earliest
records complete. Like the town's original charter, the earliest record books have been
deacidified, restored and rebound.*

tax to pay Rev. Daniel O. Gillette his salary for the present year." The meeting voted to raise such a tax and then quickly adjourned.

But it is evident things were not running smoothly about these days, for we find a town meeting called for June 17, 1799, at the same school house, "to see if the town can agree with said Mr. Gillette on terms of discontinuation between the town of Charlotte and the said Mr. Gillette's ministry in said town."

At this meeting, in regard to a "discontinuation," Hezekiah Barnes was moderator. The following committee was appointed to confer with Mr. Gillette: Abel Newell, David Hubbell, William Williams, Lyman Hurlbut, William Powell. The meeting adjourned for an hour so the committee could consult. After report of the committee, it was voted to adjourn to June 19. On June 19, 1799, the town meeting was called to order at two o'clock in the afternoon, and the committee made report "that Mr. Gillette has agreed to refund to the town two hundred pounds in demands against the inhabitants of the Town of Charlotte in due bills and notes." The town accepted the committee's report, and the committee was continued "to wait on Mr. Gillette and receive the obligations and deliver them over to the selectmen." It was also voted "that the Rev. Daniel O. Gillette be dismissed from his pastoral relations to the church and from his ministerial labors in the town of Charlotte upon his complying with the proposals which he has made to the town." Thus the "discontinuation" became operative.

From 1799 to 1807, the church had no pastor, and the membership was reduced to eleven, but in 1807 a revival occurred and the church had an addition of forty members, and Reverend Truman Baldwin was installed pastor, continuing until 1815. In 1816, Reverend Doctor Austin, president of the Vermont University, supplied the pulpit. In October 1817, Reverend Calvin Yale became pastor, and remained until 1833. During the winter of 1833-34, Reverend F. B. Reed occupied the pulpit. Reverend William Eaton was installed in September 1834, and dismissed in 1837. After him came Reverend E. W. Goodman, who remained until October 1845. The pastorship was held by Reverend Joel H. Bingham from October 1846 to November 1851. In December 21, 1851, Reverend C. M. Seaton commenced his pastorate, and continued it until January 1863. Reverend Charles W. Clark was pastor until 1871; Reverend C. C. Torry until 1878; then Reverend H. B. Putnam, Reverend A. W. Wild, and the present pastor, Reverend Hervey Gulick. It will be seen that this church has already passed its century by five years.

As early as 1789 the people were wrestling with the question where to build the meeting house, and on March 17 of that year at a town meeting held in the house of Hezekiah Barnes, a committee of six was appointed to "set a stake for a meeting house." The committee consisted of Charles Grant, Daniel Hosford, Ebenezer Hovey, Col. Barnes, Isaac Cogswell, and David Hubbell. The committee was empowered to "pur-

The Congregational Church was built in 1848 near the site of the first one which burned the same year. This early 1900's postcard shows the horse sheds and the much smaller vestry. The field between church and parsonage was used for growing hay and during the Civil War by militia as a shooting range. Floor joists in the Memorial Museum have scorched areas, an indication they may have been recycled from elsewhere and perhaps came from that first church building. Charlotte Memorial Museum.

chase five acres of land for that purpose." It wasn't that simple.

It seems the committee had trouble in finding where to "set the stake" or it wouldn't stay "set," for at a regular town meeting in April 1790, it was voted to "pass by the building of a meeting house for the present." At this meeting in April it was voted "to have the committee put the town to no expense to hire a minister before Rev. Mr. Newell comes to town." It seems that in July of the previous year it was voted to "hire Rev. Mr. Read to the 1st of September," and

this meeting, April 19, 1790, reversed the action of the town. At a regular meeting held September 7, 1790, the committee reported that "Rev. Mr. Newell will take twenty shilling per Sabbath," and Mr. Newell was hired until the next March.

In April 1791 a town meeting was held, in which it was voted "that a committee procure 10,000 feet of white pine boards, 8,000 feet of short pine shingles, and 150 feet of window frame stuff, and that the above stuff be delivered at or near the sign post in this town."

Town meetings continue in New England. The 1987 Charlotte meeting was the last in the town hall which opened in 1939. Top L.: Town clerk Hazel Prindle and assistant Margaret Therrien checked voters at the ballot boxes. Top R.: Voter Nancy Menard made a point during a discussion of town business. Bottom L.: Don Ross, Eugene Shlatz and Selectman Robert Mack during a break. Bottom R.: The traditional lunch was served by Virginia Armell, Ethel Atkins and Wilma Preston, maintenance chief Don Armell in the background. Photos by Carolyn Bates. Courtesy of Peter Bergh.

Where the "sign post" stood is perhaps not entirely clear, but it has been pretty authentically stated that the materials for this "meeting house" were moved three times before being fashioned into a building. It was first laid down on the corner south of Mrs. Wilbur Foote's,[33] then taken to the Four Corners, and finally to about where the Congregational church now stands. In an early day the dividing political line between "East and West" was sharply drawn, and it may be these things crept into "meeting house" matters to a limited degree.

On January 31, 1805, at a town meeting called for that purpose (Hezekiah Barnes, moderator, and Jeremiah Barton, town clerk), it was voted "to form into an ecclesiastical Congregational Society in said town, by a number of twenty-seven legal voters, who voted in the affirmative, and negatived by none." The following society officers were elected: clerk, Zadock Wheeler; treasurer, William Niles; assessors committee, Samuel Rich, Hezekiah Barnes, James Hill; collector, Zenas Clark; society committee, Nathaniel Newell, John Hills, James Hill.

It should never be forgotten that these sturdy men of former generations, our forefathers, were solicitous for us as well as themselves. Alongside of their interest in the church was their careful oversight of the common schools, and hardly a town meeting was warned but contained some reference to perfecting school district organizations. They were solicitous to leave us a road well lined out to good morals and good education. Their work was faithfully done, and as we walk among their graves it should be with increasing reverence.

The New England town meeting should never be eliminated from our scheme of government. In every state, each town is a little republic, governing itself, but always in conformity to general law and with the good of the state constantly in view. The town meeting is an educator. It "learned" us how to govern ourselves. In it we learn the majority must rule. By it we learn that men, trusted by the people, stand or fail, as they are competent or incompetent, honest or dishonest. In it we learn the lessons of economy by voting our own taxes; and through it we have made New England a synonym for rugged uprightness and unflinching patriotism.

The town hall which replaced the brick 1850 building in 1939 and was last used in 1987. It is now the central school library. From a half-tone plate. Charlotte Mem. Museum.

IX

The War of 1812, Indians, and
Myths about Treasures

29 January 1897

Among the English land transfers, as before spoken of, is the deed from Ethan Allen to Charles McNeil, embracing land now owned by James B. McNeil, a son of Charles McNeil and Julia A. Spear. The farm owned by Julia A. Spear is the one on which was located the famous Ferry, and the old wharf is still in use for occasional landing of canal boats in the shipment of apples, potatoes, etc., to the city markets. During the War of 1812 the British fleet in passing at this point,

Barrelling apples at the Reuben Parker farm in Ferrisburgh circa 1900. Front L. to R.: Reuben Parker, Bert Parker; Harvey C. Martin, grandfather of Gertrude Chioffi. Courtesy of Gertrude Willard Chioffi.

fired on a lot of men, women, and children assembled in the way of curiosity on the bank of the lake, fortunately with no fatal result. The company threw themselves flat upon the ground at the command of Captain Charles McNeil, the grape shot hurtling over their heads instead of through them. It turned out that the British commander was more filled with rum than patriotism for King George in this effort to massacre women and children.

At all events no one was hurt; but Captain McNeil afterwards found a round shot in his meadows that served for years as a weight to close a garden gate; probably the British government contributed this much to the convenience of Charlotters.[34]

A sand and gravel beach on the south side of the bay was a favorite camping ground for several Indian hunters and fishermen who frequented these shores forty-odd years ago, and their expertness in handling their birch canoes could hardly be excelled, if indeed equaled, by the boatmen of modern times. These Indians were probably of the St. Regis tribe, as they came from Canada way. They were, doubtless, fathers and grand-

Indian artifacts from the Charlotte Memorial Museum. Points and tools are from Harold Root's collection. Though such finds are not as common as when the plowman walked behind his plough, evidence of Indian civilization is still to be found. The last Abenaki Indians in town, the Obomsawin family, lived at Thompson's Point as caretakers. They wove baskets with the native grasses and William Obomswain made the chair. Some baskets are gifts of Robert and Madge Hawley, the chair is a gift of William Mott Hall.

fathers of those who regularly petition the legislature for compensation for a tract of land along the lake in Franklin, Chittenden, and Addison Counties that they claim was obtained through some fraudulent hocus-pocus of the pale-face. At each session of the legislature this or a similar petition is solemnly presented, generally by request according to the journal, and is with equal solemnity referred to the committee on claims.[35]

About thirty-five years ago a small band of Canadian Indians camped near the "Cove"[36] for a while, trapping and basket-making. The late John G. Thorp, who had gained their good will by some kindness, visited their camp accompanied by William Castle, a lad and descendant of the Williams family carried into captivity in the Deerfield Massacre.[37] Mr. Thorp gave the Indians to understand by words and signs that this boy was a descendant of the "Deerfield Williamses."

At the mention of these names two of the old Indians became much interested and examined the boy closely,

exchanging comments as they carefully scanned the lad's features. It was
evident their keen senses detected
some family resemblance, the details
of which may have been impressed
upon their minds by tradition only.
Mr. Castle readily recalls the close
scrutiny and subdued excitement his
boyish face occasioned when he met
these dwellers in tents.

There is no doubt the fine fishing
along the lake and good trapping
grounds in the cove and along the
brooks and Lewis Creek made this a
favorite camping ground for Indian
tribes in an early day. There are
several acres of meadowland along the
brook on the writer's farm, where it is
no unusual thing to plow up flint ar-
rowheads, and it has been said the Indians had a clearing and a cornfield at
this point. The soil is a rich loam,
clear of stones, easy to till, and was,
doubtless, selected on that account.
The Indian brave, having tender
regard for his "dusky mate," of course
sought an easy place for her to dig up
the soil and hoe the corn, while he
was looking up a scalp or two to hang
on a pole in front of his wigwam. It
was as fashionable then to decorate
with scalps, bear claws, wolves' teeth,
and porcupine quills, as now to sport
bangs, frizzes, "bussles," and the
"scholarly" eyeglasses, and to cover
hats and bonnets with entire or
despoiled song birds. It is questionable
if the history of the Indian race from

Charles McNeile of Ethan Allen Esqr

Know all men by these presents that I Ethan Allen of Bennington in the County of Bennington and State of Vermont Esqr for the consideration of one hundred and fifty pounds lawful money already received to my full satisfaction of Charles McNeile of Litchfield in the County of Litchfield and State of Connecticut the receipt whereof I do hereby acknowledge Do therefore give grant bargain sell alien and forever quitclaim unto him the said Charles McNeile and to his heirs and assigns for Ever all my right title interest property and Demand of in and to two certain lots of Land in the Township of Charlotte one of said lots or tracts of Land is No 122 and originally contained by Estimation two hundred acres be the same more or less a part of the north side thereof I have already deeded to John McNeile and the other lot or tract of land is No 119 and originally contained by Estimation one hundred acres be the same more or less the northerly part I have also deeded to John McNeile that is to say I have deeded to him the said John McNeils one hundred acres or the Northerly parts of those lots reference to the Description in his Deed being had and the remainder of the Lands contained in the said lots of land No Numbers 122 and 119 be it more or less is included in this deed to Charles McNeile the Names of the original grantees were John Ferguson and Josiah Bull and the Township was granted by the former Government of New Hampshire — To have and to hold the said Bargained and quitclaimed premises with the privileges and appurtenances thereof unto him the said Charles McNeile and to his heirs and assigns to his and their own proper use benefit and behoof for Ever so that I Neither my self my heirs or assigns nor John Bronson or Josiah Bull their heirs or assigns or any person or persons whomsoever claiming from by or under me or the said Original grantees shall ever hereafter have any lawful right or legal title to the said released premises but by these presents shall be wholly excluded and Debarred in witness whereof I have hereunto set my hand and seal this 10th day of September 1783 Signed sealed and Delivered in presence of

Moses Robinson
Noah Sawnlette

Ethan Allen & seal

Deed from Ethan Allen to Charles McNeil for portions of original lots numbered 122 and 119 filed on September 10, 1783. From the Charlotte town records.

Columbus down shows many instances in which they sacrificed the innocent songbird to feminine taste in dress. It seems left to the civilized and enlightened women of this age to outdo the barbarian.

Probably Captain Kidd never troubled himself to pole his way through the Champlain Canal to bury his ill-gotten gains in Charlotte, but we have our little tradition of buried treasure just the same. It entertained the children to hear how a very, very old squaw piloted some of her tribe to the foot of an ancient pine tree standing in "Mud Hollow," and that after their departure a square hole was found, out of which the credulous assumed a box of money had been taken. One can hardly be called upon at this late day to state accurately the amount of money abstracted, and it may be that no one ever saw the "square hole," but it is well authenticated that such a legend existed, whether the money ever did or not.[38]

Speaking of money recalls an instance, stated by an old resident, in which an individual emptied his pockets in great haste, throwing silver by the handful into and over a stone wall on the west side of the old stage road,

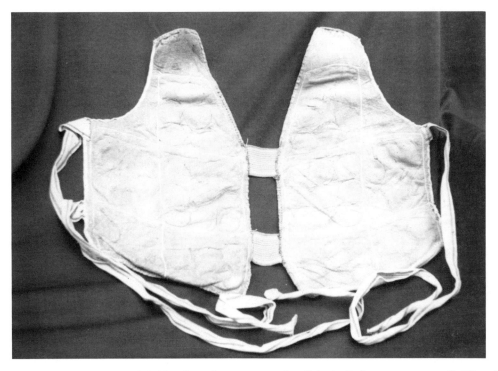

Vest used by one successful Charlotte "treasure seeker." A. A. Byington went to California in 1853, worked hard and saved his money. He brought back gold pieces in this suede vest made for the job. The imprint of the large gold pieces can be seen on the lining. With the money he bought the original Byington farm on Route 7. Donated by Anna and Ethel Byington. Charlotte Memorial Museum.

a little south of J. B. Williams'. The occasion for this extraordinary liberality was ascertained to be an officer of the law, some distance in the rear, who was making earnest efforts to pat the gentleman affectionately on the shoulder. The counterfeiter, for such he proved to be, was too speedy, however, and made his escape after casting his seed by the wayside.

During the War of 1812, a load of silver to pay the troops on the northern frontiers, commencing north on the stage road and escorted by the usual guard of soldiers, stopped for the night at the tavern kept by Jeremiah Barton where the writer now lives. The money was in kegs, and a portion, if not the whole of it, was unloaded and rolled into the bar room for safe keeping.

It was only a few years ago that Mr. Hathaway, living on the lakeshore north of the Meech Bay, found a number of gold sovereigns that had evidently been recently washed out of the bank. It is supposed the money was secreted there in an early day, probably about the time a party of British and Indians were defeated in their locally famous attack on the Shelburne block house.

Older residents recall how excited some of their neighbors became over the supposed finding, or at least the eager pursuit of a great treasure hid in a cave somewhere in the line of mountain towns east of us. Rocks were blasted and dirt dug to amazing extent, but the "treasure" failed to materialize. It is a commentary on human nature that many an individual who is too lazy to chop an armful of wood ten minutes ahead of its immediate use will toil early and late, even raise a blister, in quest of "treasure" hid under stump or tree.

Round shot, souvenirs of the War of 1812. The larger one is said to be the gate weight from the McNeil property and the one that Higbee owned. A modern treasure--a dime-- indicates their size. Charlotte Memorial Museum Collection.

X

The Allens, First Town Meetings and
the Newell-Barnes Rivalry

5 February 1897

The lover of nature, the poetic soul of some "Leather-Stocking," as, a century ago, he swept the horizon from the summit of Mount Philo, must have felt an expansion, a going-forth of himself. The solemn stillness of the endless forest, the magnificence of the rugged mountain chains east of him and west of him, the mile on mile of the glorious Champlain are all around. Perhaps the early sunrise, lighting up the green of those far-away mountains, or the golden sunset paint a picture of lake and wood and plain more vividly beautiful than the cunningest hand has ever transferred to canvas.

East, north, west, everywhere the boundless woods; perhaps the curling smoke of a wigwam, the camp fire of some hardy adventurer like himself, nothing else to denote that anything human but himself existed. I hazard the assertion that this has been seen and felt, that he who could not write his name, perhaps could not read a single line, who lived a simple, un-lettered hunter, and whose place of burial no one knows, has looked abroad from these very rocks and felt this expansion of soul.

But the trouble is, it would never do to keep so much good soil growing nothing but trees; so at it went the axe-man and the mill-man and the charcoal-man and the pearlash-man. Through these works Charlotte and Ferrisburgh and adjoining towns soon developed an agricultural prominence so pronounced that New Hampshire wanted some of us and New York hankered after us, and we, that is, Vermont, became of such importance that we "stood off" the entire party and ran business for ourselves for a considerable period of time.

In order to do this, the Green Mountain boys, supported and en-couraged always by the Green Mountain girls, formed a combination under the leadership of one Ethan Al-len, who came later to be quite well known by several sheriffs and deputy sheriffs from New York.

Of course, Dorset and Sunderland and Bennington and numerous other towns in the southern part of the State were mainly the theaters of war, and probably the "seal" was used more frequently in those sections.[39] But it is safe to maintain that the dwellers in either Charlotte or Ferrisburgh at that time were ardent patriots and would have whacked a New Yorker over the head with a blue beech gad instanter[40], had he manifested an intention of jumping their claim.

There used to be several Allens in Charlotte, and there is a discharge of a mortgage on the margin of one of our earliest records in the handwriting of Ira Allen, so long associated in diplomatic matters with Governor Thomas Chittenden.[41] The Allen family are numerous in Ferrisburgh and other Addison County towns and the given names Ethan and Ira are still largely preserved.

There is a peculiarity about the early grants of several towns in this vicinity, that the grantees are somewhat identical; and it is possible the names of some of the grantees were more fictitious than real. It is indeed possible that the spirit of speculation, to a certain degree, permeated the Puritan as well as his descendant, and the same name may have figured in several places with no detriment to the signature of his worthiness, Benning Wentworth who seemed, as Governor of the Province of New Hampshire, to represent his Majesty, King George the Third.

One thing is certain, this same Benning Wentworth was in no sense left out in the cold, as each of the newly-granted towns had some five hundred acres or so reserved as the "Governor's right," and it is entirely supposable that the "Governor" received substantial benefit from the same, as such faithful officials should. The "Governor's lot" of about five hundred acres lies in the southwest corner of Charlotte, and was bid off years ago for taxes by George Thorp.

It seems these original grantees were no more prompt in tax paying than their sons and daughters, for the early records are full of "tax sales" in which the collector at "public vendue" is continually disposing of their grants to satisfy the demands of an exacting public. If the "Governor" had only paid his taxes promptly, he could have saved for his heirs and executors the "Cove" and its surroundings, being one of the best places to shoot muskrats and pickerel in this vicinity.

The original grantees of Charlotte, numbering seventy, held their first meeting at the house of Daniel Merritt, on the Oblong, Dutchess County, New York, July 29, 1762. This meeting was called under charter regulations by Benjamin Ferris and only a little routine business was done. The proprietors' meeting held May 9, 1763, also at the house of Daniel Merritt, in Dutchess County, New York, voted Benjamin Ferris Jr., proprietors' clerk.[42] It was voted to lay out two hundred acres in each share, and that Benjamin Ferris, Jr., be paid 18 shillings per day for surveying and plotting the same. John McCune, Asahel Hitchcock, Zeronah Ferris, and John Phillips were voted ten shillings a day as assistants.

At this meeting it was voted to "lay out four rights," one for the "incorporated society," one for the "glebe for the Church of England,"[43] one for the "first settled minister," and one for "free schools." It was voted that lots be drawn for town rights. David Ferris and Reuben Southgate drew the lots, and a record of them was kept by John Connor. In the first division Lot No.

A descendant of George Thorp, Susie Tremblay and her niece, Judy Morse in the private cemetery at Thorp Cove. Harland Thorp left the farm after his wife and two younger children died of smallpox in 1895. Because of the quarantine he had to bury them there. Photo taken in 1989.

81 was for the Church of England; No. 75 for the free schools; No. 32 for the incorporated society;[44] No. 51 for the first settled minister. A town plot was also reserved, located on what is now known as "Guinea;"[45] but our forefathers not being up to the West in incubating "cities," the land in question was subsequently divided into 2, 3, or 4 acre lots, one for each proprietor, and reverted to the commonplace business of general farming.

In 1785, Daniel Hosford, also a surveyor, became proprietors' clerk. Charlotte was then in Rutland County. Up to this time the proprietors held their meetings mainly in Dutchess County, New York; but at a meeting held in Bennington, March 29, 1785, it was voted to adjourn to the first Wednesday of July at the house of Moses Yale, in Charlotte. At this meeting in Bennington, held at the house of Jonathan Robinson, it was voted to apportion the remaining lands in a second division of 145 half-acres each, among the seventy original proprietors.

According to the records, the adjourned meeting at Bennington was convened at the house of Moses Yale. He was the great-grandfather of our

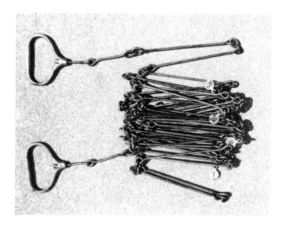

A Gunter chain such as was used by Benjamin Ferris, Jr. and Daniel Hosford in their surveying of Charlotte. The chain has 100 links and is 66 feet (4 rods) long. The brass markers indicate one-rod sections. Charlotte Memorial Museum Collection.

William Lyman Yale and his sisters, the grandchildren of Moses Yale.

First Settlers coming to Vermont. From "Barber's History and Antiquities of the Northern States," by John Warner Barber. 1842.

The second division of lots in the town in a composite map with the first lotting out to the original proprietors. Drawn by Frank Thornton from information in the town records.

67

townsman, William S. Yale, and to him belongs the distinction of furnishing the place for the first town meeting. Moses Yale came from Connecticut as did many of our earliest settlers. He had come some time in March, 1785, on the ice from Whitehall, and it was a cold day when he drove off Lake Champlain and looked around for a place to locate his log cabin. He built on the point of land now occupied by Frank K. Converse. It was here on July 6, 1785, our forefathers held their first town meeting. This was over one hundred years ago, and here and there a "settler" had made an opening in the woods.

Moses Pierson was chosen moderator; Daniel Hosford, clerk. This first meeting, without further business, adjourned to July 21, at the same place, when it was voted to accept the report of the committee on the second division of land, and to raise a tax of one pound and four shillings on each proprietor's right to pay for surveying and lotting out the same. At this meeting, John McNeil was elected treasurer.

In the second division, lot 11 fell to the incorporated society; No. 1, glebe for the Church of England; No. 3, the first settled minister; No. 38, for free schools. In 1785 Ira Allen, then of Sunderland, deeded two hundred acres of land in Charlotte to Abel Newell of Litchfield, Connecticut. This is probably the commencement of the Newell holdings here. Abel Newell subsequently removed to Charlotte, and others of the same name long exercised a commanding influence in church and town affairs.

Indeed, at one time the Newells owned about half the town. It is said that Nathaniel Newell and Hezekiah Barnes were political rivals, and it was catch as catch can between them year after year. Occasionally, somebody else would slip up to Montpelier as representative, but it was more frequently either "Nat" Newell or Gen. Barnes. The former being rather the more agile of the two distanced his competitors, and I think has the credit of more Assembly elections than any other in the history of the town. He is said to have been a very able man.[46]

Lakeview Seminary, built in 1881 by public subscription to serve as a public school. John Dewey was its first principal. Used as a school until 1949, it is now a private home. Photo taken in 1979.

XI

Sectarianism, the Battle of Plattsburgh, Haying and Canadian Workmen, Wheat, Rye and "Indian"

19 February 1897

It is a noticeable fact that theological leanings have been plainly marked since the earliest history of this and adjoining towns. Since 1805, when a town meeting was called in Charlotte for the purpose of forming an "Ecclesiastical Congregational Society," Congregationalism has been largely dominant.

In Ferrisburgh, the Methodist Episcopal church seemed more nearly to meet the minds of the people. In an earlier time Shelburne had a strong Episcopal society and it has today one of the prettiest of churches with an active membership. The Methodists of Shelburne predominated and have a fine stone church, built some twenty or twenty-five years ago.

In 1847 a Methodist church was erected at the "Four Corners" and regular service was held here for a series of years. It is a sacred place to many of our people whose fathers and mothers worshipped there. The Breakenridge family, who were strongly attached to this church and were among its pillars, has no one of the name now remaining in town.[47]

One of the latest, if not the last of its regular pastors, was Reverend B. D. Ames; and there are many, the writer among the rest, who pleasantly recall their school days in the old "Seminary" taught by Mrs. Ames who possessed the rare faculty of inspiring her scholars with a love of study and an earnest enthusiasm for good things. It may not be out of place just here to emphasize the importance of the teacher's vocation, and point out how strong is that influence on the after life of the pupil. The common schools are attended by those whose minds are the more readily impressed for good or ill. Mrs. Ames possessed enthusiasm and could inspire it in others. She was a born teacher and "her works do follow her."

This is no place for discussions on theology, but it may not be improper to recall the experiences of our forefathers who sat through two long sermons a day in a building without a fire save a few coals in the "foot-stove," generally reserved for the mother and grandmother. There were the old box pews, with the back coming just about

The original Seminary Building on South Greenbush Rd. at the Four Corners, built in 1836. It served as a Female Seminary then a Methodist School until 1880 when it burned. Charlotte Memorial Museum Collection.

THE BOY VOLUNTEER.

An Old Man's Story of the Battle of Lake Champlain—A Young Artillerist's Service.

[Special Correspondence of The Boston Globe.]

MARLBORO, N. H., May 28.—Colonel Cyrus Frost of this town is a gentleman of nearly four score years. He is an old military commander; has represented Marlboro and his native town, Dublin, in the State Legislature, and held other important offices.

"History fails to give any account of who fired the first shot at the battle of Lake Champlain fought at Plattsburg, September 11, 1814," said he to THE GLOBE correspondent. "It was fired by a young man calling himself the Volunteer. I will give you the story as it was told to me by John Nutting, one of the participants in the battle."

"At the time the British sent word to the Americans that they were coming to take tea with them our best war vessels were at Whitehall, Commodore McDonough in command. Our squadron numbered eighty-six guns and was composed of the Saratoga, of twenty-six guns, the Eagle of twenty, the Ticonderoga of seventeen, the Preble of seven and ten galleys. The Ticonderoga was the flagship. As the fleet sailed along a youth of dark complexion, 19 or 20 years old, stood on a sand bar and hailed the Ticonderoga, asking to be taken on board.

" 'You?' demanded the commodore.
" 'Yes, me.'
" 'What do you want?'
" 'To enlist.'
" 'What can you do?'
" 'A little of everything.'
" 'Well, come aboard and we will try you.'
"The youth was soon on deck.
" 'Now, then,' said McDonough, 'let's see you manoeuvre that gun,' and as he spoke he pointed to the largest gun of the Ticonderoga.

"The stranger quickly executed all the gun manoeuvres, showing himself a perfect master of the art. 'You are accepted,' exclaimed the commodore, "and may take charge of that gun. Who are you?'

" 'No matter; call me the Volunteer.'
" 'The Volunteer?'
" 'Yes.'

"A short sail brought the fleet to Plattsburg, where the American army was stationed. Here it anchored, remaining some two days. When word was received that the British were advancing, McDonough sailed down the lake to meet the hostile fleet. The British fleet was commanded by Captain Downie, and was composed of the Confiance, a frigate of thirty-nine guns, a brig of sixteen, two sloops of eleven, and several galleys, mounting in all ninety-five guns. Captain Downie was aboard the Confiance, which grounded on the sand bar, being much exposed to the American guns. Commodore McDonough had given orders that no one should fire until he gave the word.

"The Volunteer heard the commodore's order, but immediately sighted his gun and fired at the Confiance. The shot carried away the mast, killing Captain Downie, and the next minute the guns on both sides were brought into play, the Americans thinking they had been ordered to commence action. The British fought desperately in spite of their loss. The guns of the Ticonderoga, with the exception of the one in charge of the Volunteer, were dismounted, or had become unmanageable, and the British cheered at the advantage they had gained. Suddenly a cock among some fowls on the Ticonderoga flew to the top of his coop and crowed. It was heard above the din of battle, and, taking it as a good omen, the Americans fought with renewed vigor, soon turning the tide of the battle. The Confiance was soon compelled to surrender, the rest of the fleet, of course, following her example. The American loss was fifty-two killed and fifty-eight wounded, while the British loss was eighty-four killed and 110 wounded.

"When the American fleet arrived at Sackett's Harbor the Volunteer left, refusing to take any part of the prize money. He was never heard of again, and it was never learned who he was."

"The Boy Volunteer," a newspaper clipping from a scrapbook with no date given, but it was probably after 1883. Truth or folklore? Charlotte Memorial Museum Collection.

the middle of a small boy's head--a sharp-eyed beadle ready to poke a young fellow with a pole if he whispered, or punch him twice if he fell asleep under the various divisions of the pastor's learned discourse.

It seemed to the small boy that the best time for sermonizing was in the summer when it wasn't so cold, and the beadle more likely to fall in the doze himself, forgetting all about his prodding pole. But when the summer came and the woods about the meeting house were full of song birds and chipping squirrels; or later, as the ripened nuts clattered among the dry leaves, the frost grapes hung so temptingly in the branches, and garrulous blue jays said all manner of things to each other; then the boy wished they

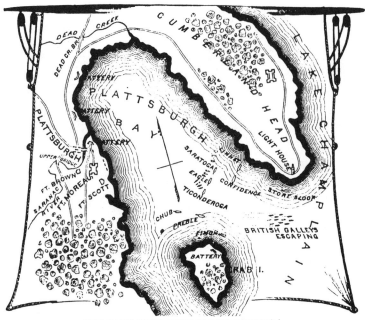

PLAN OF THE NAVAL ACTION ON LAKE CHAMPLAIN.[1]

The Battle of Plattsburgh. Plan of the action on Lake Champlain. Medal awarded to Thomas MacDonough from "The Pictorial Field-Book of The War of 1812" by Benjamin J. Lossing, New York. 1869. Courtesy of the Lake Champlain Maritime Museum, Basin Harbor, Vt.

would confine preaching long sermons to the winter season when he had less to do.

But the boy lived through it all; and, anon, came to Sunday School with a little modern thought and modern warmth and modern books and papers. An old man today, he recalls the years that slipped by, one by one, and the sternness of the old times seems to him in exact harmony with the rugged nature of the hearts that loved him.

In 1814, the day of the Battle of Plattsburgh, Mount Philo was a lively place. A company had been raised in Charlotte, or partially raised here; teams had been pressed into service, I think by General Strong of Vergennes. All minds were turned northward and all ears were listening eagerly to the sullen boom that meant so much; for the trained soldiers of Wellington, fresh from Waterloo and the overthrow of Napoleon, were pitted against the armed peasantry of America.

From Mount Philo, some thirty years before, the fleet of Arnold had been seen hurrying southward, after the defeat at Valcour, and the British flag cast an ominous shadow on Lake Champlain as it followed in pursuit.

Was this to be repeated? The mountain was crowded with people straining the eyes northward to catch the first glimpse of disaster and ruin. Along the lake rolled the echoes of cannon, meaning fire and pillage and liberty overthrown, or a country saved, a nation free.

Who should be the first to catch a glimpse of flying ships, of a dismayed and vanquished soldiery? Revolutions do not go backward. Mount Philo has never yet since Arnold's day seen a beaten American vessel hurrying southward. Mt. Philo has looked down on no hostile army since Burgoyne, baffled, bewildered, surrounded, dropped his sword point.

The day waned; the thunder far to northward ceased. The people could do no more than go to their homes. But the stars and crimson stripes hung at the masthead in Plattsburgh Bay.[48] The plowman-warrior, the hunter leaving his wild game to take his place in the ranks, had met the proudest troops of the proudest nation on earth and had beaten them. But what else could the people have expected who stood on Mount Philo that day? How in the world could the English from England have thought for a moment they could come over and whip the English in America? It was one of England's mightiest who exclaimed, "If I were an American, as I am an Englishman, I would never lay down my arms--never! never!"

Sixty years ago there was no railroad line through these lake towns. There were no telegraphs. All heavy freighting to and from markets was done by boats. Cities and places along the Hudson were known as "down country." Albany and Troy were headquarters for most of our merchandise, and a fleet of canal boats tied up for winter in the slips of New York or in favorable localities further north, waiting for the spring trade that always accompanied the spring freshets.

There were no mowing machines, twine binders, self-dumping horse rakes, sulkey plows. The young farmer of today has little conception of the way work was done at that time.

Every acre of grass was cut with a scythe whose propelling power was the strong muscles of the man who swung it. And he must come up to "two acres a day," or fail to receive the seventy-five cents to a dollar that compensated him from "sun to sun."

The old way.

Haying in the old time.

Field after field of grain was harvested with the sickle until some unquiet genius invented the grain cradle, injecting a new element into the service of agriculture. Everything in field and meadow, in the line of gathering the crop, was done with the hand rake. The lines of men and boys, often girls and women too, marched up and down in haying time, rolling up long lines of fragrancy--the boys and weaker ones

ahead, the stout of limb bringing up the rear to "closeup" the windrows. In time the same or some other genius, equally as unquiet, conceived the idea of doing it by horse power.

And so the dump rake came first; about eight feet long, ten feet of rope running from each end attached to the propelling power, the horse. When the windrow was reached, the engineer stopped the horse, pulled the rake back a little, threw it over the windrow, and away again, to be repeated in the next twenty to fifty feet, according to the "yield."

Then came the "revolver"--not the dangerous implement of Colt and Smith & Wesson fame, but something that has done far more for humanity though perhaps its inventor may not be remembered beyond the little neighborhood in which he lived. Here was business. The rake dumped itself, or "revolved" by raising up a little on the handles, setting the end of the teeth in the ground by means of a spring. No stopping at windrows, but a constant round of triumphal marching and piling up of hay. Only now and then, or sometimes more often on rough ground, the teeth would do a little catching of their own, revolutionizing matters out of the regular.

Perhaps you ran into an anthill, unexpected-like, and before the fly-tormented horse came to a standstill, out came a tooth or two with a snap like a pistol. Sometimes the man at the handles got a little too fast-gaited, hitting his toes on the end of the teeth, but generally found it out in season to keep from running over the concern.

In an early day the hill towns east of us afforded extra and excellent help

Revolving hay-rake as pictured in 1846.

in haying, but later on they had work of their own and we came to depend on Canada for a supply. Haying was not done as early in the season then as now, and from the first to the middle of July the Canadian workmen rattled by in their old two-wheeled carts, happy as kings, all talking at a time and every one smoking the strongest kind of pig-tail, home grown tobacco, in a pipe black as the ace of spades and not two inches longer than the end of his nose. The price used to be a dollar a day, and it was an extra hand who got more. It was nothing unusual to count twenty of these carts in a string, and generally each cart had two passengers.

The tough little Canada ponies were in a perpetual trot, and the only springs the cart riders seemed to get was an occasional jump upward from an inch board running across the box. Not one in ten could talk English, and if the official interpreter failed to be on hand, it was the quaint combine of jargon, pantomime, and mutual guess work that consummated a trade. The fine meadows in Addison County were usually their objective, and, as the same men were employed year after year, it was difficult to stop most of the old hands this side of Addison, Bridport or Shoreham.

They were tough as whit-leather[49], and calculated to earn their money. Their return, with a season's pay in the little round leather wallets, was accompanied with song and cheer; and many a night dweller on the main road listened to songs that were utterly unintelligible to those not adept in the patois of the Canadians.

Above: Threshing wheat at the Kingsland farm circa 1900, a scene familiar to Higbee. Below: The kitchen/dining room fireplace at Rokeby, such as pioneer mother Van Vliet used for making those buckwheat cakes. Courtesy of the Wheeler/Kingsland Collection.

Threshing was done by hand, and the "dull thunder of alternate flails" occasioned no surprise in the neighborhoods. The first horse power machine that appeared in these parts was a sweep power[50]; and the grain, taken out of the straw, was shoveled into a fanning mill run by a belt from the main cylinder to be cleaned.

Perhaps the boys and possibly a good portion of the men of 1897 have little idea of what a "Hand fan" was. Imagine a circle some four feet across --say an immense cheese box, for example. Put on a couple of handles, one on each side, so a man can hold the box in front of him. Now cut the front side or the side opposite the man square off about one third the way back. Your box, with its circular sides, is the old hand fan. The separator filled this box with a bushel or two of grain in the chaff, stood with his back to the wind, generally at an open barn door, and by deft tosses and shakes, and wriggles and twists and dodges caught the grain in the fan, the chaff floating off into the viewless air. It took a smart man a long while to "clean up" a small pile of grain, but that's the way they did it, until somebody electrified the world with the fanning mill.

It is said when the first fanning mill appeared, the fore-fathers would congregate for miles around to see it work. That and the grain cradle came nearly together, and they revolutionized farming methods as effectively in their day as the steam thresher and twine binder in this.

There was a time when the chinch bug practically precluded the growing of wheat, its place being taken by corn, rye and buckwheat. Wheat bread was a rarity, but "rye and Indian" made pretty fair living preceded, of course, by a healthy appetite. Buckwheat pancakes cut no small figure in daily life, cooked on a long-handled frying pan over the coals in the wide-mouthed fireplace. One good mother, who was an adept at turning them with a twist

Buckwheat in the shock.

A threshing device as pictured in 1845 (Warren's horse-power and thresher).

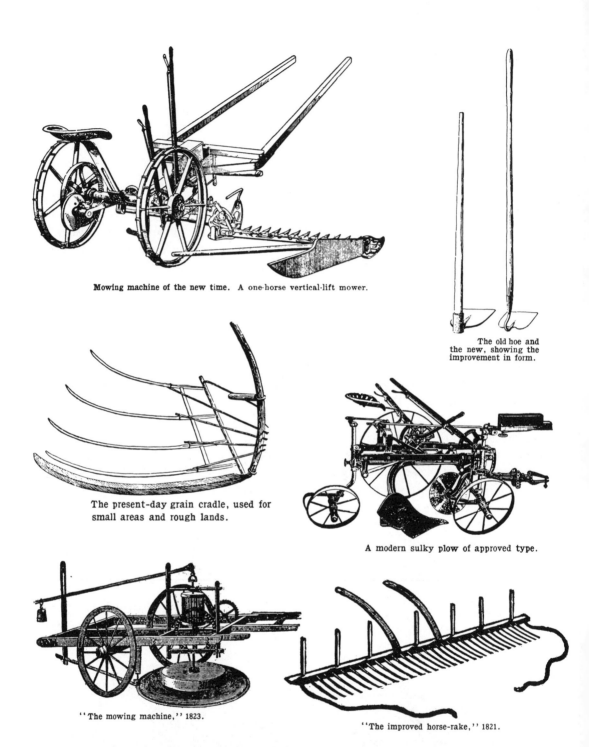

Mowing machine of the new time. A one-horse vertical-lift mower.

The old hoe and the new, showing the improvement in form.

The present-day grain cradle, used for small areas and rough lands.

A modern sulky plow of approved type.

"The mowing machine," 1823.

"The improved horse-rake," 1821.

Farming tools and equipment such as Higbee describes. From "Cyclopedia of American Agriculture; Vol I, Farms and II, Crops." Edited by L. H. Bailey. MacMillan Co. 1907.

of the wrist and upward throw of the cake, was said to have kept a steady stream going up and coming down the chimney for half an hour or so before meal time. But then she had fifteen children to feed beside herself and Uncle Peter and it is no wonder the Van Vliet farm on the south side of Mount Philo took the cake in this particular industry.

It is said about 75 years ago Jeremiah Barton had fifteen to twenty acres of wheat on the lot south and west of Michael Fleming's and help being scarce just then, he posted notices offering a bushel of wheat for a day's work. It had to be done with sickles and it was cut in a little over two days. Before the soil became exhausted most of our farms bore repeated crops of wheat.

Charlotte is not a clay town, but there is enough found in most sections to give strength and durability, and with frequent rains the clay lands are the best for pasture or meadow. Clay is found in "Guinea" more than

anywhere else, and the magnificent beef cattle that used to find pasturage here in the days of the Meeches testified to the quality of its grasses. Kentucky with its blue grasses can hardly surpass Vermont, and indeed it seems she goes to the front today as naturally as when her brave sons defied her enemies and traducers of long ago.

It used occasionally to happen that Vermont was spoken of as a state where the crops had to be fired into the ground with a shotgun, and sheep held up by the heels to nibble a blade of grass from among the stones. Such things amused the jokers, but did not disturb us in the least. In a short time they were all coming here for our Black Hawk[51] horses and Merino sheep so we pocketed the cash and developed the State and finally loaned money enough to the West and South to have built a dozen pyramids and have plenty of it yet remaining to go largely into home industries this time, it is hoped.

FEEDING THE SHEEP
THE OLD VERMONT WAY

How one Charlotte artist envisions a Higbee story. Courtesy of Charlie Lotz.

79

THE LONG SERMON.

The boy's life as portrayed in "Harper's New Monthly Magazine," Dec. 1854. Higbee's boy would hold a candle straight up "so as not to grease the floor."

DONE UP.

XII

Household Lighting, Blacksmith Shops, the King's Pines and Monkton

26 February 1897

Sixty years ago Vergennes, Burlington and other populous cities did not luxuriate in electric lights, telephones, trolley cars and similar accessories. Tallow candles and whale oil lamps illuminated the dark places, and "dipping" candles was as much a part of household routine after the fall butchering as the making of sausage and head cheese. Round tin

A one-candle power tin lantern with glass sides to keep it from going out.

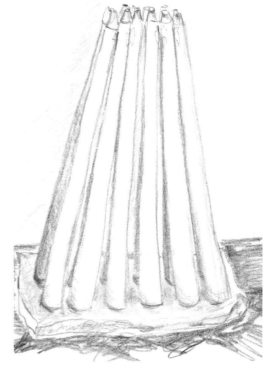

A 12-candle mold with tops soldered together. Sketches by Shirley Thompson. Charlotte Memorial Museum Collection.

lanterns with conical tops and punctured with numberless holes emitted feeble rays from a tallow dip, always running down in confined quarters and constantly clamoring to be "snuffed" or liable to go out altogether. If the bump of economy, as phrenologists would term it, happened to be largely developed, as was not infrequently the case, a rather small detail of tallow candles stood marshalled on the kitchen table after nightfall, flanked by the indispensable snuffer tray and snuffers.

If the small boy started off almost any direction with one of these illuminators, he was generally charged to

A brass kerosene lantern about eight inches high that was used for ice skating.

"hold the candle straight up" so as not to grease the floor. And "see you don't drop sparks." There was little danger from the dripping grease, but there was danger lurking in the hard "spark" generally ready to tumble from the wick should it happen to strike in the right, or rather, the wrong place.

The whale oil lamp was no great improvement. It was a light, and that is about the whole of it. When the round wick was not "pulled up" with a hairpin or some like implement, or the clinkers being brushed off the top, it would get on in an indifferent, flickering sort of a way, seeming entirely satisfied to go out by the tiny amount of light it made. Then, the fluid lamp with a bright flame, and dangerous as bright, for one might as well have gone around with gunpowder and live coals in conjunction. "Coal oil" afterwards bubbled to the top, a thick, smoky material for a while, but now the purified kerosene, almost as essential as daylight.

About as frequent as taverns, sixty or seventy years ago, were the blacksmith shops. There were good reasons for this. None of the innumerable things now made by machinery and sold everywhere in the line of hardware, nails, etc., existed. The blacksmith forged out his shoes for oxen and horses. He wrought out his own nails, and his anvil furnished the building supplies for frugal neighbors. Even the door latches and hinges came from the local blacksmith. What would you think now of placing with him an order for a pound or two of nails to do a little repairing, or, if

A blacksmith shop, or in the original caption, "a manufactory." As Higbee states, blacksmiths made many things besides the horseshoes we associate with them. He mentions sixteen different shops in Charlotte and Ferrisburgh, most smaller than this one pictured in a 19th century textbook.

about to build a house, contract with him for a complement of house furnishing hardware?

Hay and manure forks, shovels and spades were hand forged. Manure forks were generally three-tined, the tines about a quarter of an inch thick, half an inch wide at the big end and coming to a point, possibly as sharp as a sled stake, but not much more so. The hoe had an "eye" somewhere near the middle into which the farmer thrust a homemade handle. It was not a very neat or agreeable tool, and it is no wonder a certain son of toil, years ago, thus apostrophized this instrument on his return to the field from dinner, hoping by some good luck not to find the hoe, "I see you, blast you, but I'd rather see the devil." Shovels, spades, plows, axes, all partook of the same nature as to finish and adaptability. But they somehow dug up the soil, cut down the forests, laid out the highways, built the school houses and churches, fenced the fields, educated the children, established the banks, founded the colleges, made New England what she is today: the fountainhead of national prosperity. To say that Shelburne, Charlotte, Ferrisburgh, Monkton failed in doing their substantial part in the rugged early days is stating what is not true.

The townships of Charlotte, Ferrisburgh, and Monkton "corner" near where Lewis Creek afforded water powers for the Sherman and Leavenworth mills. The latter were further up the stream where in an early day, Nathan Leavenworth, the father of Burke and the grandfather of Henry C. Leavenworth, converted the tall pines and lordly hemlocks into "stuff" for the forest homes around him. The up-and-down saw that tore its rasping asthmatic way through the great logs was a slow coach compared with the modern mill, where the great circular burns through bark and knot, lopping off boards faster than a man can carry them away.

Along the creek valley and up the side hills to the lake was an abundance of the finest timber. The good King George in the Charlotte charter and probably so with sister towns reserved the "white and other pine trees" for "masting the royal navy." If the king had taken a little tour through hereabout those days he

83

Scene in Monkton with two of the roads that Higbee found so numerous and Monkton Pond (now Cedar Lake). Courtesy of Jessie Thomas.

Monkton Ridge, looking north. Courtesy of Jessie Thomas.

The Methodist Episcopal church in Monkton Boro. Horse sheds show behind the church. The Boro school is to the far right with the John Bushey slaughter house back of the school. Charlotte Memorial Museum, gift of Rod Baldwin.

would have found a tree or two could have been spared with no detriment to his "navy." It is true, however that large quantities of masts were shipped from this vicinity to Canada. It has been stated that some of the timber was obtained from this vicinity in the building of Arnold's fleet.

For reasons plain to understand the early settlers sought the highlands for homes and highways. They had plenty to do without building "corduroys"[52] through the swamps if they "slashed" land enough for a field of wheat or corn. And that is probably why so many of our roads climb plumb over the hills instead of going round them. Towns have been wrestling with this change in highways for years--and only a short time ago Monkton went into the business by wholesale, running roads from Ferrisburgh to the Boro and the Ridge so there are few hills now to check the speed of the United States mailman as he hustles along on schedule time.

Monkton Boro and Monkton Ridge both with stores and a church and hotels, but only one town house between them, separated by the Pond, a placid inland sea perhaps a mile long and half a mile wide, would be ideal places for the romantic dreamer to while away his summer days. If the sojourner wishes to hide himself from the sun, let him penetrate the fringes of cedars found everywhere--and among them he finds the darkness of twilight at the hour of midday.

These lands have been sold off in strips for the timber. It is more than likely that ancient landmarks and trees bearing mysterious letters have

long since succumbed to the ravages of time, making the town clerk's office frequently the scene of patient and often impatient searches for a piece of "cedar swamp."

But these things need not disturb the placidity of our summer sojourner

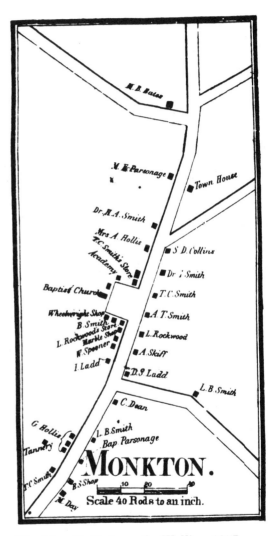

Monkton P. O. from the Walling 1857 map of Addison county. One of the "Ladd" places is the hotel. Higbee wrote more about Monkton in Chapter XXXIX. Courtesy of Bixby Free Mem. Library.

85

A Monkton group at a camp meeting: l. front seated Richard Dean; children behind him, Louis Dean and __?__McClerins; Mrs. Ellen (Collins) Thomas, wife of Dr. Thomas; Alma Dean; girl in front not identified; Fred Skiff and Lindley Dean; back row, left; unidentified; Dr. Thomas; near tree with hammock, Jane (Collins) Skiff; unident.; John Thomas; Ernest Lawrence. Others not identified. Courtesy of Jessie Thomas.

as he goes up and down the long single street, looking from the bright residences of modern times to numerous weatherbeaten dwellings that seem dreaming of the days they knew almost a century ago when they, whose names are now found at the head of scores of graves, were calling to each other.

Our sojourner can launch his boat and try his hand at fishing should he be so disposed and if the fish are not hungry that day, or he wearies of the sport, a tramp of a mile or two brings him abreast of an elevation known as "Hogsback"--while a little to the north of this a lesser hill would, if it could, answer to the roll call as "pig's back." One of them being larger than the other doubtless settles the vexed question as to where a pig ceases to exist and becomes a hog. What could be more appropriate than to locate "potato hill" in an adjoining town--and then, "buckwheat street" in Ferrisburgh? If our sojourner could properly put things together, would these suggest the appetizing qualities of the excellent dinner waiting for him at Ladd's over in the Boro?

If our sojourner cares to delve among old records, let him gratify his tastes by picking out the puzzling handwriting of some long ago clerk whose disregard of capitals and punctuations towered to sublimity.[53]

The Smith, Collins, Dean and Barnum families appear to have figured prominently in Monkton land transfers, and the rule seems to yet hold good. Many of our elders recall the numerous lawsuits that used to incubate about the "Boro," wherein "Cute" Smith, as he came to be known far and near, used to contrive more smart dodges and wily traps in one day than his average opponent could pick himself out of in a year. Monkton has its telephone, and one of these days, when a trolley line runs through there and so on to Bristol, the numerous summer boarders will bustle among its quiet old homes and clamber around its mountains.

Ladd's Hotel "over in the Boro" where there is an "excellent dinner waiting." Charlotte Memorial Museum, gift of Rod Baldwin.

Portrait of a Farmer, attributed to Sheldon Peck, about 1835. This portrait of an unidentified farmer is thought to have been painted in Charlotte. Local legend indicates it may have been used to advertise the dairy products of the farm. Courtesy of Mr. and Mrs. William G. Crawshaw.

XIII

Vermont Wives and Mothers, Pioneer Hospitality, Bees and Teamsters

5 March 1897

Nature seems to compensate and make good in one direction what is withheld in another. From Hinesburgh southward a line of beautiful ponds, begirt with hills and affording fine fishing for lovers of angling, in large degree takes the place of Champlain. The shores of these ponds are coming more and more to furnish summer homes for those whose duties relax as the heat waves undulate over the land.

It may seem paradoxical, but the quietest time in all the year for the "cousins" in the city is the busiest of all seasons for his country relative; and I herein enter a plea for the faithful helpmate of the Vermont farmer who finds herself called upon to "entertain" when every energy is already in full play to furnish three meals a day to hungry men who gather about her table in haying and harvesting.

Conceding everything to American chivalry for women, the American housewife is hardly credited with what is due her in this "scuffle for existence," as it has been called. To plan and furnish three wholesome meals a day would drive the average man to his wits' end. Perhaps he never thinks

about it, yet it seems somehow these meals "grow," and the wife trips around, brushing away the flies as a sort of reaction.

Since the days of the New Hampshire Grants, the wives and mothers of Vermont have done their part in the development of the State. It was no small thing for a girl to leave home and kindred and the comforts of the southern colonies. But the instinct of the human race to "have a home of its own," and a loving trust in the true-hearted man of her choice compensated for the isolation and danger of a life in the woods, until, finally, these woods were lessened about the log house door. And the girl, grown gray in the years of toil and care, sat smiling among her sons and daughters, a queen in her little realm.

As before stated, the first town meeting in Charlotte was held at the house of Moses Yale, July 6, 1785, only two days after a date so famous in the history of the United States. It would have been the romance of history if our first town meeting could have convened two days earlier. But it is the antiquity of things that counts. Perhaps the forefathers never thought July 4 would ever come to be such a date for the American people. When the years slip by, events stand out with increased prominence. The writer of these papers seeks to perpetuate the memory of things that might, somehow, drop out of mind, and his reward may possibly be a hurried thanks from a future generation.[54]

The nearest mill for grinding corn was "Skenesboro," now Whitehall, and you paddled your way up[55] the lake or went by marked trees along the trail. Going to mill meant something in those days. It was exposure to storm and delay and danger, and no wonder the people of early times were hospitable, and the latch string hung out, for who could tell when it might come his turn to seek shelter and a bit of food. There was less "culture" then than now; but hearts were just as honest, and common sense just as essential. The hard lot of the pioneers put people more nearly on a temporary level, to say the least, and that equilibrium was not disturbed for years. Of course, the gossip found convenient opportunity, and the back-biter was, no doubt, a present quantity, but kindliness and hospitality was the rule and not the exception.

Imagine a scatter line of cabins from here to Whitehall, sometimes along the line of marked trees, more frequently off of it--a little clearing for an acre of two of grain and garden, possibly a cow, a few sheep, or a pig. These were realities when our forefathers came to Charlotte, Ferrisburgh,

Shelburne. They "slashed" the timber during the winter and spring, felling it in rows as much as possible. In the fall, after a summer's drying, they fired the "slash," burning away the small stuff and limbs. After that the "log rolling," when the remaining tree trunks were put into great piles to again be fired.

Those were the days of "bees"--not the little insect always on the sting-- but when neighbors for miles around came to the "logging," with strong muscles and cheery hearts, helping each other right royally. It is possible certain individuals, politically inclined, took advantage of these gatherings to "drop anchor to the windward," and hence came down to us the term "log rolling" in politics. It is not my province to discuss these things and a single suggestion suffices.

West of the old Fonda place the plain had been cut for rafting timber to Montreal, and later the dry tops, fired to clear the land, encircled with flames several men, the grandfather

90

of the writer among the rest. It was possible to distinguish them fighting their way to life through the hot smoke, until a lull in the flames enabled them to break through, scorched and blackened, but alive. It was a close shave, and afforded topic for comment among the pioneers for many a day.

The marketing expeditions of some time ago were accomplished by team work. Wheat, pork, and pearlash were marketed either in Montreal or Troy, generally at the latter point, and an entire community would delay butchering, one for another, until a certain time, so they could go to market together.

Solomon W. Hubbell, father of our townsman, Luther R., gave the writer a somewhat graphic description of these marketing expeditions in which, as a young man, he participated. It was no unusual thing for fifteen to twenty loaded teams to start together, about the middle of January, for Troy, loaded with anything and everything that could be exchanged for "barter." Frequently the farmers would contract with local traders to bring back a load of merchandise and thus make the trip pay a little both ways. These teamsters always stood by each other through thick and thin; and it is surmised that New Yorkers sometimes thought of them as green mountain "boys" by their queer pranks and original ways. In those days taverns were not hard to find, and it was the custom for everyone to sample the drinkables, and it may be a stalwart Vermonter occasionally

Butchering was a part of farm life. In Monkton someone took a photo of the work being done. From left, __?__ Meader, Sam Siple, Frank Tracy, John Thomas. Courtesy of Jessie Thomas.

claimed more than his share of the highway, and according to Mr. Hubbell, he generally succeeded in getting it.

It was another thing, in comparison with our day, this transaction of business with Troy and Albany and so on to New York. The merchant wrote out his letters and memoranda with a quill, and let the ink dry or sprinkled sand over it to keep it from blotting. It cost fifteen to eighteen cents to send a letter to Boston or New York, and twenty-five cents to Washington. It took eight to ten days to a fortnight for our caravan of farmers to sell their produce in Troy and return, provided things were favorable. The route used to be mainly through Skenesboro, and then along the Hudson.

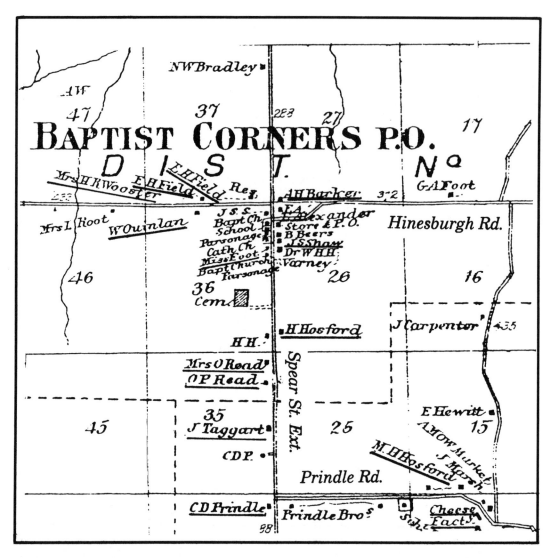

Portion of a modified Beers 1869 map of Charlotte showing locations in Baptist Corners. The Westcott/Read/VanVliet house south of store is shown as the J. S. Shaw house. The A. H. Barker house was first the Reuben Martin tavern. The William O. Barker house was southwest of the tavern and indicated here as belonging to J. S. Shaw (J. S. S.) The numbers in the marked-off squares are those of the original lots of the proprietors; numbers on roads are the lengths of the sections in rods; dotted lines are the boundaries of school districts.

XIV

East Charlotte

12 March 1897

East Charlotte since an early day has been known as "Baptist Corners," and will doubtless be so designated in a local way through future years. Probably the theological leanings of its people had much, if not everything, to do with this christening, and the final "setting the stake" for the "meeting house,"[56] that agitated repeated town meetings in years past, may have had no inconsiderable influence in the establishment of the Calvinistic Baptist church organized there May 6, 1807, with the following members: Abel Gibbs, Samuel Hyde, Daniel Hosford, Henry Straight, Solomon Powell, Eliza Powell, Reuben Powell, Archibald Gibbs, William Sheels, Anna Sheels, Abigail Niles, Jerusha Powell, Ruth Powell, Mary Gibbs, Betty Hyde, Hannah Sheels. Their pastor was Reverend Isaac Sawyer. The first church was of wood with the usual square box pews. The

Baptist Corners. The view south from Hinesburgh Rd. around 1910 with the Charlie Johns store on the left, the William. S. Baldwin/Beech Beers house behind it, the church on the right. Gift of John Holmes. Charlotte Memorial Museum.

93

The Baptist Church at East Charlotte in August of 1906. The building is now a second home whose owner encourages its use for community activities such as an art show with the annual Grange strawberry festival. Gift of John Holmes. Charlotte Mem. Museum Collection.

pulpit, standing at one corner, was reached by a flight of stairs, and the minister was an elevated personage in point of fact. The present brick church was built in 1839.

The road running through the Baptist Corners from Shelburne Falls continues in a southerly course through Charlotte, Monkton, and New Haven, and possibly on to Massachusetts, by way of Rutland and Mount Holly, over which the New Hampshire troops marched to Bennington. This route was an early Indian trail, and many a party on the warpath has flitted along its winding course.

After getting into Monkton, it has been called the "Barnumtown Road" for a period of time when the memory of man runneth not back to the contrary, and it has rather of a tough time of it climbing over hills and plowing through long stretches of clay, stiff enough for the children of Israel to have made brick of, straw or no straw. But the fathers had to keep on the high lands to avoid miles of cedar swamp stretching, dark and somber,

The interior of the Baptist Church in 1909. Gift of John Holmes. Charlotte Memorial Museum Collection.

View looking west from Jackson hill, east of Baptist Corners. The white building on the right horizon was the E. H. Field farm of which filled-in cellar holes now remain. The collection of buildings on the extreme right are on the site of the Barker tavern, the area where the barns of the Sheehan farm are now. A lilac bush by the barns marks the site of a house. The Jackson Hill road was the main road then, but was replaced by the present Hinesburgh road up the hill. Gift of John Holmes. Charlotte Memorial Museum.

The store at Baptist Corners around 1910, now much changed and operated by the Sheehans. Courtesy of Eugene Shortsleeves.

Eugene Shortsleeves as he delivered groceries for the store at Baptist Corners. Store steps on the right. Courtesy of Eugene Shortsleeves.

to the east. Barnumtown used to have its mill and was an important local center, but time has wrought its changes, and the wrecks of an old dam, twisted iron, or a broken mill wheel, indicate where the busy former generation converted the logs into boards and the corn into meal. The hillsides and hollows that boasted the tallest pines and hemlocks and the lowlands whose cedars vied with those of Lebanon remain. The woodsman would say their glory had departed, but the farmer points to his crowded barns, his sleek cattle, his comforting creamery check, and insists that the Barnumtown of today answers his purpose far better than the Barnumtown of long ago with its woodland glory.

Some seventy-five years ago in East Charlotte John Westcott owned the farm where Curtis L. VanVliet lives. Westcott sold this to Amos Read, who built the brick house now standing. Michael Read owned the farm occupied by E. H. Field, and probably built the old wood-colored dwelling that Mr. Field replaced with the present fine farm home.

The large house on the corner of the road, now owned by Mrs. Clayton, was built by Reuben Martin for a tavern. Mr. Martin was, I think, one of the seven brothers of that name who settled in this vicinity and Ferrisburgh, and tavern-keeping came as naturally to them as to some of the famous hotel families of modern times. Native tact, a certain indefinable way of dealing with the public, seems to have been an inheritance--and a successful hotel man, like the poet, must be born, not made. In connection with other business, Mr. Martin had a tannery and shoe shop on the north side of the east-west road, near the spring.

Calvin Powell lived where J. A. Harris is, but later, that farm, with the Martin House, was owned by William O. Barker, father of the late Alonzo H. Barker. William was a lover of fine horses and his place was headquarters for down-country buyers who then regarded Vermont Morgans as among the choicest roadsters.

Isaac Foote used to live at the now John R. Taggart's house, and Samuel Hyde, grandfather of Herman Hyde of Monkton, lived on the present O. P. Read farm. Orrin Read, brother of Amos, lived in comparatively more recent day in the old one-story house south of O. P. Read's. The two brothers, Amos and Orrin, will be recalled by older readers as shrewd and successful businessmen, dealing heavily in cattle in connection with their large farm.

Leonard Sherman, one of George Sherman's sons, used to be engaged largely with the Reads in cattle buying, going into Canada to pick up droves. During one of these expeditions, Mr. Sherman was taken sick with a fever and died in Fairfield in the north part of the state.

The farm occupied by Ezra Hosford and his son William E. has been in the same name for years. Heman Hosford, the father of Ezra, spent a long and successful life here. A son of his, Holcomb Hosford, is pleasantly recalled by lovers of good reading, as they delve among the books in the Baptist church library, placed there through his liberality. Mr. Horsford spent his business life mainly in Lowell, Massachusetts, and accumulated a large fortune. The Hosford name is connected with the history of Charlotte almost from the first. Daniel Hosford, elected clerk at the first meeting held in town, as has been previously stated, lived in a house that stood east of the present stone farmhouse of the late Myron H. Hosford. Alonza Bingham sold Herman Wooster the farm now owned by the Wooster family. David

Atwood built the house on the farm of Mrs. Melinda H. Read, and he owned adjacent timber lands. Norman Atwood, one of David's nine children lived on the John Taggart farm.

Solomon Johnson owned the farm where George W. Prindle lives and after selling it, he and his seven sons moved to Michigan, all locating in one place, calling the place Johnsonville. Thus Vermont was putting her imprint on the West years ago.

Frank Colt owns the place where Simon Foote used to live. There was once a blacksmith shop on the east

The George W. Prindle farmhouse and family around 1900. Seated from left, George W. Prindle, Jennie (Byington) Prindle; back from left, Jessie, Lester, Leon. Leon was the father of the late Mark Prindle, Charlotte representative from 1985 to 1987 who operated the farm until 1968. Lester became professor of classical languages at UVM. Jessie married Gaylord Baldwin and lived in Hinesburgh. The Beers map lists the farm as C. D. Prindle's, father of George W. Courtesy of Representative Hazel (Mrs. Mark) Prindle.

side of the highway from the William O. Barker house, conducted by a man named Prentice, and others. The remains of an old lime kiln are still seen on the north side of the road and a little east of William Quinlan's; it used to furnish an excellent article, though limited in quantity. Wood in plenty was found in the hemlocks to the north of the quarry; for in the days of the fathers a tree was looked upon almost as an enemy. Not a kernel of grain, not a blade of grass appeared until the shadowy woodland was subdued; and this meant days of grimy toil, something more than even Puritan faith, to remove the stumps and stones, converting into green meadows and sweet pastures the uplands and lowlands of Charlotte.

It is not my intention to discriminate in the calling of names, neither shall I be fortunate enough in the gathering of information to meet my own demands in honoring our sturdy progenitors. But the will for the deed must suffice in the effort to perpetuate the memory of some who these many years have slept the sleep of the grave.

George E. Prindle, brother of Cyrus G. Pringle, is dressed to haul butter to the Burlington market. His team is protected against the flies. His farm was at the corner of Prindle and Garen Rd. Courtesy of his granddaughter Elinor (Prindle) Benning.

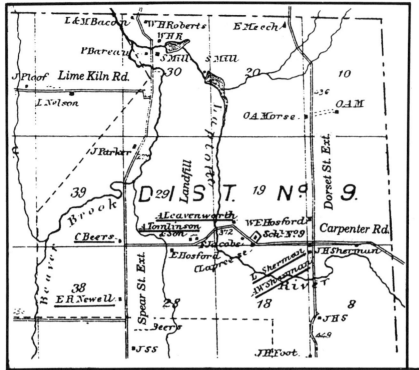

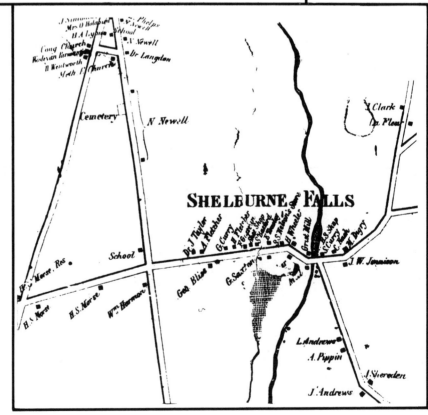

Higbee's short trip to the LaPlatte river valley, the northeast corner of Charlotte. Below: Shelburne Falls, from the Walling map. Two mills and a blacksmith shop were on the river here.

XV

The La Platte River, Abolitionist Sentiment and the Mud Church

19 March 1897

North of the farm occupied by Willys Newell, a descendant of the family so long and intimately connected with our history, and in the brick house where E. B. Beers lives, his grandfather, Benjamin Beers, spent a good part of a long and active life. "Uncle Ben," as he came to be known by everybody, was an extensive buyer and seller of beef cattle, stocking up in the spring to sell during the summer, according to the thrift of the animal. This called him into adjoining towns, where he was recognized as a typical New Englander in speech and manner, whose rugged and absolute integrity was no more questioned than the rising and setting of the sun.

Amos Tomlinson spent a long and laborious life on the farm now occupied by B. H. Carpenter, where industry and economy made him a prosperous, well-to-do citizen.

The bridge across La Platte at the foot of the hill near the Abel Leavenworth place figured more or less in Charlotte records since the earliest days, and the minutes of town meetings contain numerous suggestions as to needed repairs at this point. A former generation saw the streams larger and more rapid in high water than now and bridges, like men, found it easier to go with the current than against it; and so it not unfrequently occurred that "the bridge near Amos Tomlinson's" became the object of public solicitude.

The ancient farm house north of the present A. S. Sherman place was occupied, if not built, by Leverette Sherman, where he lived and died. A son of his, and brother to the late Alfred W. Sherman, was buried and suffocated in a pit along the highway east of the Abel Leavenworth place, where he was getting sand for a house being built for a prospective bride.

The La Platte, in its wandering course to the lake, afforded numerous fairly good water powers and the best of them was at Shelburne Falls where the river took an abrupt tumble of many feet. Various water wheels have been hurrying round and round at this point these many years, turning the mill stones, the up-and-down saws of the fathers, the big circulars, that now and then lop off a leg or cut a man plumb in two, and the numberless contrivances for cabinet or wheelwright work. Now, finally, the saw mill

101

The Marcotte/Hutchins farm on Carpenter Rd., just east of the LaPlatte river bridge. This was the Abel Leavenworth farm. Drawing by Paul Marcotte.

and grist mill alone remain to call up the energies of this ancient stream whose waters are forever new.[57]

After the reckless hurry-skurry of the Falls, the river assumes a sedate and solemn air, and most of its way to the lake is shadowed by willows and water elms, beneath which moves the same sluggish current that bore the bark canoes of a party of Indian warriors who, at least two generations ago in their effort to exterminate the pale face, were themselves annihilated.[58]

From Martin's south [see Chapter III], sixty, seventy years have made changes such as we note in the woodlands, as one comes upon the mossy trunks of old trees, whose death and decay inaugurate the advent of new and fresher vegetation. This rule holds good with trees; and mankind, with his feeble hold on life, has not been able, thus far, to effect a change. One generation gives place to another, as the leaves of autumn make way for the luxuriance of a coming May.

In the stage-coach days, and indeed some time after, John W. and Carlos C. Martin, sons of Squire Martin, kept a public house where Stoddard Martin now lives. The post office used to be there, and it was one of the most central places along the main road between Vergennes and Shelburne. The Martins were speculators in various farm products. In one way or another they managed to set the current in their direction, paying the producer a fair price and themselves a just profit; so between them all, the old stand held its own year after year.

About those days, the slavery question was the prominent feature in politics, and a newspaper printed in Washington, called the *National Era*, published *Uncle Tom's Cabin*, by Harriet Beecher Stowe in weekly installments.[59] I remember as a boy being sent, sometimes on foot, sometimes on horseback, to Martin's when the *Era* was due; and we never went to bed after the paper came until every word of *Uncle Tom* was read to us all. It is impossible, at this day, to adequately express the impression of this life work of Mrs. Stowe. It came when the mind of the nation was intensely occupied with a question of right and wrong. And it did more to free the slave than its gifted author ever dared to dream.

South of Martin's, Joseph Allen had a blacksmith shop, not far from where William Noonan's house now stands. Mr. Allen, by some unfortunate accident, injured one of his legs so it resulted in an amputation. I recall the telling how, in his case, grit and suffering took the place of anesthetics in surgery. Julius Seguin used to work in Allen's shop, and later on conducted one of his own near his present dwelling, but time and decay has laid its heavy hands on muscle and brain. Amasa Phelps, father of Mrs. Stephen Ball, lived in the house now owned by Joseph Fonda.

The old school house occupied very nearly the present site, with a floor sloping to the center; here the boys and girls obtained the major part of education, and it is safe to assume that in solid worth the common schools of sixty years ago would in no sense suffer in comparison with those of today. When spelling school night

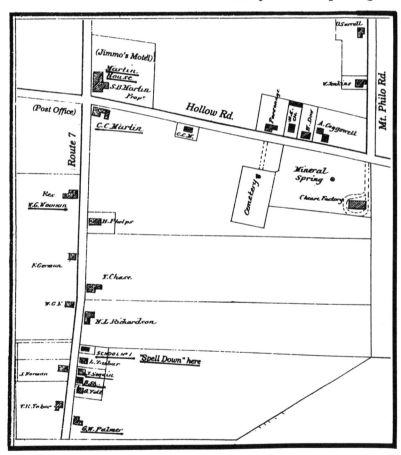

Part of the Beers insert map of North Ferrisburgh. Sites from Higbee's writing are underlined and the present-day post office and Jimmo's motel have been added. Names of three major roads supplied.

103

A stereograph of the Mud church. Some sort of group meeting is going on. The people in front are three pairs of boys and men who appear to be doing square dance figures while the others watch. Courtesy of the Wheeler/Kingsland Collection.

The Mud church in the Hollow was located east of the present fire station. A sign marks the place. This summer-time photo from about 1890 shows the deterioration of the unfired mud bricks after the plaster coating cracked away. Because the congregation gave up its active existence in 1853, there is probably no photo of the church in its Wesleyan Methodist days. Courtesy of Inez Willard Chioffi.

came, there was always a large attendance on the "stage road," and as frequently happened, the teacher's *Webster* had a tough time of it before the last one was "down" in the grand finale of the evening.

"Choosing sides" generally opened the session when the best speller among the boys and the best among the girls took opposite positions on the long benches. The toss of a penny usually decided the first choice, and then came the marshalling of hosts. It

was good generalship, of course, for each leader to enlist the best spellers on his side; but it not unfrequently happened the leader of the boys had a choice in the one to sit next beside him, and some blushing maiden slid into the coveted place, hoping in her tender heart that she wouldn't miss a word; and her leader not caring a straw whether she did or not, for the girl was of more importance to him than the spelling. Some boy who always stood either at the foot or next to the foot in spelling, but whose jollity and wit were not at all discredited thereby, was hesitatingly bidden by the girl leader to the post of honor at her side, for, with strange inconsistency, she had rather be vanquished with him than victorious without him. The closing scene was usually oratorical in character, when "Rienzi's Address to the Romans," or "The Boy Stood on the Burning Deck," or, sometimes, appreciated offerings of visiting scholars but more frequently the result of home talent, dismissed the happy laughing crowd.

Across the road from the school house and farther south lived "Father" Labor. He was an Englishman, a strong Methodist, and used frequently to preach in the Mud Church at the Hollow. This little one-storied edifice has rather a stirring history. At least the hearts of a former generation were stirred when it came into existence. When the abolition of slavery came into American politics to stay, it made division in Church as well as in State, and when times were ripe certain sturdy abolitionists built this little church out of unburned brick and worshipped therein according to their consciences.

Father Labor preached not in a regular way as settled pastor, but when a pulpit vacancy occurred. "Father" Labor had several children, among them a daughter, Caroline, who once taught school in the old 7th district, when the house stood on "the rocks." She was passionately fond of flowers, and her favorite was the lily of the valley, growing in abundance in a mossy glen south of the Pettibone place, now owned by Herbert Wells. It afforded the scholars many a delightful run in the woods to gather them. Some of the sons were rather eccentric, to say the least. One was a doctor, and another stood ready to take contracts in rat catching, claiming to own a certain powder possessing the power of alluring a rat to inevitable destruction.

It took money, as well as patriotism and holy impulses, to run churches then as now. Samuel H. Tupper, who removed from Ferrisburgh to Charlotte, frequently occupied the pulpit, and I recall as a boy hearing him make a prayer that had the rhythm and swing of poetry--and perhaps naturally enough, too, for he was a good deal of a poet in his day.

Those were stirring days when Cyrus and Lyman Prindle hurled their shining spears at the brazen front of slavery. But with the war came the death of slavery, and the Christian hearts united again, and so the little church is only a recollection. But it did glorious work in its day, and many an inspiration for human freedom had here its birthplace.

Connected with this church was a Sunday school, and its literature from leaflet up, was on fire with the hideousness of slavery. The parents were abolitionists, the minister, the teachers too; and how could the children be anything else? They drank in the sentiments of freedom for the slave at the mother's knee; and tell me, will you, how to eradicate from the boy what the mother teaches, as she looks down into his earnest eyes. The mothers of the nation, sooner or later, make the nation's laws.

XVI

Mostly about the Hollow
and Fugitive Slaves

26 March 1897

About where George W. Palmer lives, Nicholas Guindon kept a temperance tavern at a time, too, when everybody did more or less drinking; and he must have been one of those rare souls who possessed the courage of his convictions. He was in addition an ardent abolitionist and erected a liberty pole near his home that some mischievous parties one night cut down with augers. But such things did not daunt Uncle "Nick" in the least nor abate in any degree his enthusiastic love of liberty.

His house was an important station on the "underground railroad," that older readers so well understand, in connection with the escape of runaway slaves. There was a general law imposing fine and imprisonment for aiding in the escape of a slave, even making it obligatory to assist in returning them to slavery. This might do in the border states as they were called, but when the "chivalry" attempted to force Vermonters to catch their runaways, it came again to be known "the gods of the valleys were not the gods of the hills," and scattered all along to Canada were those who secretly aided these fugitives in their race for liberty. Such points

were known as "stations on the underground railroad" and many a slave was passed over this when it would have been a sorry day, financially, for the man who "passed" him, had it become known to the law.

"Uncle Nick Guindon," as everybody seemed to know him, had a way of pleasing the public and he was everybody's friend. He was an abolitionist through and through, but he so mingled shrewdness with boldness that no officer of the law ever succeeded in getting a twist on him for his underground railroad activities, though it was often tried.

It is said that one time a couple of runaways were hidden in his home barn, and the pursuit was unusually sharp. In fact, only an hour or two behind were the searchers, armed with all sorts of legal "whereases" and "be it knowns." Up came the officials to find "Uncle Nick" busily at work mowing away a "jag"[60] of hay in the home barn loft. No one could have evinced more surprise than he at the suggestion of any stray property being around his premises. The officers were invited to look things over, which they probably did with considerable thoroughness.

In the meantime the landlord was

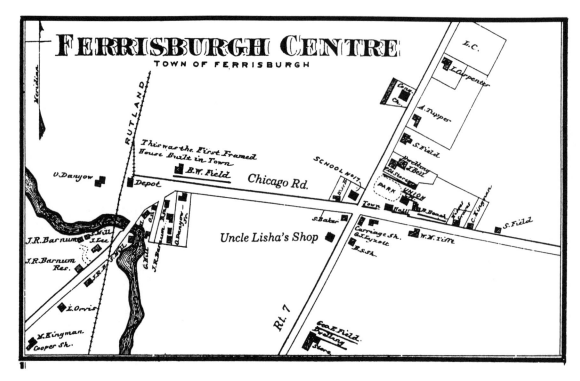

Ferrisburgh Centre from the Beers map with Higbee's places suitably marked.

mowing away hay very leisurely and it was not until the searching party was at a perfectly safe distance that a couple of half-smothered but thoroughly delighted darkies were dug out of the hay mow in the barn loft, and they went north, not south, after leaving "Uncle Nick's."[61]

The significance of such incidents may be more thoroughly realized when it is understood that a finding of these runaways under the circumstances would have subjected Mr. Guindon to a fine of not less than one thousand dollars and imprisonment or both. It took both grit and wit to carry the thing through successfully, and he had plenty of both. At his death he was buried in the west [Barber]

cemetery in Charlotte where a monument marks the resting place of himself and his wife.

Dan Miller lived on the George Yott place. There were several of the Millers who were carpenters and most of them were large, powerful men, and almost incredible stories have been told of the short space of time taken by two of them in putting up the frame of a barn from trees standing in the "Greenbush woods." Nathaniel Martin, grandfather of Harvey C. Martin built the brick house owned by C. C. Taft. South of where Russell S. Miller lives, and on the west side of the road, was the old Enoch Woodbridge sawmill. The well defined outlines of the old dam are still seen at

108

The story of three roads. The first (original) Rt. 7 crossed Lewis creek from the bend in the road seen across the creek in this photo, the second crossed downstream (left), the third (present) is at the same location as the first. The house barely visible on the hill was the Nick Guindon/George W. Palmer house and still stands as the second north of Hanlon's store. In this picture the W. Miller house is next to the Creek. Hanlon's now at the top of the hill is the old Quaker meeting house from near the Quaker cemetery on the south side of the creek on the second location of the Rt. 7. Courtesy of Rokeby Museum.

the north end of the bridge. Years ago, the bridge crossing was further up the creek and above Miller's house; but it was hard of access in high water, and so the road was changed from the little valley on the Dakin farm to the harder climb as it now is. Enoch Woodbridge was father of the late Hon. R. E. Woodbridge of Vergennes.

Connected with this mill was a pail and tub factory, run by Wardwell & Frost, where were made the old-time sap buckets, big at the bottom and little at the top, and the pine wash-tubs of our grandmothers, with a

longer stave on each side for a handle. A man by the name of Sargent built the Russell Miller house, and at one time ran the sawmill. But high water carried off the dam and the mill property got into litigation and what the lawyers left after the lawsuit, being smaller than a grain of mustard seed, the industries at this point vanished many years ago.

North of the watering trough and up under the bank, Roswell Hopkins kept a tavern. Wing Rogers was innkeeper here at one time. Nathaniel Martin had a tannery and shoeshop

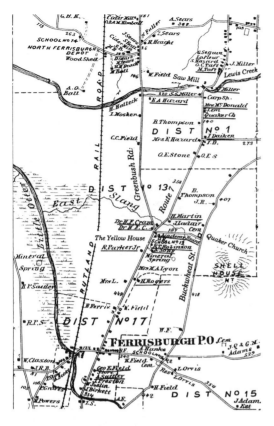

Beers map of Rt. 7 through the northern part of Ferrisburgh with the site of The Yellow House added. The upper right corner is the intersection of Rt. 7 and the Hollow Rd.

below the sawmill on the north side of the creek. Further to the west, and on the same side, lives Moses Taft and Benedict Champlin. Thomas Hazard lived where Ezra A. Hazard now does, and he established a kind of private post office by putting up a box on the corner near the brick house, now owned by Mrs. Allis, into which the post rider dropped his mail. Alonzo Kimball, father of Noble Kimball of Ferrisburgh, owned the present John Thompson farm. Timothy Dakin,

grandfather of Peter Dakin,[62] John V. Dakin and Mrs. Lydia Macomber lived where Peter now does, and I think put up the original farm buildings. Sarah Fish, mother of David Hazard and widow of Robert Hazard, lived in the present tenant house owned by W. H. Dean. Robert Hazard was the first of the name to settle in Ferrisburgh. David Hazard, who afterwards built the brick house owned by W. H. Dean, used to live on the east side of the road near where William Williams lives, in a house built by young Wing Rogers. Old Wing Rogers, as he was called, lived south of the Dean place and on the west side of the road. Simeon Miller, father of the late Sheldon Miller, built the house where Mrs. McDonald lives. The main part of the house now owned by Mr. Field used to stand across the road from Dean's. Peter V. Higbee was born in this house in 1811.

James Aiken owned the John Wheeler farm, now belonging to Lucius B. Martin. This house was a tavern. The Cram place seems to have taken to medicine from the first. Dr. Hatch occupied it, followed by Dr. Jonathan Cram, and he in turn by his son, Harvey C. Later another man skilled in the science of healing, Dr. Reynolds, moved in and he will doubtless continue to make it the Mecca of the ailing. North of the Cram place stood a blacksmith shop where Nathaniel Varney, grandfather of Dr. Varney and George W. Varney of Charlotte, used to work. Later the shop was run by John Clark and John Stevens. Further south, and on the

Dakin farmhouse in the early 1900's. It is located at the northeast corner of Rt. 7 and Dakin Rd. in Ferrisburgh. Courtesy of the Wheeler/Kingsland Collection.

The David Hazard house from the Walling Addison county map. It is now the 1810 Farm-house and Restaurant on Rt. 7 with the covered bridge from the Hollow on this property. Peter V. Higbee, the author's father, was born in a house that was across from this one.

111

The Kingsland school of Charlotte's old District No. 6 at the intersection of State Park Rd. and Rt. 7 as it appeared in 1979 when owned by Guy Cheng.

Robinson Academy which was at the southeast corner of Robinson Rd. and Rt. 7, opposite the intersection of Greenbush Rd. The then Cram place is at the left and the H. Martin house beyond the bend on Rt. 7. Bricks from this building were used in the Simmonds Precision Products plant in Vergennes and one shows the Robinson name. Courtesy of Rokeby Museum.

east side of the road, Raymond Reynolds had a cooper shop where he put up cheese casks. These casks, made of pine, were about as high as a flour barrel, though with much less bulge, and cheeses were packed into them for transportation.

One tavern at the Wheeler place seeming hardly to suffice, another came into existence and had for a series of years a prosperous life, on the site of what came to be known by a subsequent generation as the "old yellow house." William Gage, George Pease, Calvin C. Martin, Asa Henenway, and probably others were among its genial hosts.

The old two story brick building, standing on an elevation east of the road, was spick and span and new in 1839, when Rowland T. Robinson and other earnest men erected it for an academy Its first teacher was Joel Bingham, who had a flourishing school here until about 1843, the tavern being a boarding house.

There are many now a long way past middle life who recall the school days under Mr. Bingham. After him came Lucien Cheney with varying successes, until about 1846, when the rooms became silent, the seats (or some of them) came up into school district No. 6 in Charlotte, and the

J. R. Barnum's saw mill below Frazier's Falls and the railroad bridge on the Little Otter west of Ferrisburgh Center, site of the first mill in town. The roof of the covered railroad bridge which burned in 1901 is in the background. Courtesy of Karl Devine.

bell, vacating its commanding tower, clanged for a time with equal cheerfulness from the top of the Mud Church in the Hollow.

On the north and south road next east of the stage road and a little south of Noble Ellsworth's stood a plain two story wooden building, the upper floor being so arranged that it could be taken up in the center, leaving a row of seats, gallery-like around the outside. This was the meeting place of the Quakers, who, prior to troubles that grew out of certain doctrinal points, congregated here from Peru and other New York points, holding two quarterly meetings here and two in Peru. About 1828 the congregations were large, but twenty

years later the building was taken down and some of it used in the present Society of Friends church in North Ferrisburgh.

It must have been a little trying to the fathers, whose worship was so largely silent and meditative, this adjustment of vexatious questions propounded by the Hicksite to the Orthodox, and with equal firmness flashed back from Orthodox to Hicksite. Although by ancestry a pronounced Quaker, with a grandfather lying now in the old meeting house burying ground, it would be best not to hazard an opinion upon a matter that sundered so great a body of devoutly pious men and women.[63]

Rowland E. Robinson with some of Rokeby's sheep. At one time there were thousands of sheep on the Rokeby farm. Courtesy of Rokeby Museum.

XVII

From Rokeby to Vergennes

2 April 1897

The Robinson farm, with its beautiful meadows stretching away like a prairie, still remains in the name, an instance rare enough to occasion comment.[64] And a little further south, about the same distance from the road, with its long, steep roof and low sides almost hidden amid the ancient trees that exist among the rocks, the old Rogers homestead has its title deeds still untransferred. Thomas Richardson Robinson first settled in Vergennes, but came to Ferrisburgh about 1794, living first on the old Keese farm. The Keese place was afterwards occupied by Captain Gideon Hawley, who luxuriated in tavern keeping, making the third tavern in about a mile.

Thomas Robinson at an early day became interested in the Spanish Merino, and Rowland E. Robinson has a bill of sale dated November 7, 1819, in which it appears his grandfather, Thomas, and one Jonas Minturn were jointly purchasers in an importation at prices that seem well up in figures for nearly ninety years ago. The invoice embraces six half-blood ewes, $300; one three-quarter blood lamb, $150; one full blood ram No. 21, $485; one full blood ewe No. 149, $245; one full blood ewe, $115; one full blood ewe, $125. Several would be glad to make such sales today. Rowland T. Robinson, succeeded the father, making additions to the old family home; and finally only one of his sons remains, testifying with whitened hair and beard to the passing of the years.

The district school house used to stand on the east side of the road, opposite Reuben Parker's and the spirit of unrest must have animated this building to a remarkable degree, for it had four distinct removals. Commencing on "Buckwheat Street," south of the old Quaker church, it first came part way to the main road, and then in successive stages, hitched along southward until, east of the Center, it finally developed into a blacksmith shop where it doubtless stands today, possibly meditating still other moves. Seventy years ago the house on the Frisbie place was the only building between the Rogers farm and the Town House, and here lived David Fish. The old Town House was a wooden building that came to be the blacksmith shop recently standing north of the George Field place.

From the pounding of candidates to the pounding of iron, the transaction may not have been so very great. Warren Bard lived on the present Abram Sattley place. Burr Beach lived east of the old brick church, where he died. The "Union Church" east of the village green with its old-time architecture and beautifully proportioned tower, its outlook far to westward over green fields and lake and lordly mountains, and its old association that should be tender as a mother's twilight song, stands silent, empty, neglected, and will doubtless so remain.

Cyrus Collins built up the George Field place, and this was a tavern. The old building, recently removed, standing on the corner below the Town House, was used for wheel wrighting by Ethiel Collins and Goodrich & Lyzott. Henry Rogers and Heman Barnum were prominent movers in, if not builders of, the brick store now owned by Mr. Avery, that at a later period became the "Union Store," offering alluring prosperity to its originators, but finally resulting in a dead loss to numerous enthusiastic promoters. This project was something like Longfellow's highway, that beginning in the thrifty villages and fertile meadows, lessened as it continued, finally dwindling into a squir-

The brothers Rowland E. (on left) and George Robinson on the porch at Rokeby. The farm remained in the Robinson family until it became a museum in 1968. The collections of the family artists, many artifacts of farm life, books, diaries and papers make this a remarkable exhibit of the 19th century life which Higbee has written about. Members of the family were also town clerks in Ferrisburgh with the office at this house for over one-hundred years. Courtesy of Rokeby Museum.

rel track, running up a tree. Norris Day, who will be recalled by the older ones as an enthusiastic and perhaps mesmeric evangelist, modeled over the house now owned by Mr. Frisbie.

On the west side of the road, south of the Center, stood the Blacksmith shop of Elisha Green, and perhaps few men whose business was the forging of horseshoes and nails and early contrivances of the fathers, has had a more skillful pen to perpetuate his humble life than that of Rowland E. Robinson, whose *Uncle Lisha's Shop* may have drawn its inspiration from the diminutive building of the worthy Mr. Green, so small that only part of a horse would be accommodated in it at any one time.

The Byron Field house, near the depot and supposed to be the oldest frame house in town, was built by John Frasier, whose name appears upon the records for the first time in 1791. Near this house was the "official post," where were placed warnings for town meetings and elections, sheriff sales, etc. In an early day, before the streams lessened so much in size, the Little Otter afforded an unusually fine and continuous water power and for a long time two sawmills and a grist mill were run by Mr. Frasier and others at those falls.

The place now owned by Joseph Birkett was occupied by one of that name at an early day. The brick house on the hill known as the Bragg place stands on the farm formerly owned by Alpha Tupper, and here was another tavern. For a number of years town meetings were held at "Tupper's

Section of the Beers map of Ferrisburgh with additions related to Higbee's travels.

117

Above: The brick store on the north side of the green in Ferrisburgh Center, when it was operated by Kimball and Cushman. It was also the post office and a feed store. The store complex burned down, leaving only a garage, which still remains and is located behind the house now on the site. Courtesy of Bixby Free Memorial Library. Below: The same place several years earlier with several people barely visible. The man standing by the window of the garage is Burr Beach. Courtesy of Karl Devine. Photos undated.

An early photograph of the Union church and the town hall on the green in Ferrisburgh Center. The house that belonged to Burr Beach is behind the town hall. Courtesy of Bixby Free Memorial Library.

The Union Church on the east side of the green in Ferrisburgh Center when it served as town hall. The church was last in use in the 1970's. Charlotte Mem. Museum Collection.

Tavern"; and it is among the possibilities that herein lies an explanation for some of the animated scenes that the fathers say used frequently to occur when the stalwart freemen of Ferrisburgh differed a little as to who should "run the concern."

The farm now owned by Henry T. Booth has long been in the name, and there was no house between here and the Meigs place, a little north of which stands the stone marking the limits of the oldest city in Vermont. Beyond this stone no imprisoned debtor could pass when out "on Limits." In an early day a man who could not pay a debt was as promptly imprisoned as one who could pay and wouldn't, until the fathers saw that shutting a man up in jail did not ordinarily increase his earning powers, and so imprisonment for debt became a thing of the past.

From Martin's to Vergennes, the writer has mainly followed the old "stage road," and if these enumerations, imperfect as they are, add anything in fixing the names and habitations of those long since returned to the dust from whence they came, it will have afforded him perhaps more pleasure in the writing than you in the reading.

A drawing by Rowland E. Robinson used as the title page of one of his books. Photographic negative from Sylvia Sprigg. Courtesy of Rokeby Museum

XVIII

Lewis Creek and Its Mills

16 April 1897

There are now in existence in this vicinity several smooth bore rifles and regular shot guns made by Zimri Hill, and so substantial was his work that a "Hill" gun was always its own advertiser. Solomon A. Williams owns one of them that his father carried during his hunting days, and James B. Williams is the possessor of another shot gun, almost as long as a rake handle, that used to annihilate foxes at incredible distances. Zimri Hill was grandfather of Abel C. Palmer and owned the Palmer homestead. His shop stood in the southwest corner of Mr. Palmer's dooryard, and a little digging will today unearth debris and cinders from the ancient forge and shop. Mr. Hill's foreman, a remarkably expert workman, was a pugnacious little Englishman named Tommy Jones, who would no more tolerate a slighting remark relative to either his country or his guns than a mad bull the red flags in a Mexican bullfight. The result was that Tommy had to fight it out on this line a good many times, according to tradition.

In 1815 Mr. Hill in company with Sadoc Martin moved to Chautauqua County, New York, where the "Holland Purchase" held out alluring promises to settlers. At that time Western New York was West and Ohio was the Far West. Ahira Hall, a

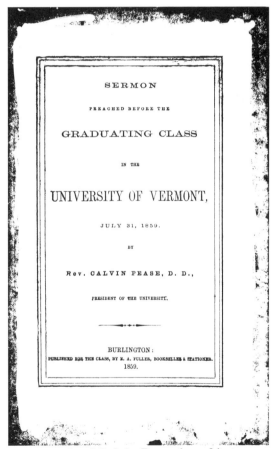

A souvenir of Calvin Pease from his tenure as president of the University of Vermont. Charlotte Memorial Museum Collection.

Lewis Creek near the site of the Nathan Leavenworth mills. No signs of the mills remain beyond an occasional piece of iron found beside the creek.

brother-in-law of Hill's who was drafted from this town into the War of 1812, started for the "Purchase" after the war. He went with an ox team and was forty-one days in arriving at the tavern of Daniel Barnes, another Charlotte man who had preceded him to that place. I think Mr. Barnes owned the farm where Andrew Franklin is, and he sold it to Solomon Pease, father of Peter E. Pease, now of Burlington. Calvin Pease, so long the head of the University at Burlington, was a son of Solomon Pease.[65]

Mention has been made of the colored people on whose account a certain section came to be known as "Guinea." Three brothers, Peter Freeman, Edward Shelton, and Amos Morocco, each of them taking the name of former masters, settled in an early day west of the Malinda H. Read farm and on land now owned by Sarah and Kirk Palmer. For a time these brothers were prosperous, had a farm paid for and a comfortable home, but they became involved by some un-fortunate speculation, and finally lost their land, and all of them drifted away. A sister of the brothers, named Lemon, came with them, and she planted a few chestnuts on an elevation that is known today as Chestnut Knoll, on which is now standing a chestnut tree that has borne fruit for more than fifty years. The great tract of land now in pasture and meadow in this section was a pine and hemlock forest, and a sawmill used to do a flourishing business on a small stream west of O. P. Read's.

The streams were larger and more reliable water powers in the early days when great stretches of evergreen forests retained the snow and moisture and the uncultivated and undrained low lands were reservoirs, constantly supplying the brooks and springs, and one stumbles upon the foundations and ruins of old mills in unexpected places.

Charlotte afforded several excellent mill sites along rapids in Lewis Creek, already spoken of, but possibly

The Leavenworth bridge over Lewis Creek below the mill sites located a few rods from the Hinesburg line. Photos taken in April, 1990

it may be of interest to refer to them again. General Nathan Leavenworth, who originated and gave name to the mills on this highest water power, came from New Milford, Connecticut, in 1787 settling in Hinesburgh. He was a man of marked capacity, going immediately to the front in a business and political way. He represented Hinesburgh twenty times in the Legislature, twice in the Senate, and was Presidential elector in 1833. The mills, located a few rods downstream from the Hinesburgh line, consisted of a grist mill, clothing mill, and a sawmill. The grist mill was a good one for those days, and a brother of Dorman Leavenworth, grandfather of our townsman Henry C. Leavenworth, cut one or more of its stones from a granite boulder found in the fields. One of these ancient stones is now used as a doorstep by Walter W. Parker. At one time this was the only grist mill between Winooski and Vergennes and it had to run sometimes night and day to keep up with

the demands of customers.

Of course the woolen mill was a much less pretentious affair than those of modern times, but its carding machine for making rolls, cloth dresser and press, its coloring vat and fulling mill were fully abreast of the wants of those who spun their own yarn and wove their own cloth and made their own clothing some two generations ago. Ready-made clothing stores were then unknown, at least in these parts, and the chest full of kersye[66] blankets, snow-white linen, and other substantials, the bride of seventy years ago took to her new home, and they were generally the result of her own skill and industry.

Stored away in garrets the curious will find the great spinning wheels she whirled with just the required speed: a step or two forward, then back again, the spindle singing its monotonous song hour after hour as she deftly drew the rolls into miles of yarn. Occasionally the flying curls of some careless youngster came in contact

123

An early "mother or maiden" spinning flax. Drawing by Rachel Robinson. Courtesy of Rokeby Museum.

After the spinning, came the weaving. A barn-frame loom used for weaving wool, linen and later for rugs is displayed in the Charlotte Memorial Museum.

with the whirring spindle, resulting in a sudden stoppage all around and an intricate untangling. So many knots, told off by the sharp click of the "reel," indicated the spinner's day's work; then transferred to the "swifts," from which the hand loom with its rattle and steady pound finally completed the yards. The fathers grew the flax, pulled it, let it lay exposed to rain and sun a certain length of time, and when the fiber was sufficiently softened, at it they went with the "swingle" and

"breaker" and "hetchel" until the piles of sandy colored tow were ready for the flax wheels, and the mothers and the maidens rested not until the linen, from brown to the whiteness of snow, was added to the household store.

The cloth mill burned down about seventy-five years ago. The house now owned and occupied by Joseph Carpenter once stood near the creek and was moved to its present site by James Barton. In an early day it was owned by a Mr. Header and was occupied by William Killam and Isaac Sherwood who worked in the clothing mill.

The old mill house south of the bridge, also owned by Joseph Carpenter, was occupied by John Moses, who tended the grist mill. Previous to this, Dorman Leavenworth lived in

The Sherman (Quinlan) bridge and the Lewis Creek valley. Beef cattle graze and hay is in plastic bags. Photo taken April, 1990.

the same house, ran the grist mill, and either built or repaired the sawmill. A man by the name of Joseph Hall lived where Fred Thomas's dwelling now is, and he ran a blacksmith shop there for years.

The winding valley of Lewis Creek, from Leavenworth's down, is fair to look upon, as the stream works its way among rocky cliffs and along reedy banks, sometimes dashing with rapids terminating in a deep quiet pool. It turns here and there upon itself, as though minded at times to run back again to its parent hills; hardly a half mile and possibly not a quarter, does it continue a straightforward course, but loiters under the shading elms and willows as loath to leave them.

Below Joseph J. Quinlan's it turns an oxbow of half to three-quarters of a mile, when a straight cut across could have been made in twenty rods, reminding one of the great bend in the Connecticut, seen from Mount Holyoke, only less pretentious. The several acres of the greenest of sward

and sweetest of feed included in this bow are the gradual deposits of hundreds of overflows; and tradition has it that this was an Indian cornfield in the years when beavers were busy in most of our streams, and the silver salmon flashed in the sunshine or hid himself in the shadows of the overhanging forest trees.[67]

Before the woodsman with his axe, before the mill man with the rattle and clash of his saw and wheel, this stream ran full-banked to the lake, its only navigator the red man, whose birch canoe swept along the water like a floating leaf. He owed allegiance only to his tribe, loving the stream for what it gave him, loving the dark forests for the game found therein and his wigwam because it sheltered him; loving his tomahawk and scalping knife for the protections in war, and his forefathers for their fierceness, fighting to the last for their graves--all this, and more than this, the stream has known.

125

Month of August 1896	No. of Cheese Made Daily.	J.A. Foote	E.A. Hicks	J.L. Shaw	C.D. Prindle	N.H. Hoxford	G.C. Prindle	H.C. Clark	J.M. Dean	G. Willoughby	Mrs. Howlett	W.S. Bradley	C. Livermore	D. Hoxford	O.P. Read	E.O. Prindle	A. Lawrance
1	9	371	401	236	322	199 / 293	184 / 220	223 / 264	403	213	281	306 / 266	205 / 209	98 / 103	76 / 105		
2	9	377	392	233	319	182 / 242	173 / 220	203 / 257	403	204	274	271 / 291	192 / 234	100 / 104	86 / 91		
3	10	390	399	243	345	216 / 255	179 / 226	240 / 261	394	219	280	253 / 155	195 / 233	105 / 125	86 / 108		
4	8	370	377	235	326	205 / 293	190 / 208	216 / 262		208	269	267 / 268	191 / 216	101 / 105	73 / 109		
5	9	377	388	238	158	212 / 232	202 / 233	224 / 274	404	203	280	278 / 308	199 / 237	119 / 96	76 / 104		
6	10	405	417	248	164	244 / 259	194 / 240	236 / 267	418	215	275	274 / 254	790 / 112	114 / 85			
7	10	392	402	244	361	202 / 259	191 / 288	230 / 271	407	210	282	545 / 288	95 / 119	109 / 85	95		
8	10	402	374	250	344	211 / 263	176 / 227	213 / 261	409	206	282	568 / 243	209 / 115	95 / 88	92		
9	10	404	442	248	355	217 / 259	183 / 220	233 / 257	423	217	304	543 / 240	206 / 111	93 / 87	64		
10	10	405	414	250	344	211 / 261	176 / 210	234 / 258	404	206	303	583 / 250	191 / 107	94 / 94	71		
11	10	396	395	253	360	221 / 195	191 / 252	218		221	305	550 / 214	202 / 102	112 / 88	81		
12	10	405	402	235	360	222 / 248	194 / 190	231 / 267	700	217	296	554 / 223	194 / 106	89	76		
13	12	410	403	247	358	225 / 250	184 / 214	222 / 265	399	212	318	559 / 242	260 / 102	97			
14	12	403	399	244	372	221 / 264	176 / 214	234 / 265	408	213	314	558 / 226	194 / 106	100 / 86	74		
15	12	379	396	247	366	215 / 254	177 / 216	222 / 283	418	215	316	557 / 195	195 / 102	101 / 98	92		
16	10	390	387	245	379	241 / 257	191 / 213	234 / 270		212	311	570 / 254	429 / 121	97 / 104	82		
17	9	390	403	247	363	232 / 242	182 / 196	229 / 259		224	308	558 / 218	206 / 95	93 / 90	74		
18	9	399	398	240	356	225 / 189	220 / 256	227		203	306	531 / 206	104 / 118	76 / 101		102	
19	9	379	382	220	350	241 / 230	194 / 185	230 / 257		204	296	576 / 240	186 / 108	106 / 90	81	101	364
20	10	391	396	234	152	219 / 248	195 / 200	240 / 267		208	291	521 / 218	190 / 118	106 / 84	79	102	362
21	10	379	380	240	174	228 / 257	170 / 196	229 / 268		222	303	545 / 260	214 / 100	101 / 92	91	100	358
22	10	401	372	253	353	223 / 237	169 / 173	232 / 259		204	302	571 / 103	196 / 86	114 /	79	104	345
23	10	406	379	222	341	236 / 239	205 / 240	231 / 255		214	293	489 / 202	402 / 103	114 / 88	85		331
24	10	396	400	241	366	242 / 262	200 / 207	244 / 276		198	304	536 / 191	221 / 111	104 / 80	85		315
25	8	451	416	249	357	238 / 221	229 / 193	237 / 235		229	807	535 / 195	220 / 117	110 / 85	82		
26	8	420	400	253	353	241 / 215	189 / 253	238		195	310	624 / 214	195 / 110	104 / 79	93		
27		409	384	237	334	235 / 224	166 / 212	226 / 264		184		570 / 191	185 / 110	105 / 81	81		928
28	9	418	378	258	381	243 / 252	163 / 203	226 / 260		218	287		187 / 198	102 / 119			
29		398	390	248	359	228 / 244	168 / 185	226 / 253		220	306		177 / 101	101			
30	8	383	398	253	348	239 / 247	182 / 202	230 / 249		196	301		360 / 193	114 / 90			
31	7	392	371	240	354	219 / 239	159 / 190	218 / 257		208	295		170 / 200	114 / 92			

"The View toward Camel's Hump."
Oil painting by Daniel Folger Bigelow (1823-1910), around 1870.
Courtesy of an area resident

XIX

Mountain Views and Railroads

14 May 1897

The miles of circling drives at "Red Rocks" near Burlington have afforded boundless pleasure to thousands, and the wealthy gentleman who thus contributed to the health and happiness of the public proclaims himself a benefactor of his race. But this spot, beautiful as it is, is not to be compared with a drive we shall see when some generous hand encircles Mount Philo or Pease Mountain with winding highways[68]. Here, too, we have the woods, the birds, the springs, miniature plains, where the young pines and cedars crowd each other as they grow, or quiet glens up whose rock sides clings a wealth of bush, and tree and vine, from whose retreat the soft-eyed rabbit stares in wondering surprise and the partridge startles you with booming whirr of wings as he shoots from under your feet.

Drives such as these will afford not a rod of sameness, but a continual, delighted enjoyment of a scene that cannot be surpassed in New England.

The view from either Mount Tom or Mount Holyoke of the Connecticut Valley is something like it, but it lacks in magnitude compared with ours. That is beautiful; this magnificent.

Nothing here is indistinct from being at too great an elevation, as it is from Camel's Hump or Mansfield. The brooks and rivers that flow into the lake from the Little Otter south wind their silvery way, marking out the lesser valleys and watering the fertile farms that stretch away on every hand. Each farm with its patch of woodland, and now and then an outlot growing up to hard wood or young pines, leads you to think the forest days are not yet passed, for the woods seem multiplied as one looks down upon them from the hills. A sunrise in summer, heralded an hour before by hundreds of birds, will well repay you for an early climb, and a sunset with its broad horizon of gold, tempts you to linger again and again among the fragrant cedars and whispering pine.

In August, 1878, sixteen farmers from East Charlotte produced milk for the cheese factory at Prindle corners. Some made two deliveries per day, among them M. H. Hosford, G. E. Prindle and H. Clark. C. G. Prindle (probably Cyrus Gurnsey Pringle) did not produce much milk--his farming was more in fruit crops, his livelihood from being a plant collector. Charlotte Memorial Museum Collection.

The view from Mt. Philo in 1974 photographed on infra-red film. Higbee's favorite views remain much the same.

It is not quite fifty years since the first train ran through here on the Rutland and Burlington road, but from the changed condition of things since 1848, one would suppose that a century must have elapsed. We have not advanced by steps and strides, but by bounds. Hardly a farm implement of today but then would have been an object of amazement. Imagine our dairymen talking about cheese factories and creameries then. What would have been said of a modern Buckeye buzzing its way through the meadows, or a twine binder kicking out bundles at the rate of twenty to the minute, or the plow boy making his rounds on the spring seat of the sulky plow.

Compare the vehicles of today, the team wagons, buggies, carriages, sleighs, harness. The telegraph was a crude affair in comparison with present uses of electricity. Trains of loaded cars, going forty miles an hour, with no visible propelling powers, belong to this age most decidedly, and the horseless road wagon will soon be taking nobody's dust. Bicycles pass in every direction, factory and mill hands go to and from their work on them; postmen, school girls, school boys, merchants, bankers, tourists, college students, lawyers, minister--all the

The Lakeview Creamery by the railroad station made blocks of butter "printed" with its name. These are rubbings of two of its prints, each about eight inches wide. Charlotte Memorial Museum Collection.

world on wheels, except the farmer. Not being able to pasture his dairy in the highway, the latter has to forego the pleasure of driving up his cows on a "bike" and hunting the wild-eyed kine out of bush lots in fly time rather calls upon him to foot it. But the farmer of today keeps his place in the procession, and the products of his toil and care feed the world.

Only a few days ago a prominent official of the Boston and Maine system, testifying before a legislative committee on transportation, said it was only a question of time when steam would be superseded by electricity as a propelling power. His road had experimented with a third rail, dispensing with overhead wires and supporting poles, and they were satisfied that the thing was practicable. This may result in cheapening the operating of railroads and may increase speed, something the commercial world is always looking for. It may not be so many years before electric lines for passengers and light freight will run along on main highways, connecting the rural districts and thrifty villages in all directions.

From Burlington south through Shelburne, Charlotte, Ferrisburgh, and east through Monkton to the beautiful village of Bristol, a rich and thickly populated section would furnish a large amount of local business. It would seem that an electric road running from Vergennes to the southwest and west and taking the travel and traffic of Panton, Addison, Weybridge, Bridport, and other towns would be of great advantage to Vergennes, and an immense accommodation to the towns in question.

129

Vergennes is the center of a magnificent farming country, but surrounded by a soil that rivals Virginia in sticking qualities at certain season. It has a famous market and can afford to look this thing up a little and see if an electric railroad would not bring a boom to their economy in a healthy, businesslike way.

Suppose the money that Vermonters have dropped in Western and Southern bubbles had been employed in some such way as this right here at home, during the last twenty-five years, would as fine farms as Addison or Chittenden counties boast be looking for buyers at less than half their real worth? Prices of farm products here and in the west show conclusively there is no occasion for grumbling on the part of the Vermont farmer. The trouble has been: surplus capital has for years back been looking "away off" for investments. Home enterprises were no good. A captivating per cent--on paper--blinded the eye to a probable vanishing of the principal.

It was a cross. Take Vergennes, for instance, with both boat and railroad communication, and as magnificent a water power as the State affords. Within a radius of twenty miles--a territory that naturally seeks her markets--enough money has probably been dropped in unfortunate out-of-the-state enterprises to have originated business along the stream below the falls that would have employed hundreds of workmen.

Mankind, after all, is a good deal like boys fishing--the rock "over yonder" is always the place where fish are going to bite the best. The West has been developed with Eastern money, and Vermont has been as lavish with her dollars as with her sons, who are found everywhere in the highest seats in the world's synagogues and capitals. Notwithstanding our losses, statistics show that Vermont is rich today--richer in proportion to her population than perhaps any other State in the Union, and if home enterprises are properly fostered in the future, the "abandoned farms" will be a thing of the past.

"A magnificent farming country" as sketched by Rowland Robinson in 1880. Courtesy of Rokeby Museum.

XX

Joseph Hoag: Quaker Visionary

14 May 1897

Perhaps one of the unique characters connected with our earlier history was Mr. Joseph Hoag, who settled in the southeast part of the town about on the line between Charlotte and Monkton. He cleared off a large farm, part of which was owned by the late Rufus Eno and Oscar Hazard. He built nearly a mile of road through his holdings, setting out maple trees on each side: but subsequently the farm was divided, a portion of the highway discontinued, and a good share of the maple trees cut down, leaving a portion of those trees near the highway close to Mrs. Sarah Hazard's.

Mr. Hoag was a successful farmer and a recognized local authority on gardening and fruit growing. He was a distinguished member of the Society of Friends, coming here at such an early day that he found only three families in these parts of similar beliefs. His remarkable vision has been commented upon through the press for years; only recently an article appeared in the *Burlington Free Press* from a public address on "Joseph Hoag and his Vision."[69] He was an evangelist, going north, south east and west preaching the gospel of peace, good will toward men. His work was not for pay. He went with neither script nor purse into the busy markets of the world, into the wayside cottage; a cup of cold water, a mouthful of bread, a resting place for the night, a consciousness of trying to do good to his fellow man--this seemed to be enough.

The imprint of his work will remain. He was an enthusiast. The lonely woods, the deep valleys, the high mountains, the swollen streams, hardships and dangers added to the fires of the soul and obstacles but increased his fervor. Coupled with practical business sagacity, was the dreamy nature of the poet, and sights floated before his eyes and words were spoken in his ears that came not to all.

It is said he was the first minister to settle in Charlotte and was offered a section of land on that account, but he declined to accept it as he did not believe in taking pay for preaching. Right or wrong in the matter of being the "first minister," how much the world owes to the stern and sturdy virtues of those long dead.

The Joseph Hoag House. Oscar Hazard bought the farm from Hoag. His son George, leaning on his rake on the right, and family are seen here. In more recent times the farm belonged to Rod Baldwin and now is owned by Dale and Lucille Garvey. Charlotte Memorial Museum Collection.

The field where Joseph Hoag had his famous vision. It is between the farm house and the Quaker cemetery. The Quaker meeting house was then near the cemetery and Hoag often went this way to the meeting house. Photo taken in April, 1990.

A Quaker Prophecy

The Strange Vision of Joseph Hoag.

There is a large Quaker settlement at Salem, Iowa. Years ago writes a Keokuk, Iowa, correspondent of The St. Louis Globe-Democrat, Joseph Hoag was of their number. He was blessed with the gift of visions, and the Quakers had great faith in him. The most noteworthy of these visions was one happening in South Carolina in 1803. In it was imparted to Joseph Hoag, the knowledge of the coming war in the church and that of the revolution. Monarchical form of government founded on religion and thereafter events, are yet to come. Copies of this vision are most carefully preserved by most every Quaker family in the vicinity of Salem. From one of these copies, which the owner declares to have been in his possession for over thirty years, a Globe-Democrat representative secured the prophecy. It is as follows:

In the year 1803, probably in the eighth or ninth month, I was one day alone in the field, and I observed the sun shone clear, but a mist eclipsed the brightness of its shining. As I reflected on the singularity of the event my mind was clothed with silence, the most solemn I ever remember. My faculties were laid low and unusually brought into silence, I said to myself: 'What can all this mean?' I do not remember ever to have been sensible to such feelings, and I heard a voice from Heaven saying: 'This that thou seest, that dims the brightness of the sun, is the sign of a present and coming tim. I took the fathers of this country from the land of oppression. I planted them here among forests. I blessed them and sustained them and while they were humble I fed them, and they became a numerous people, but they now have become proud and lifted up and have forgotten me who nourished and protected them, and are running into every abominable and evil practice which the old country was guilty of, and taking quietude from the land, and have suffered a dividing spirit to come among them. Lift up thine eyes and behold.' I saw them dividing in great haste. This division began in the church on points of doctrine. It commenced with the Presbyterian society, went through various religious denominations, and its progress and close were nearly the same. Those who divided went off with high heads and taunting language and those who kept original sentiments appeared exercised and sorrowful, and when the dividing spirit entered the Society of Friends it raged in as high a degree as any I have before described and as before those who separated went with lofty looks and taunting, censuring language; those who kept ancient principles retired to themselves.

"It next appeared in the lodges of Freemasons and set the country in an uproar for a long time. Then it entered politics throughout the United States, and it did not stop until it produced a civil war, and abundance of blood was shed in the course of the combat. The fourteen states lost their power, and slavery was annihilated from their borders.

"Then a monarchical government arose and established a nation of religion, and made all societies tributary to support its expenses. I was amazed at beholding all this, and I heard a voice proclaim. 'This power shall not always stand, but with this power shall I chastize my church until they return to the faithfulness their forefathers. Thou seest what is coming in thy native land for their iniquities and the blood of Africa, the rememberance of which has come up before me. This vision is yet for many days.'"

More of the Hoag vision. This undated clipping from the St. Louis Globe-Democrat places the scene of the vision in South Carolina. Historians of local Quaker activities have a stronger case for the site shown here. Charlotte Memorial Museum Collection.

A Quaker meeting at the John Gove farm around 1871. This became the Eugene Aube farm on Dorset St. Ext. The house burned in 1918. Gift of Hazel Hoskam. Charlotte Memorial Museum Collection.

XXI

Sherman's Sawmill
Varney's Iron Working Shop

21 May 1897

Downward from Leavenworth's not very far as the crow flies, but a long way if you follow the meandering of Lewis Creek and a little east of the old house now occupied by Henry Lesor, stood the Sherman saw mill. Two brothers, George and Edmund Sherman, located in the valley and cleared up farms together, George on the south side of Lewis Creek and Edmund on the north side. Edmund's house stood northeast of the bridge and north of the highway as it now runs. Probably the house on the south side, saving an occasional modernizing, is the one that was built by George Sherman.

The saw mill was a valuable adjunct to the early settler as it rasped along the pine and hemlock logs in a persistent and if not over-rapid manner until 1843. A freshet cut a channel between the mill and the bank and a bridge had to be constructed before the sawyer could get home to dinner, unless he swam for it. William J. Scott[70] was mill tender at that time and before going home to his meals

A saw mill in Monkton Ridge after steam replaced water power and mills moved away from streams. Courtesy of Jessie Thomas.

135

some fifty rods away, he would set the saw going in a fourteen foot log getting back in time to lug off the board and "gig" the ponderous carriage into position again. In time the river cut queer pranks and newer courses until the mill fell into gradual decline and was finally torn down or washed away.

Still further down stream, and on the north side of the creek, Nathan Varney, who came from Berwick, Maine, had a trip hammer and iron working shop. Connected with him at one time were Alpheus and William Varney, his sons. They built the W. J. Scott house now owned by J. J. Stapleton, to point nails in.

Iron came to the shop in "pigs" or rough blocks, was pounded out by the trip hammer, and the nails were hand-forged. After forging, they were taken to the pointing shop, placed in dies, and hammered out to proper shape. The Varneys made axes, shovels, hoes, spades, scythes, and carpenter tools . I think George W. Varney, a son of Alpheus, has one of their scythes. Nathan Varney lived in a house that stood south of the old Stapleton place, near the bend in the road. In 1833, Alpheus Varney built the house and shop on the old homestead where he died. Hezekiah Varney, a brother of Nathan Varney, lived just over the Monkton line on the place now owned by Nathan Perkins, and he made spinning wheels for both wool and flax: reels, swifts, hand fans for cleaning grain, window sash, and probably numerous other handy contrivances.

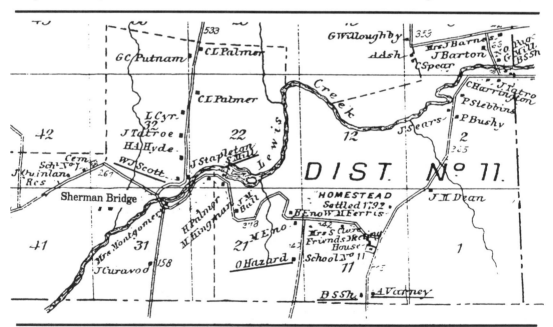

Beers map of the southeast corner of Charlotte with Scott's house and mill, Alpheus Varney's shop and home, the Sherman bridge and Oscar Hazard's (Joseph Hoag's) house located.

The remains of the Alpheus Varney blacksmith shop on Roscoe Rd. just north of
the Monkton town line. In 1921 Clifford
and Allen Cole posed in the window.
"Shop" still shows in the triangular stone
lintel. That stone is now in the Shelburne
Museum collection. Courtesy of Dorothy
and Allen Cole.

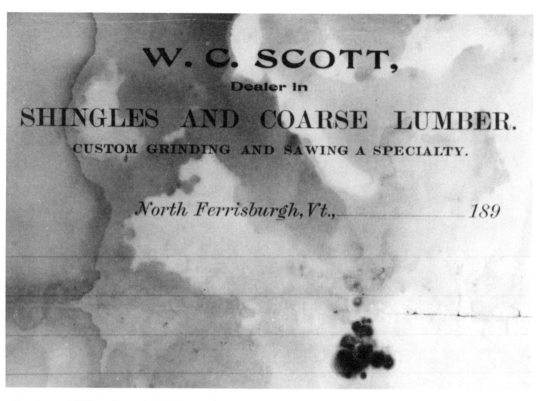

W. C. SCOTT,
Dealer in
SHINGLES AND COARSE LUMBER.
CUSTOM GRINDING AND SAWING A SPECIALTY.

*North Ferrisburgh, Vt.,*_____ *189*

Business billing form for Scott's mill in the 1890s. This was probably the last water mill to operate in Charlotte. Courtesy of Marty Illick.

Dr. William Henry Harrison Varney, the youngest child of Alpheus and Phila (Palmer) Varney. He studied at Uncle Ben's academy in Vergennes, received a medical degree from the Berkshire Medical school, practiced medicine in East Charlotte, held many town offices. In the 1911 town meeting he made a motion of commendation to W. W. Higbee on his 39th election to be town clerk. Photo from a group picture of Masons circa 1906. Charlotte Memorial Museum Collection

XXII

Thorp Finds a Whale, Marble Tombstones, Potash Business, the Stage and Greenbush Roads and the Post Office

28 May 1897

When the Rutland and Burlington Railroad was being built William Wright had a contract for some three miles of the grading commencing south of the Thorp crossing and running north through Barber's swamp. The late John G. Thorp was one day going along the "fill" and some workmen called his attention to some bones lying in the freshly dumped earth. Mr. Thorp saw directly that something out of the ordinary had been struck in the cut from whence the dirt was being taken and he asked contractor Wright to shift his gang of shovelers so he could investigate, resulting in the finding of the almost perfect skeleton of a medium sized whale. Mr. Thorp invited Zadock Thompson, then connected with the Burlington University, to inspect the find and he gave Mr. Thompson the bones. The bed from which they were taken was of quicksand and minute shells. The credit for the preservation of this remarkable find is justly due to our early townsman, Mr. Thorp.

The skeleton now occupies a place in the state museum at Montpelier. What particular attraction ever called

a whale into Vermont is and will likely remain a mystery. It may be that even in remote ages Vermont had a pro-

What a place to find a whale. The approximate location where the Charlotte whale was found on the railroad north of the Thompson's Point crossing. Photo taken in April, 1990.

139

tective fish and game law, and the whale was seeking to benefit by the escaping to its protection.

Dr. Strong, father of the late John Strong, at one time carried on the marble business, where Mrs. Celinda Heard and Miss Flora J. Foote now live, and many of the stones in the old south [Barber] cemetery were made and placed there by him.

Samuel Hurlburt, who lived on the homestead of Mary E. Jones, was a wheelwright and his shop used to stand on the present site of S. E. Russell's house. Jarvis J. Bouton was a wheelwright and the house now owned by Joseph Manor and moved by Michael Naylor from the Bouton place was used by Mr. Bouton as a shop.

Across the road there used to be a potash, and a large business was done there at one time, though the writer has been unable to find out who originated it. There was also a potash on the place owned by Miss Minerva Wing, standing north of the house on the little bay. The leached ashes from both these works were loaded on boats at McNeil's ferry and taken to Long Island for fertilizing purposes. Drawing the immense piles to the lake gave

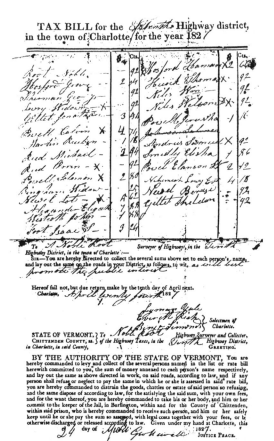

The tax bill for Highway district #10 for 1827. Noble Root was the surveyor and with his father, Gad Root, in that same year had bought a farm located beside Bingham Brook on the Hinesburgh Rd. Charlotte Memorial Museum Collection.

employment to a large number of teamsters, some of them coming here from the York State side. So large a section of hardwood land as was being rapidly cleared and fitted for cultivations furnished great quantities of the best ashes and making potash was a very profitable industry.

Sand clams such as were found with the whale, shown at actual size. They can be found in several sites in town. Sketch by Jennie Cole.

140

The records of a town meeting held some eighty years ago show that a committee was appointed to see what the town would do about "repairing or rebuilding the bridge near Dr. Strong's saw mill." Inquiry has thus far failed to locate this mill exactly, but it was probably in the east part of the town and may have been on the stream near what has for years been known as the Abel Leavenworth bridge. Probably some of our oldest citizens may be able to settle this point for us.

The "stage or post road" from Vergennes to Burlington, as by act of the legislature, was surveyed and laid out in July 1787 by William Niles, Samuel Strong, and Joseph J. Tobias, committee. The road at that time was established to be six rods wide but it seems a change was subsequently made in this width.[71]

In 1802 a road was opened leading south to Ferrisburgh, commencing "at a stake and stones the south side of the east and west highway about three rods southerly of Mr. George Thorp's store in Charlotte." This is what is now known as the Greenbush Road, intersecting the old stage road near the Dr. Cram place[72]. William Niles, Samuel Rich, and John Cobb were selectmen at that time. An effort was made to get the stage line transferred to this route and it is said the stage did run as far north as the Four Corners, going from there to Burling-

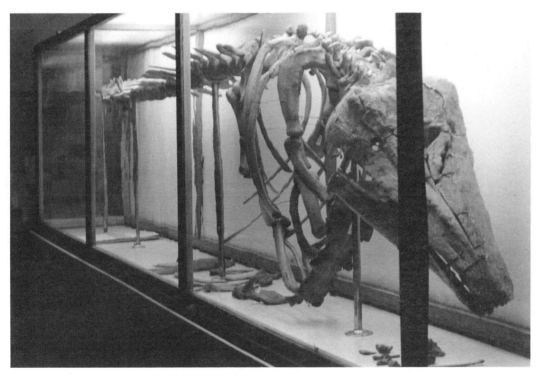

The Charlotte whale now in the Geology Museum of the University of Vermont.

ton on the old line instead of up the "Lake Road" through Shelburne, as certain individuals hoped it would. Considerable rivalry existed about the regular stage route and numerous wires were pulled and disappointments endured on these accounts.

It is a difficult matter to locate very many old highways for the want of a starting point.[73] In a majority of instances, the surveyor started a certain distance from a "corner" of somebody's "log house" or so far from near a "garden fence" when the log house and garden both ceased to exist perhaps seventy-five years ago and no living person can now point out their ancient location. The roads would have to run wild in a certain sense, only that length of years has established their rights. At an early day, and indeed down to a comparatively recent period, there was but one post office in town--located for years under various postmasters at the old Barnes-Alexander stand where James Toner is now in trade. Private individuals doubtless arranged for the distribution of mail in neighborhoods but there was much less governmental interest taken in the public than characterizes this age.

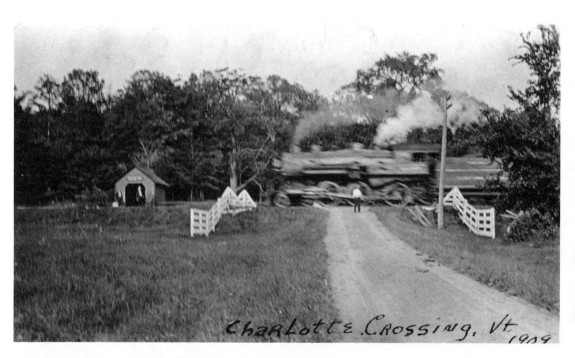

Charlotte Crossing, Vt. 1909

The railroad crossing at Thompson's Point Rd. in 1909 when it had a station. One regular passenger stopping here many years ago was a teacher at the Emerson School. Charlotte Memorial Museum Collection.

XXIII

Postmasters and Branch Post Offices, the Monkton Red School, the Hoag-Palmer Sawmill

4 June 1897

We should remember that when Hezekiah Barnes built his famous log tavern near the spring, supplementing it with a store and cider mill, there were perhaps not a dozen newspapers printed in Vermont. Now and then an ambitious city like New York, Boston, Troy or Albany supported a small sized daily. It was a rare thing for a weekly city paper to have a subscriber so far away as Vermont. When it cost ten to twenty-five cents to send a letter through the mail, people did not write, only as it became necessary. A weekly or even a monthly visit to the post office to collect the mail was doubtless sufficient as a rule.

As nearly as the writer can ascertain, Noble Lovely was the postmaster before Samuel H. Barnes; then Mr. Barnes, followed by Abial Lyon. Caleb E. Barton received the appointment under Buchanan's administration and the office had a brief removal to the building now occupied by David Dugas as a wheelwright shop at the Corners, kept by Cyrus B. Martin. Advantage being taken by certain informalities of the removal, the office went back to the old stand again, and Mr. Burton was succeeded by the late John Quinlan, and Ezra Alexander had charge of the office under Mr. Quinlan. After Buchanan came a change of presidents, and Ezra Alexander was appointed postmaster.

At that time the political pot was boiling over, and a little less than a wagonload of weekly and semi-weekly *Tribunes* discussed the issues of the day with sons and daughters of Charlotte.

Probably no single man ever imposed himself more strongly upon the

HORACE GREELEY.

American people than Horace Greeley through his *Tribune*. The editorial page of that paper from about 1850 to the election of Abraham Lincoln was on fire. It was a broadside from a seventy-four gun frigate. It was the jagged lightning, and so near, that the thunder crash came with it.

About 1868 another or branch office was established at the depot called West Charlotte with Luther R. Hubbell, postmaster. The office remained at the station and at West Charlotte, some seven years. After the failure of Ezra Alexander[74] the office was kept at the Congregational parsonage for about a year and a half by Reverend C. C. Torrey. In 1875 Mrs. Nancy C. Pope, now Mrs. Bush, was appointed postmaster, and an office was established at East Charlotte, Ezra Hosford, postmaster. Mrs. Bush has held the office through various administrations since 1875 and this certainly speaks well for her capacity and faithfulness. Several changes have occurred in East Charlotte appointments. Joseph S. Shaw succeeded Mr. Hosford, then Anna Quinlan, John R. Taggart, and the present incumbent, Joseph J. Quinlan. Mrs. Bush was Mr. Hubbell's assistant four years giving her a continuous post office service of twenty-six years. John H. Knowles, now of Ferrisburgh, was the first contractor for carrying the mail to East Char-

Setting the records straight about Mrs. ▶ *Bush, "Charlotte's Postmistress." Undated clipping from a scrapbook in the Charlotte Memorial Museum Collection.*

Charlotte's Postmistress.

We are pleased to print this week a new and correct picture of Mrs. Nancy Bush, for 37 years the popular and efficient postmistress at Charlotte. The article and cut recently published from the Boston Daily Globe was correct except in one particular, the picture did not do Mrs. Bush justice, because it was not her picture but another lady's, her sister, several years older. As soon as we

MRS. NANCY BUSH.

discovered that the Globe had made a mistake we took steps to procure a new and correct likeness of Mrs. Bush as we felt sure all the readers of this paper would like to see a picture that did Mrs. Bush justice, as far as any half tone cut printed on common newspaper stock can do any one justice.

All that the Globe said about her record and popularity we find is strictly true and much more might be added. The people of Charlotte are proud of their post misstress and her record, and we doubt if all New England can furnish her equal.

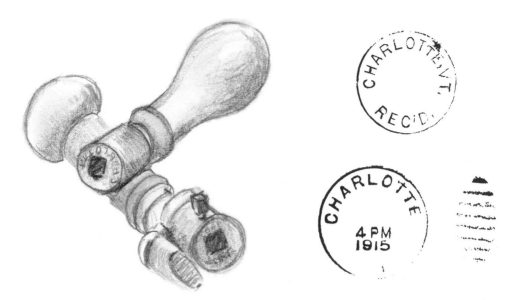

Two hand cancellation devices from the Charlotte Post Office, and the text printed by them. Sketches by Shirley Thompson. Charlotte Memorial Museum Collection.

lotte. The present carrier, William Quinlan, has been in the government service twenty-one years, and during this time, through mud and snow and storm, the mail has seldom, if ever, failed of delivery. Fifty years ago April 22, Mr. Quinlan landed at "Martin's" from the stage and he has witnessed the burial of scores of those who were active businessmen when he came to this new land.

The road leading south from Sherman's mill, past the old Hezekiah Varney place, and so on into Addison county, was surveyed and laid out years ago under act of the legislature-- and this was designated as a "stage road"--but it is doubtful if the stage ever ran over this route.

The site of the red schoolhouse in Monkton has been used for school purposes these many years, and the present building was put up by Sheldon Miller. South of the schoolhouse Elijah Carr lives on the farm that was occupied by John Knowles who was a wheelwright as well as farmer. Andrew Austin lived on the hill east of the schoolhouse on the farm now owned by Peter Bushey. Herman Hyde lived on the farm occupied by Herman Jewell. West of Mr. Hyde's and on the south side of the road, a house used to stand owned or occupied by Eli Barnum and afterwards by Lewis Barnum. Warren Partch lived on the farm now owned by A. W. Mead, where Daniel Bull lives. The late James Higbee spent a long life where George Cross now lives. The Nathaniel Higbee farm now occupied by his son, Fred Higbee, was owned by Enoch Palmer.

A road used to run north from the Enoch Palmer place, crossing the creek by a bridge near the Quinlan

145

Possibly the "Quinlan Ford" on Lewis Creek. In the left foreground are some remains of the Scott mill. A former resident remembers taking logs to the mill on the far side (north side) of the creek and fording the stream at the right in this photo. However, Higbee's text seems to locate the ford further downstream below the bridge. Photo taken in 1990.

ford, and so on north into "Guinea." This being a bad place to maintain a bridge, the road was discontinued, and crossing was had at Sherman's, higher up the stream. John Moore used to live on the old road north of Enoch Palmer's. It seems the Hoags and Joseph Palmer had a saw mill near or on the site of Winfield C. Scott's mill somewhere about 1830. This mill burned down.

Later, Henry Miles established a mill where Scott is now, making sash, doors, and blinds, and he also connected with it a foundry for plow points, cultivator teeth, etc. Mr. Miles bought the mill of Solomon Pease who used to run a saw and shingle mill on the little stream east of William Lasor's, where there is an abrupt waterfall of several feet. This mill was in existence somewhere from 1830 to 1840 and William J. Scott recalls making repairs on the mill while it was owned and run by Mr. Pease. Mr. Scott made and painted the "1849" on the Sherman bridge. It appears that Jesse Ball succeeded Miles, and then Henry Montgomery, Mitchell Kingman, and Winfield C. Scott, the present owner. This has always been a valuable water privilege, and in times when the creek is low, Scott has a chance to play a dry joke on the "Hollow" folks by shutting down his gate.

146

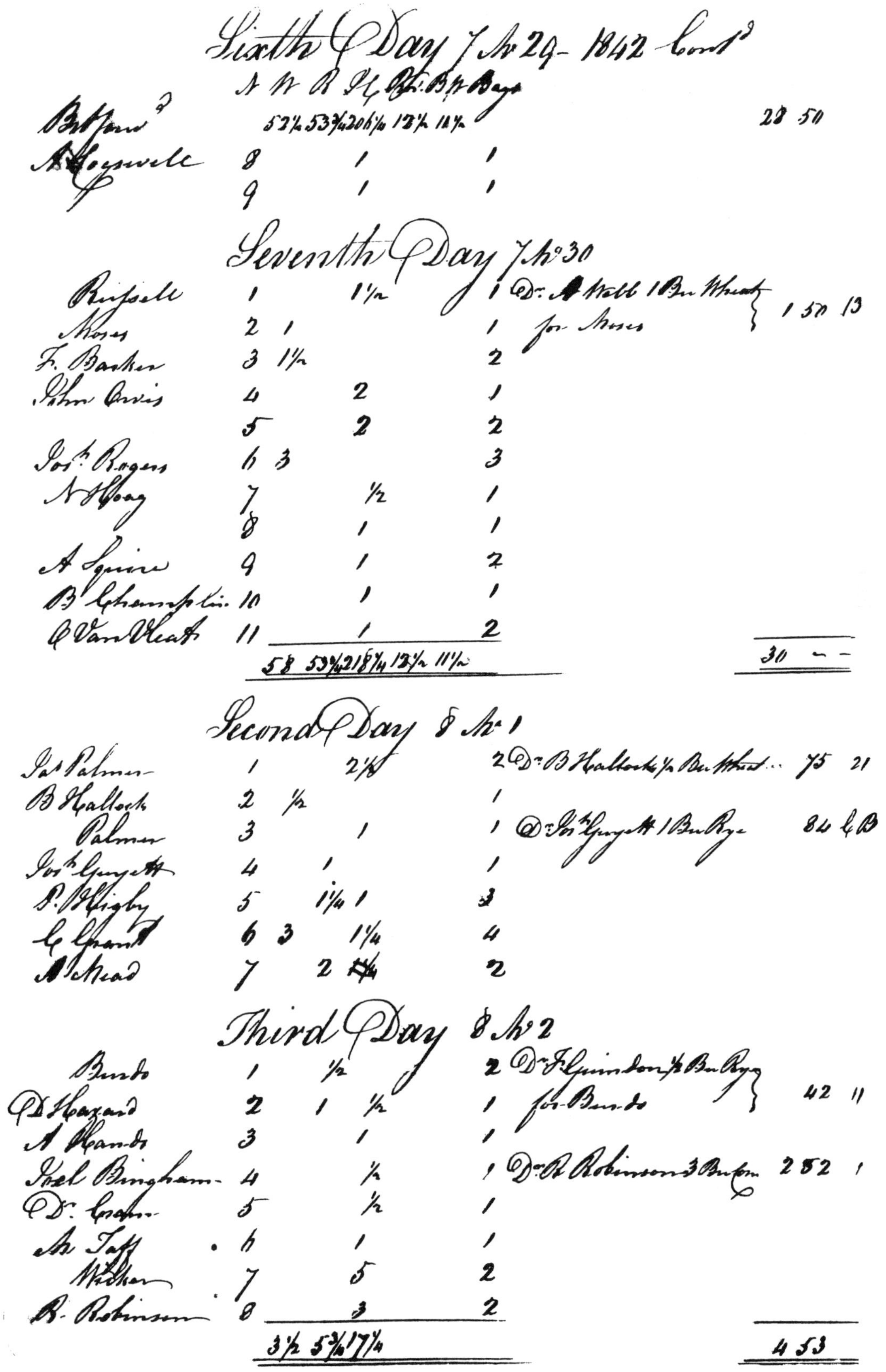

Sixth Day 7 Mo 29 - 1842 Cont^d

Bt forw^d		53½ 53¾ 206¼ 13½ 11½					28 50
A. Hopwell	8		1	1			
	9		1	1			

Seventh Day 7 Mo 30

Russell	1		1½	1	Dr A Webb 1 Bu Wheat for Moses	1 50 13
Moses	2	1		1		
F. Barker	3	1½		2		
John Orvis	4		2	1		
	5		2	2		
Jos^h Rogers	6	3		3		
N Hoag	7		½	1		
	8		1	1		
A Squire	9		1	2		
B Champlin	10		1	1		
O VanVleat	11		1	2		
	58 53¾ 218¾ 13½ 11½					30 — —

Second Day 8 Mo 1

Jas Palmer	1		2½	2	Dr B Hallock ½ Bu Wheat	75 21
B Hallock	2	½		1		
Palmer	3		1	1	Dr Jos^h Gurgett 1 Bu Rye	84 CB
Jos^h Gurgett	4	1		1		
P. Higby	5	1¼	1	3		
C Grant	6	3	1¼	4		
A Mead	7	2	[illegible]	2		

Third Day 8 Mo 2

Burds	1		½	2	Dr F Quimby ½ Bu Rye for Burds	42 11
O. D. Hazard	2	1	½	1		
A Hands	3		1	1		
Joel Bingham	4		½	1	Dr R Robinson 3 Bu Corn	2 82 1
Dr Coan	5		½	1		
M Taff	6		1	1		
Walker	7		5	2		
R. Robinson	8		3	2		
	3½ 5¾ 17¼					4 53

A record from a Henry Miles mill. This page from his account book for 1842 with days listed in the Quaker way indicates that he was sawing lumber and also grinding grain. His book does not list which mill he owned at that time. Peter Higby [sic] and O. VanVliet were among his customers. Courtesy of Miles' descendant, Marylee (Mrs. Forrest) Rose.

Left: At Scott's Pond. Remains of the dam and a wing dam on Lewis Creek above the Sherman (Quinlan) bridge. Photo taken in 1990.

Below: Breakfast for 'the boy' in the mid-1800s: buckwheat cakes and eel. Courtesy of Georgina Hurd.

Eels.

Eels must be very fresh to be good. Clean nicely, cut off the heads, skin and cut into five-inch pieces, roll in meal or flour, and fry in beef drippings salted, or pork fat. They should be nicely browned and well done. Serve on a napkin.

RAISED BUCKWHEAT GRIDDLE CAKES

One pint milk, one pint warm water, two dessertspoons melted lard, two dessertspoons molasses, half teaspoon salt, half yeast cake. To the pint of sweet milk add warm water, molasses, melted lard and salt. When cool add yeast and three cups buckwheat flour. Sponge in a pitcher at night and let rise. In morning beat down and fry on very hot griddle.

Reserve one cup batter for next lot of cakes and it will take the place of yeast. Other ingredients will be the same. Then soda must be used, as sponge will be sour; it may be added just before frying.

Griddle cakes are better when sponge has been started for three or four days.

XXIV

The Flood of 1830, the Boy Goes Eel Fishing, Squirrel Hunting and Trees a Coon

11 June 1897

The great freshet of 1830 flooded the flats in the Sherman neighborhood, and came near taking away the bridge. Fences became driftwood, and it is said Mr. Sherman had several swarms of bees on stands near the house carried downstream. One of those hives was found washed up on the bank at the "Hollow," filled with sand and dirt, but strangely enough the comb was but little broken and after being washed, the honey was found to be "lickin' good."

In 1830 a woolen mill stood where Besette's shop is in the Hollow. It was in July of that year that the great freshet did such damage along Lewis Creek. Bridges were piled in heaps along the intervales, and the farmers could hardly find their fences by advertising. During the greatest rush of water Samuel Coughlin and Edward Boynton attempted to cross the creek in a row boat. The boat upset and both the men were drowned.

The drive up the creek to "Leavenworth's" does not follow the stream closely, but winds around in curves and turns that are said to constitute lines of beauty[75] Under elms and apples and among scented evergreens, one finds here and there an outlook to the far away hills, and beyond them the loftier mountains. Downward to

Adventures of "the boy." Sketch by Jennie Cole.

149

Rowland E. Robinson fishing in Lewis Creek at the covered bridge of the older Route 7. Courtesy of Rokeby Museum.

Successful hunters of East Charlotte in the early 1900s when hunting included more than squirrels, coons and foxes. From left: Tom Hart, Floyd Foote, Art St. George, Dan St. George, Louis Poulin, Frank St. George, Burr Palmer, Cyrus Horsford, Charles Dow, Walter St. George. Courtesy of Eugene Shortsleeves.

the flashing waters, Lewis Creek hurrys along among the stones and over the sands or stands apparently still in the deep pools where the boys come to fish for "chubbs" in the daytime, or to set their poles for eels at night.

This eel is a cunning fish. He sleeps in the shadowy places by day and nightfall finds him ready for a substantial meal. So he frequently happens along where the boy has dropped in his tempting lump of angleworms, expiring on the carefully concealed hook. Down go worms and hook and some six inches of line before the fish discovers that something out of the usual has happened. It is then a tug and plunge and infinite twists for liberty, but unavailing until, finally, a squirming two feet of tawny skin and tangled line lays upon the bank. It is an indistinguishable and twisted mess, until the boy's jackknife severs the backbone "just back of the ears," and an eel, dead as a doornail, is ready for a late breakfast.

Along the immediate bank and intervales is the natural home of the hemlock, and further up and away the pine towers into the sky, with an evident desire to look over the heads of its fellows. The intruder among these quiet retreats not unfrequently disturbs the chipmunk, who scurries away among concealing roots with a coughing, chuckling note of surprise, or the red squirrel, who scratches his retreat to an overhanging limb, and with his tail beats time to the oddest combine of cackle, choke, and gurgle that ever entered into the heart of squirreldom to conceive. If there is anywhere an odder song than seems struggling to get out of a red squirrel in a musical mode, it is yet to be developed, generally ending with a "skuff" that ought to take all the breath out of his little body.

But, unless the boy has just come into possession of his first gun and has a consequent grudge against animated nature in general, he gives the chipmunk and his cousin a go-by and tiptoes towards the "grey" who is quacking on a maple limb away up on the hillside. Now, it is to be a trial of wits, unless the hunted has been shot at so many times as to be unduly suspicious and so goes jumping from limb to limb for his particular hollow tree.

Up creeps the boy, until he sees the gray tail jerking and twisting-- stopping all at once, and like a flash an object flies to the opposite side of a protecting limb. Now comes in the boy's wit, and he does well if he creeps around carefully enough among the leaves and snapping twigs to get a shot, for the squirrel moves as the boy moves, only the end of that gray tail remaining in sight to tantalize the young hunter into renewed and still more cautious activity.

The squirrel grows bolder, and the boy wiser, and after a little a black nose and a pair of sharp eyes come peering cautiously around the limb until the squirrel's head affords a fair mark for embryo Leatherstockings. What a pot pie they have at home, and how the woodshed is decorated with gray tails, perhaps arranged fantastically around the stretched-out skin of

151

a coon or two; for the boy is going to have a great fur deal some day with the local buyers and money will be plenty to fill his pockets.

A funny fellow is a coon, combining foxy cunning with unlimited stupidity. He is a lover of fish and frogs, and you see his tracks along the sandy brook banks where he has taken moonlight strolls in search of a morsel of food. But his chief delight is the young corn, just out of the milk, and he pulls down hill after hill, taking a bite or two out of an ear here and there, utterly regardless of waste, seeming to take more pleasure in the damage he does than in the corn he eats. In this respect he is first cousin to the brown bear, who used to pester the forefathers and tug off the young pigs at both and the same time. By and by the depredations are too numerous, and so the boys are allowed to "go cooning." This is often a doubtful expedient, for their "roastings" often exceed the incursion of the coons; but the boys will generally make only a night of it, and if the hunt is successful, a gain is made.

So away they go. But for genuine fun and hunting excitement, if the boys do not own a hound, they will find one to borrow. If it is a cur dog, who understands his business, he generally finds the coon in the corn, and a rough and tumble of coon and dog and boys is pretty sure to follow. The dog never barks on the track, and the first intimation of trouble the coon has is the bite that, ten to one in this case, precedes the bark.

Here is business. Back and forth goes the nosing hound, caring not a whit for the coon until he finds the track. An excited, muffled yelp or two tells the boys he is somewhat encouraged, and the heart of every boy beats a mile a minute. Hark, he's found him, and the night echoes to the excellent music of the dog as he follows the winding trail. Back and forth dog and boys--no matter about the corn--out of the field into the pasture, through the meadows. The dog is getting a fresher scent, and he tells the boys all about it by his more eager yelp. The boys let out another link, and it is a smart dog and a hot track that outspeeds them now. Into the woods, pell mell. A long drawn howl, a short yelp or two, a whine, a look upwards, a wagging body, tell the boys the "coon is treed."

A dark bunch or two on a big limb may mean something or it may not. No matter, light a fire, pile on the brush. With a satisfied "sniff" the hound lays at the root of the tree, he has done his part, and the boys with fun and frolic are doing theirs, until daylight and a shotgun gathers in the harvest of the night, and one family of coons will no more haunt the maturing grain. An old fat coon will outfight a dog sometimes, but he stands no chance with both dog and boys; and, as in the case of Davy Crockett, he might as well surrender at the outset.

The long, yawning cry that comes after nightfall, some say, is the call of the screech owl, and others the calling of the coon to her young for a forage on the fields. It seldom if ever comes save in September, and so we will assume it as a challenge to a night of sport. And if he fails to find the game, the rest of the hunting will not be lessened thereby an iota, for what is one boy without a hunter's instinct? After all, were the Indians so far out of the way in holding their green-corn dance in some secluded clearing along Lewis Creek, when a kettle of succotash, a haunch of the wild deer, dozens of salmon, and fat bear meat to match graced the festive board? The bill of fare was not so nicely printed perhaps, but it saved the old Indian the trouble of getting out his nose glasses to read it for himself and squaw. He knew for sure no room need be reserved for pie or pudding at the end of the feast.

The "corn dance" came with autumn, and the maples were all on fire and the birches a pyramid of gold, the beeches a staid and quiet bower, the pine, the cedar, the hemlock in the dark green they have worn since time began, all these were there, glorifying the closing year, and the soft winds, sighing through a thousand miles of trees.

After all, history is only tradition written out; and perhaps the legend of how Lewis Creek came to get its name has been all these long years floating in somebody's brain, and only accident or an unusually happy guess of the long ago brings it to modern eye or ear. When all the hillsides were in the shadow of the woods, and all the lowlands answered back the whisper of the leaves, and the silence of the forests dwelt throughout the land, up from the lake came a pale-face hunter, his birch canoe his ship of state, the rifle in the bow, the long knife in his belt, the strength of youth, the courage of a brave heart, his title of ownership to the stream, the valley, the upland, the mountain.

The red man welcomes him, the wigwam shelters him, the Indian maiden smiles upon him out of her dark eyes, and the romance of life commences on the banks of a stream that ever after bears his name, where his sons and daughters grew to love their pale-face father and listened with burning eyes to the mother's legends of brave deeds done long, long ago when the whistling arrow, the red tomahawk, the dripping knife, and the torn scalp lock settled the disputed rights of her tribe.

THE FOX HOUND.

THE BEAGLE.

Hunting dogs of "the boy's" time. "Harper's New Monthly Magazine," Apr., 1855, pp. 621-2.

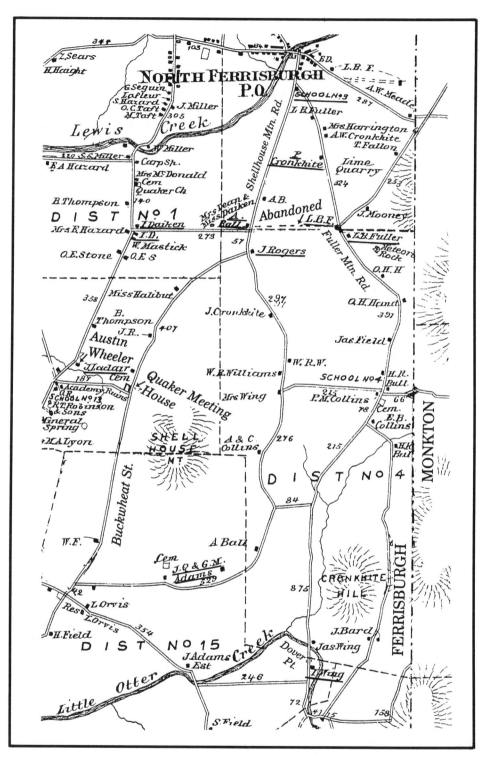

Beers map of some of the east side of Ferrisburgh showing Shellhouse Mountain Road, Fuller Mountain Road and some of the sites mentioned in this chapter and the next.

XXV

The Patient Reading Public,
the Little Otter's Intervale,
Dover Point Manufacturing Center,
Cannonballs and a Hoax at Barnumtown,
Life in the Woods Two Generations Ago

23 July 1897

Somehow these papers have outgrown my original intention, just as a chip of a boy wriggles along until he becomes an ungainly and full-grown man--a matter of surprise to the writer, and he should probably add, of mortification also. But now and then a word of commendation, a kindly volunteer of information sets the wheels whirring again, and it will probably be somewhat like your grandfather's old clock in the corner, running so long as wound up, until an entire collapse occurs; perhaps like the end of the deacon's one horse shay. One good thing, the public will patiently submit to numerous inflictions on its good nature, and if the writer or the printer makes mistakes in names and dates and distances among the long agos, those who detect the error will kindly rectify it.

So many mistakes are erroneously piled upon the printer the writer cheerfully assumes any error as his own exclusive possession, and thereby earns the gratitude of the faithful compositor, who feels his way through manuscripts wherein the common eye could not distinguish a continuous sentence for the life of him. Since Guttenburg and his wooden type and hand press, what a stride has been made for the literature of the world. The city dailies with steam cylinder presses, folders, and typesetting machines are marvels of speed. But the compositor at his case, click, click, click,--"stick" after stick emptied into the "galley" until ready for a "proof," knows there is another way of getting certain other newspapers ready for the press. After the "proof" comes the reading by "copy," and it depends upon the marginal hieroglyphics after that how many corrections are to be made.

But your good compositor is skillful as well as conscientious and the "form" is soon ready to be "locked" in for the old Washington press with its flying "tympan"[76], and a pull at the oddly angled lever, that many a strong man could not bring around, for the lack of knowing how. The pressman must

A Washington-style press here as displayed and used for demonstrations at the Ben Lane Print Shop at the Shelburne Museum. The lever, which Higbee considered unmanageable, is adjusted on this one for easy use. Photo taken in 1990.

have his "insides register with the outside," and so he can if he is careful about the "pickholes" as he lays the moistened sheets. Ah, the printer has nerve-trying work, and Saturday finds him ready with his "string" of proof, and the gold and silver and precious stones that rattle into his expectant hand are generally honorably and faithfully earned.

It has been intimated that Fuller Mountain is more than a mile south of Mount Philo,[77] and that very little of it lies in Ferrisburgh, as was stated in

a former paper, and these are doubtless the facts. But it is perhaps well to use an elastic mile in some of our measurements, one that contracts or expands, as it were, according to circumstances, and so we leave the mountain just as we found it, only the Monkton town line must continue to run along its western base, and Ferrisburgh thus loses one of the most picturesque of hills.

One would think, looking from northern elevations, that Fuller Mountain and Shellhouse are largely one and the same--but herein is a mistake, for an intervale containing numerous beautiful farms lies between; and a ride over some of the roads is romantic enough for a poet-- and over certain others of them rough enough to dislocate both the bones and the ox cart of the fathers.

Through this intervale turns and twists the Little Otter[78] and it has more rapids and short falls on its way to the lake than most of us are aware of. After the roaring chase over the rocks and through the wide gorge at the Center, its career is henceforth peaceful, but upstream it frets and foams and tumbles by spells, and used to turn numerous wheels that ceased revolving years ago at and above the falls, near the Isaac Wing place, where his son Charles E. Wing now lives.

It seems this point was called "Dover," and threatened at one time to be of no inconsiderable importance as a manufacturing center. The best obtainable information indicates that a Mr. Blood had a chain factory; that there existed at one time a fulling mill

The Sawyer's cabin at the Shelburne Museum donated to the museum in 1957 by the late Thomas Schermerhorn of Charlotte. The tower of the Charlotte meeting house is in the background. Photo taken in 1979.

and carding machine, owned by Mr. Hard, grandfather of Mr. Alvin Ball. James Sanborn ran a cooper shop, and Joseph Walker, a saw mill that turned out one thousand feet of lumber in a day, to the wonder and delight of the neighborhood. The new schoolhouse near the bridge is known as "Walkers Corners." Mr. Charles Wing says the road and bridge used to cross the creek just a little upstream from his house and so on over the hill. He is informed a man named Clark had a tannery near the foot of the falls, and that Mr. Sanborn had a forge and foundry near the old bridge and on

the east side of the creek and that cannon balls were once cast here.

A letter recently received says, "The forge was about a mile up the creek near the covered bridge on the road from Vergennes to Barnumtown and was owned by Ezekiel Barnum." If the correspondent has in mind the same property spoken of by Mr. Wing, tradition is at fault somewhere. It is said that at some forge in this vicinity, would-be purchasers were so delighted at the toughness of the iron that a "dicker" was immediately entered into, but the mine owner had dropped some forty silver dollars into

Interior of the Sawyer's cabin showing a trundle bed not quite hidden in its daytime storage place and a hollowed-out log cradle. Photo taken in 1990.

the smelter and this made the iron "lock better as she was"--to somebody's disadvantage, no doubt. Whether there were two forges or only one, it is certainly a romantic stream that tumbles over the rocks below the bridge, and it is unfortunate for all of us that through the efforts of these energetic pioneers a center like Lowell or Lawrence failed to materialize near the headwaters of Little Otter.

South of the "Hollow," and near where the old and new schoolhouse now stands the road forks; one keeping southerly and the other bearing to the southeast. To the present generation, this information has very little

newness in it, the writer is well aware, but possibly they may not know who traversed these highways in years long gone, and who inhabited the humble homes whose broad chimneys sent into the winter air columns of white smoke, like emblems of peace.

Once in a while remains one old enough to take the grandchild or the great-grandchild upon the knee and tell of the old, old days when the "latch string" opened the kitchen door, and this kitchen was dining room and parlor as well, and possibly the bed stood in a corner and the happy children clambered up the steep stairs to sleep in the "loft," except two or three of the youngest, to say nothing of the baby, who were packed into the "trundle" housed under the bed in the daytime[79]. Seldom, however, is this aged parent known and these things come in tradition. We remember them as we recall pleasant stories and the fragrance of last year's roses.

Those days had their hardships and deprivations, but I submit their lives were free from the cares and anxieties of modern times and exactions of modern society that many a man and woman would be healthier and happier could they step into that life in the woods two generations ago.

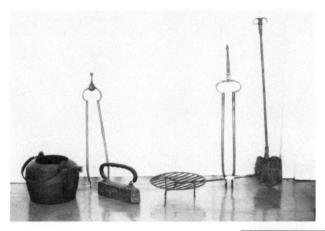

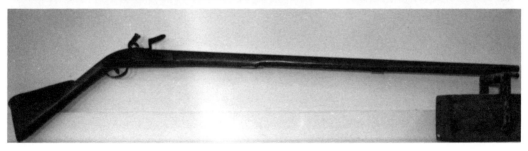

Some essentials to pioneer life: early fireplace utensils: cast-iron teakettle, flat iron, gridiron or trivet, wrought-iron tongs and shovel. Charlotte Memorial Museum Collection. A Hill gun (see Chapter XVIII). The markings on the barrel are typical of guns made by the Hill family in Connecticut. The date precludes its having been made by Zimri Hill in Charlotte and nothing more has been found about him as a gunsmith, but is of the type made in his time. Courtesy of Arthur T. Prime.

Quaker Corners, a name unfamiliar to many present residents. Looking south on Roscoe Rd. with Lewis Creek Rd. at the right and the Douglas farm on the left horizon. The Baldwin (Quaker) school was behind the large tree on the right; the Quaker meeting house was on the other side of Lewis Creek Rd. Douglas Hill, on the left across some fields, is the site of the Cave and the Oven. Courtesy of Bixby Free Memorial Library.

XXVI

Locations of Quaker Churches,
the Oldest Houses in Charlotte and Ferrisburgh,
a Panther Story,
Barker and Edgerton Apple Trees,
Naming of Shellhouse Mountain,
Benjamin Field: a Great Landowner in Ferrisburgh

10 September 1897

A tract of land of about two hundred acres on the north and south road, and south of the village was owned in an early day by a man named Hurd, and his house stood a little south of where John Harrington's house is located. A house occupied by Asa Steadman stood farther to the southwest on what was known as the "Sandlot." Possibly the foundations remain, nothing more. The Alvin Ball farm was owned by Sela Gregory and William Hazard. The Gregory house stood on the east side of the road near a spring and about opposite the north barn on the Ball place. The Hazard house occupied nearly the same site of the new house built by Alvin Ball. Bram Rogers settled on the place now owned by Ebenezer Ward. He afterwards bought the Hurd farm and the one owned by Noble Ellsworth.

After the disruption of the Society of Friends about 1828, the Hicksites held meetings in the old church south of Ellsworth's, and the Orthodox made an addition to the schoolhouse standing a little west of Abram Rogers where their meetings were held a good many years.

Joseph Rogers claimed that the house he lived in was the first frame house built in town. In point of age there is probably little difference between this and the "Frazier" house in Ferrisburgh Center. In 1790 Samuel Prindle bought at a tax sale for eighteen shillings, eight pence, the farm now owned and occupied by John H. and Almira Knowles. This he sold to Peter Cronkhite[80] in 1791 who built the house now standing. He was a mill wright and assisted in building most of the early mills in Ferrisburgh and adjoining towns.

About 1810 his daughter Mary was chased by a panther for quite a distance west of the house, and only the courage of a dog that was with her saved her life. She married Moses Barton and lived on a farm in Monkton near that of Joseph Hoag.

161

The farm is now owned by a daughter, Mary A. Jewell. Peter and Jacob, twin boys, were born in the Knowles house in 1804, and it is said they looked so much alike the mother had almost to label the little chaps or there was danger of spanking the wrong baby as occasion required. Jacob Cronk died in 1880, and was buried from the same room in which he was born. The mother of Jacob lived to be ninety-nine years old. Mrs. Knowles has a coverlid that was woven in 1690 by her grandfather four-times-removed John Wiekam of Connecticut, making it over two hundred years old. The weaver was ninety-two years old when the work was done. She also has one of the shoes her great grandmother wore when married in 1757. It was made of changeable silk, sharp pointed, the heel two and three-quarter inches high.

John Harvey took up the place south of Cronkhite, later owned by Joel Palmer and his son Peter, but now owned by John Cronk. John Dalrymple used to live north of Palmer's on the east side of the road, where Mr. Hanks now owns. Further south lived John Wing, whose house was burned down over fifty years ago. It was rebuilt and the farm was afterward sold to Jacob Cronk, and it is now owned and occupied by his son, Peter A. Cronk. Beyond this is the old John Peck farm occupied by Henry Jones; and a little south of the Jones dwelling stood a house owned and occupied years ago by Francis Barker, who afterward moved to Charlotte owning the present Timothy Stebbins farm.

Brass stencils for labelling the apples of the Edgerton orchards found in the 1812 (Newell) Tavern when it was being restored. H. D., George E. and A. Edgerton sent at least five varieties to the Boston area. The stencil copies here are 25% of actual size.

Mr. Barker was interested in fruit growing, and used to have a considerable nursery. The orchard owned by H. D. Edgerton was mainly planted by Anson Edgerton with Barker trees. In those days, barreling apples for market was largely unknown, and the orchard man who had the greatest number of varieties was a leader in his line; Mr. Edgerton used to say he should have had more kinds if the land had only held more trees. Experience gave wisdom, however, and judicious grafting brought the Edgerton orchard to be one of the finest in the valley.

Lanson Hard built a house near where the new house of Homer Ball, his grandson, now stands. Following this road south-westerly and around the south end of the mountain, John Q. Adams owns the place that was once in whole or in part the property of Martin Shellhouse, a man of Dutch descent whose name has come down to us in the mountain at whose base he cleared himself a home. We have thus far journeyed along the east side. The farm now owned and occupied by L. M. Macomber and his wife Lydia Dakin was taken up by Timothy Dakin and his house stood a little northeast of where Macomber lives. The eighty acres westerly and embracing the place where Peter Dakin lives, it seems, went from him to Isaac Dakin.

West of the Joseph Rogers homestead, Parmenus Hurlburt cleared up a tract of land and lived in the large house owned by Joseph Laclair. Near Mrs. Alvin Ball's there used to be four corners, the road from the west going on easterly over the

The Rogers Homestead on the east side of Rt. 7 in North Ferrisburgh on the ridge south of Rokeby. Sketch by Rowland Robinson. Courtesy of Karl Devine.

163

hill to the Fuller place. Stephen Hazard lived many years on the fine farm now owned by Noble Ellsworth.

A man by the name of Griffin made a commencement where Joseph Collett lives. A little to the south and on the east side of the road Mingo Miles lived in a more or less pretentious way, followed later by others.

Mention has already been made of the Friends church, south of Collett's and the schoolhouse standing hereabouts whose travels ended at the Center--the hamlet of churches. Southerly stood a large two story house owned and perhaps built by Sylvanus Austin. This might have been intended for a tavern, as modern "hotels" were once denominated--but nothing remains but a possible hole in the ground where once was a cellar. Walker B. Field owns the land, and it is known as the "Austin place."

South of this lived one of the most successful of Ferrisburgh's early farm-

ers, Benjamin Field, who became one of the great land owners of his day. Anthony Field, a brother of his, settled in the eastern neighborhood of Ferrisburgh. The Benjamin Field homestead is now owned by Harry Thomas of Burlington. The road leading northerly has for many years been known in the local way as "Buckwheat Street," and the reason for this cannot be assigned by the writer, but of one thing rest assured, nowhere is often found a more beautiful outlook over Champlain and the mountains than a drive past the old Rogers place. Health, happiness and a daily feasting on nature's beauties awaits the city man who will place his summer outing money in some of these fertile acres, breathing the sweet air of our hills, drinking the water of their springs-- catching, daily, glorious sunsets over the Adirondacks that no painter, even one with the greatest skills, need ever expect to imitate.

R. M. Shurtleff (1838-1915) painted this "View of Lake Champlain" from a point near Rt.7 north of the Charlotte/Ferrisburgh town line. Poor Farm Bay and Thompson's Point are set against a background of Rattlesnake Mountain, Split Rock and the Adirondacks on the New York side.

XXVII

Dean's Cave and the Oven
Gold in the Quartz?

24 September 1897

Ferrisburgh, Monkton, and Charlotte corner together in the neighborhood of the Joshua M. Dean farm, which his father William Dean occupied before him, and where a third generation, the late J. Richard Dean, died recently in the prime of life and at the outset of an honorable and useful career. At the time of his death, he was one of the selectmen of Charlotte, and at the town meeting following his decease resolutions of respect and regret were adopted by the town and put in the town records.

On the Dean farm are two great curiosities--one a cavern of several rooms, the other the "Oven", as it has been called. A climb over rocks and pleasant walks through little valleys bring you to the cave and one can stand within ten feet of the entrance without the least idea of its existence, so completely has nature hidden this retreat among the rocks. It is said early hunters and settlers used this place many times in hiding from Indian incursions. An abrupt turn around the face of a rock reveals a narrow cleft in the face of the bold headland running down some thirty or forty feet, with steps somewhat like a rugged stair-way. At the bottom is an opening that would accommodate a score of people if each did not want all the space and other continuations or annexes still further enlarge the hospitalities of the place. After looking the premises over, one is satisfied that primitive housekeeping could have been quite successfully established here, only getting up and down stairs would have been a trifle tiresome on occasions. An opening in the top serves the purpose of a chimney and the smoke-begrimed sides indicate that many generations here have luxuriated in the home-like comforts of a fireside.

Stranger than fiction often are the soberest truths and a mind given to speculations and wonderments finds in this cave an object of exceeding interest. How came such perfect work-- here a room, up an incline of ten or fifteen feet another, and further on a tunnel leading still on into the mountainside. The outlet, a clean-cut fissure only wide enough and large enough for one at a time, a large tree clinging somehow halfway up its sides, steps that a giant might have placed, but no other human hands; all so deftly hidden by rock and tree and bush that the keenest eye would have passed it scores of times.

A scramble down brings you to the valley far below, but the front door seems properly to face the summit of the mountain; and here the early hunter and refugee doubtless came and went, listening mayhap to the howl of the hungry wolf or the more dreadful whoop of the trailing warrior. Here, a hundred years ago, the birds mated in springtime and departed silently as the million leaves rustled to the ground in autumn. The robin with its cheer-up song; the wren; the thrush; the keen witted crow; the jay, garrulous dandy of the woodland; the red bird, with front of jet; the owl, whose wise look outdoes the wisdom of the Scribes and Pharisees; the watchful hawk, ever suspicious and alert; and over all, with stately flap of wing or majestic swoop in widening circle toward the sky, the king and symbol of our country--the eagle.

A quarter of a mile or so southward from the cave is the "Oven," the greater curiosity of the two and perhaps a no more remarkable formation exists in the Champlain Valley. Were it situated near the lake shore or more directly on the line of summer travel, it would be visited by hundreds of delighted and well repaid sightseers. The mountain ridge leads on into Monkton with the characteristic western front and eastern slope, but breaks off abruptly to the south, and in this southern front is the "Oven," or perhaps more properly the arch. It is from thirty to forty feet across the base, rising with the regu-

Some portions of the Red Sandrock series are very regularly and handsomely stratified, but other portions are much disturbed and broken, or bent and folded. One of the most interesting plications in this rock, which have been noticed, is in Monkton. The south end of this plication is represented in the figure below.

The white spaces between the curved lines represent the edges of the strata. These are all of the ordinary sandstone. The broad dark stratum, $c\,c$, is argillaceous slate, having the laminæ nearly perpendicular to the plane of deposit. The upper portion of this, which is left wholly dark, has been removed, forming the cavity called *the Oven*. The portion represented in the cut, is about 30 feet broad at the base.

Zadock Thompson's description of the Oven, from his 1848 book, "The Natural History of Vermont," pp. 265-266.

larity of the most perfect masonry and with a keystone tapering and finely outlined, enough to satisfy the most exacting architect. Zadock Thompson, in his *Geography and Geology of Vermont*, published in 1848, pronounces it "a remarkable plication of rock called the Oven which forms a very great geological curiosity."

Joshua M. Dean while living on the farm piloted numerous parties to the cavern and oven, among them men of scientific research, and he informs the writer that no one has ever been disappointed or begrudged the tramp. Especially have they been interested in this wonderful arch formation. One highly educated gentleman said, "Caves are frequent enough, but this arch is rare indeed." Some of the strata are almost pure quartz, and who knows but some day gold bearing veins will be discovered and we have a Klondike here in Vermont. To come nearer the realities of Alaska, enthusiastic miners might commence operations in January, blasting through a few feet of frozen soil.

Map of Charlotte from the 1857 Walling Map of Chittenden County. Charlotte Memorial Museum Collection.

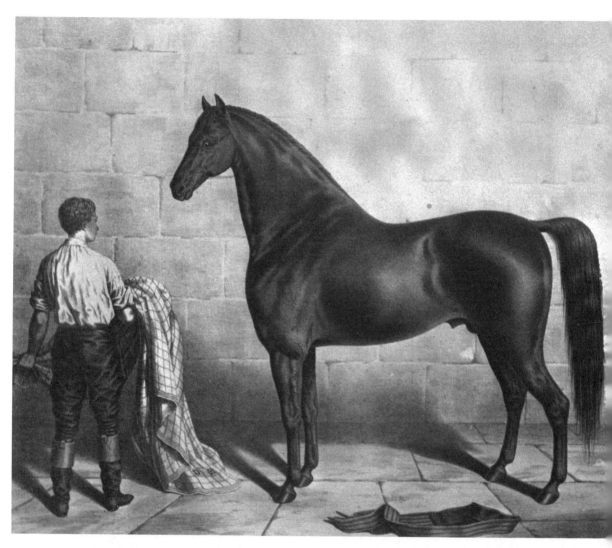

"The original Vermont Black Hawk.. sire of fast-trotting horses, Ethan Allen, Black Ralph, Belle of Saratoga, Black Hawk Maid, Know Nothing, Red Leg, etc." He was grandson of Justin Morgan and was owned by David Hill, Esq., Bridport, Vermont. Engraving from a painting by Theodore Marston, December, 1851. Courtesy of the American Morgan Horse Association Archives, Shelburne, Vt.

XXVIII

Black Marble, Slate, Early Settlement in Addison County, Full-Blooded Sheep and Horses

8 October 1897

The rock formation of this part of Addison County is largely identical with that of Rutland County where have been opened perhaps some of the finest marble and slate quarries in the world, and it is not at all improbable that the mountains of Ferrisburgh, Monkton, and Charlotte contain what may someday rival the riches of Rutland County.

On the road leading to McNeil's Ferry from the Four Corners is "Woodchuck Hill" owned by William S. Yale, and here years ago quite a business was done quarrying black marble. Dr. John Strong used to work this stone into chimney mantles and gravestones. It took and retained a high polish. Pease Hill and Mutton Hill north of it no doubt are holding in reserve a wealth of slate stone for future generations to develop. The late Alanson Edgerton, who was an unusually close observer, informed the writer that he found in the bottom of the brook on the farm of the late Luther D. Stone, specimens of slate about the size and shape of those for school children, smooth and perfect enough to frame and use. It was his opinion after further investigation, that a stripping of the soil would have revealed a fine quality of slate.

Mr. Edgerton was a builder of large experience and his judgment was probably well founded. Many older readers will associate Mr. Edgerton with bridges and other public works with which he was connected. Very many towns in the lake counties have monuments of his skillful and honest workmanship spanning their streams. His delight was some tough job that many another builder gladly shunned and he told a story with as much success as he built a bridge.[81]

Perhaps to Addison County belongs the honor of having the first civilized settlement west of the Green Mountains within Vermont's present limits. This is the town of Addison at Chimney Point. It was about 1731 that the French built Fort Frederick, afterwards called Crown Point. At Chimney Point was a large stone windmill, used both as a mill and fort, mounting a number of cannon. Early settlers would naturally seek the larger streams and the shores of the lake, as water communication was quicker and easier than packing through the woods by marked trees. There was

169

Two purebred Merinos of the Charles A. Chapman flock in Ferrisburgh being posed by farm workers. Courtesy of Karl Devine.

H. THORP'S NO. 1.
Bred and owned by HENRY THORP, Charlotte, Vt.   Residence 2 miles from depot, road 13. [See Map.]

Henry Thorp raised Atwood Merino sheep on his farm on Rt. 7. His ad was in the Child's Gazetteer of 1882-83.

more danger connected with such settlements, however, as the same waters bore the Indian's canoe, and up and down Champlain the French and English chased each other alternately until about 1760 when the French abandoned Chimney Point and the English flag alone responded to the sunset gun; until Ethan Allen and Seth Warner with their Green Mountain Boys electrified the world at Ticonderoga and Bennington.

Perhaps Addison County can also claim credit for what it has done in the way of improving the trotting horse and the fine-wooled sheep, and perhaps the town of Addison, in the person of the energetic Carlton W.

170

Read, possesses one of the most extensive wool dealers in the state. Mr. Read was born in Charlotte and so we claim the credit of infusing some excellent blood into the business veins of a sister town.

The various ups and downs of tariffs and other political wrinkles may have worked harm to the sheep interests and the price of horses has hardly kept pace with the speed of the animals. But the fact remains that this section of the state has always led in "full bloods," and why not? For back of the enterprise of its citizens, or rather under them, were the prairie-like acres stretching away to the lake where the sweetest feed and best of market hay evidenced the pushing qualities of their lands. Some people are no particular authority on horses, and seldom find one too slow gaited or sedate; some have been in boyhood so pushed by an ugly ram as to have acquired a distaste for the life of a shepherd. But it appears from Black Hawk to H. T. Booth's Little Gem, the speed standard climbs steadily upward, and henceforth sheepmen will probably be in clover, all wool and a yard wide. Sixty years ago Addison County had about 5,500 horses, over

Fort Ticonderoga was the destination for a Charlotte school trip in the bicentennial year, 1976. Stephen Groleau and Tim Armell with an unidentified soldier contemplate history.

260,000 sheep, 40,000 cattle, and the wool clip was 677,000 pounds. Perhaps some of our sheepmen can give us a comparison for 1897.

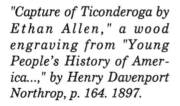

"Capture of Ticonderoga by Ethan Allen," a wood engraving from "Young People's History of America...," by Henry Davenport Northrop, p. 164. 1897.

The rich land that was so good for sheep now produces hay and a view to the west.

The Charlotte Overlook on the west side of Rt. 7 occupies land south of the former Thorp farm. Acquired by the town in 1973 as open land after cliff-hanging negotiations, it preserves a view of the lake from the highway. As Higbee might say, it defies the camera to show its beauty. Photos taken in August, 1990

XXIX

The Populations of Towns and
in Praise of Common Schools

15 October 1897

In 1769 settlers from other parts of New England came to Waltham and about this time the great falls in Otter Creek began to turn the first sawmill wheel. It seems Ferrisburgh and Charlotte were both chartered the same day, 24 June, 1762[82], and George the Third did this business through his "well beloved" Benning Wentworth, governor of the previous New Hampshire. The Governor's lots of five hundred acres were located in the northeast corner of Ferrisburgh and the southwest corner of Charlotte, that is five hundred acres in each town. If the worthy Governor was equally favored in other charters, it is possible he found himself "land poor," as mortal man is said sometimes to become. Both towns appear to have been settled permanently in 1784.

Previous to this, the French and Indian Wars and the Revolution had made such uncertain living that most of the settlers had gone back to New Hampshire and Connecticut not abandoning their claims, but waiting for more peaceable times. Some families secreted their ironware in holes in the rocks or sunk their pewter dishes in ponds and wells, to be fished out long years after. The population of Ferrisburgh in 1840 was 1,755--it is now 1501. Charlotte in 1840, 1620--it is now 1240. Ferrisburgh has forty-five square miles--Charlotte, thirty-eight. Monkton had a population in 1840 of 1310--now 847 with thirty seven square miles. These twin towns, as they may be called, are not the only sufferers in population. Addison with 1232 in '40, now has 900. New Haven had 1503--now 1224. Some towns east of us have been gainers. Lincoln has 1225--770 in 1840.

Vergennes has crowded her way from 1017 to 1773 in the last sixty years, and there is no good reason why she should not hustle along in the next half century at the same speedy rate. The beautiful town of Bristol, at the foot of the Green Mountains, has grown to 1828 from 123 in '40; and there is every reason to suppose this mountain village is just picking herself up for still more rapid development with steam car communications, telephones and telegraph, trout brooks, mountains to climb, and the sweet air of the spruce woods to fill the lungs with fresher life.[83]

Some of Charlotte's common schools. The Lyceum school in East Charlotte in 1909. The building is now the Grange Hall. Is that the teacher climbing the wall? Courtesy of Eugene Shortsleeves.

A first for these children: a real Christmas tree in the Lyceum school in 1909. The tree also had lighted candles. Cora Clark was the teacher. Courtesy of Eugene Shortsleeves.

The Prindle school that was on the south side of Prindle Rd. and west of the Horsford stone house, on the small rise near the woods. Courtesy of Elinor (Prindle) Benning.

The Emerson school at the corner of Thompson's Point and Lake Roads shown as it was about 1905. The oldest school to survive, it is now completely remodeled to a private residence. Courtesy of the Root family.

The interior of the Emerson school showing an unusual arrangement and the heating system. One resident who attended this school recalls that the playground and the outhouses were across Lake Rd. Courtesy of the Root family.

As farms grew larger in the different towns, population decreased. Let each reader take his own school district, or what used to be a school district before legislative solons conceived the idea that we did not know enough to manage our own business and care for our own children. Then see how many an old foundation can be counted where a dwelling house used to stand. Farms ranged from fifty to two hundred acres. It was seldom the latter figures were surpassed. Reference is had, of course, to the general run of farms. It is safe to hazard the statement that we should be better off today, as a whole, if there were smaller farms and more farmers tilling them. The tax list would be larger, public burdens would be borne by more taxpayers, schools would be improved, because they would be more largely patronized.

"Educators" tell us our schools are "deteriorating," and probably they do not come up to the standard of forty or fifty years ago. But the cause is plain enough. The children of the state are taken out of the common schools at a far different age now than they were then. It is not "the thing" to be educated there, no matter how good the advantages.

176

The Columbus School, Dist. No. 6, celebrating Columbus and giving us a date but no names of the participants. This was the Middlebrook school in Ferrisburgh located on the Monkton Rd. east of Rt. 7 and one report claims it is now the Bakery Lane II shop in the shopping center west of the original site. Courtesy of Bixby Free Memorial Library.

Stop a minute, some of you men and women from fifty to sixty-five years old, as good business men and women as can be found every day, and tell me how much schooling did you ever get outside of the old district schoolhouses? Perhaps two or three at some academy: Hinesburgh, Williston, Bakersfield, or with "Uncle Ben" Allen in Vergennes. The bulk of it you dug out in the district school. The tendency was toward them then, not away from them. The questions have often been asked, and perhaps are still mooted ones, whether the increased cost and more roundabout methods have in similar proportion increased the value of our schools[84]. The question remains whether the parents of the children in the old district form are not just as competent to provide for them as three men called a "board of directors," and perhaps not one of them with a child to educate. Do some of the "new methods" increase or lessen our personal interest in schools?

177

Esther Newell's house in the Hollow. It was also at one time the Post Office, and is now known as the Hicks house. Courtesy of the Wheeler/Kingsland Collection.

The grand list of Charlotte sixty years ago was $5,755, now $8,843. Ferrisburgh's was $7,133 in 1840. Records of early town meetings show that Charlotte sometimes voted a tax of two cents on the dollar "to be paid into the treasury for town purposes," and in 1837 it raised four cents on the dollar to be paid by the first day of August, and "the collector to pay to the town interest on all sums remaining unpaid at the time."

Birdsay Newell was collector and it is perhaps safe to assume he "got there" with those taxes and so saved that "interest." Mr. Newell used to live on the farm now occupied by Darwin O. Foote in Charlotte, but sold it and removed to North Ferrisburgh, buying the brick house now owned by his daughter, Esther Newell. He formerly owned and ran the sawmill afterwards owned by the late Argaius Newell, but now the property of J. L. St. Peter.

The "Dam and Bridge, North Ferrisburgh, Vt." in the early 1900s. On the left the penstock and the J. L. St.Peter sawmill. Now the dam is gone but the bridge is standing over a "stream" south of the 1810 Farmhouse and Restaurant on Rt. 7 (see Chapter IV). Courtesy of the Wheeler/Kingsland Collection.

XXX

The Formation of Vermont and President McKinley's Fish and Game Address

5 November 1897

Addison County, when incorporated on October 18, 1785, included in its limits the whole of what is now Chittenden, Franklin, Grand Isle, and Lamoille and several towns of Orleans and Washington counties. By the incorporation of Chittenden County, October 22, 1787, Addison County was reduced to nearly its present limits. Starksboro was subsequently added to Addison from Chittenden and Orwell from Rutland County. The change on county lines came from the fact that the state was settled from the south, and as settlements advanced northward, new counties were formed.

The town of Addison was, practically if not legally, the county seat for some six years. The first county court in Addison County seems to have been held there in 1786 and continued to be so held until 1792. Of the towns and counties not yet formed there was no official representation in the General Convention held in Dorset, September 25, 1776, consisting of delegates from towns on the east and west side of the Green Mountains, but it is safe to assume that wherever a

settler's cabin existed, its occupants were ready and eager to sustain the action of the convention when it voted without a dissenting voice, "to declare the New Hampshire Grants a free and separate district."

It is not infrequently the case that incidents in the career of state or nation suffer a great increase by patriotic exaggeration, to the detriment of actual historical truth. Sectional pride has to be allowed for and discounted, and dim tradition may possibly run so far into the past that the obscurity of its legends darkens the white light of the actual. But in the case of Vermont such contingency does not arise, recorded evidence of what we rely upon in maintaining the assertion already made, that nowhere in the history of this nation is found anything so heroic, so magnificently self-reliant, so successfully daring. Absolutely alone, she stood off the greed of the powerful, the rapine of war, maintained her honor when accused of dallying with a foreign foe-- protected her citizens by diplomacy when possible, by musket and cannon when necessary, until finally Congress came to see she was right, the land grabbers came to learn their course was lost; and into the Union this state of the Green Mountains carried the same commanding influence, the same lofty patriotism. Her sons were among the first to face the foe at Plattsburgh, and had the troops of Wellington marched southward in 1812, they would again have become "a threatening storm upon the flank." Such a people, such a state, is our proud inheritance. It is more than a privilege, it is a duty that these things be taught our children. It is more than education that the history of Vermont should go into the homes and schools--it is national life. The boy, the girl should know what mind conceived, whose hands built, whose courage defended this fabric of a state. It is said the "thinking bayonets" are those that win--and by this is meant the intelligent bravery of those who carry them and to such intelligence and bravery we point to our children as we account the past.

The little republic of Switzerland has been held up to the world in history, song and story as a model of heroic accomplishment these many many years and William Tell will always remain the romantic hero time has painted him. But nowhere in the annals of nations is found a more heroic act than the "declaration" of that earlier Dorset convention at its adjourned meeting in Westminster, January 15, 1777.

Harassed by New York, the title to their homes disputed, a hostile power along the northern boundary, ready, at any time, to sweep the land with English soldiers and Indian warriors, what did the delegates do? This is what our forefathers did:

This convention, whose members are duly chosen by the voice of their constituents in the several towns on the New Hampshire Grants, ought to be and is hereby declared forever hereafter to be considered as a free and independent jurisdiction or State.

An early version of the state coat-of-arms. "Barber's History and Antiquities of the Northern States," by John Warner Barber. 1842.

With the signing of that immortal document in Philadelphia in 1776, thirteen states were pledged each to the other in weal or woe. But here, on the border of the Canadas[85], a single state dared assert its rights to its own; and asserting, dared and did maintain them. Nowhere in history is a record of better statesmanship, more keenness in statecraft, more deftness in delicate diplomacy than characterized the days when such as Thomas Chittenden, Ira Allen, Moses Robinson, Jonas Fay took counsel together over the district of Vermont. In this convention, Addison was represented by David Vallance; Panton, by John Gale; Bridport, Samuel Benton; Middlebury, Gamaliel Painter; Williston, Colonel Thomas Chittenden; Colchester, Ira Allen. The New Yorkers who attempted to enforce their authority over the "grants" previous to the Revolutions divided the territory into four counties: Cumberland and Gloucester on the east, Bennington and Charlotte on the west of the Green Mountains. Probably the name of one of these early counties descended to a town, and "Bennington" remains in full force and effect until this day, complimentary to the good taste of New York forefathers in the choice of names.

After the Declaration of Westminster in January 1777, the convention adjourned to meet on the first Wednesday in June at Windsor. A state constitution was adopted and a legislative session held at Windsor, March 1778, lasting fifteen days. Business must have been pressing about then, for the legislature met again in Bennington, June 4, and at Windsor the same year. In 1781 a session was held in Charlestown, New Hampshire, but Bennington and Windsor appear to have been storm centers. Rutland had sessions in 1784, 1792, 1794, 1797-98, and 1804. Addison County "legislated" somewhat with a session at Vergennes of twenty-nine days in 1798, Middlebury in 1800, and again

in 1806. Burlington had its turn in 1802, with thirty days, with an expense of $11,483.44.

There are probably those in the ministry today who recall the early Connecticut custom of all the clergymen going to election and dining at the expense of the state. In other words, they assembled at the Capitol to witness the inauguration of the incoming governor. Readers of Hawthorne's *Scarlet Letter* will recall that the Reverend Arthur Dimmesdale, the eminently pious hero of this strange romance, was selected to preach the sermon on a similar occasion, and we are told he outdid himself to so remarkable a degree as astonished the assembled Puritan fathers; while all the time the Reverend Brother's mental vision was filled with Hester Prynne and little Pearl.

Of course, no such commingling of sin and sanctity had crept into the spiritual atmosphere of Vermont. Successful candidates for our "Election Sermons" had nothing more difficult to contend with than the ordinary theological problems.

Daniel C. Saunders preached the election sermon at Vergennes, Benjamin Wooster and Thomas A. Merrill at Middlebury, the Reverend Peter Powers preached the sermon at the first legislative session at Windsor, in March 1778. Montpelier commenced business October 13, 1808, and since that date she has been the Mecca of devout politicians, with a constantly increasing cost to the state. Her first session called for $12,000, and if somebody will inform the writer as to the

Part of President McKinley's 1897 Vermont trip as pictured in "The Vermonter," Volume 7, p. 345, Oct., 1901.

cash outlay for the session of 1896, it will save him the trouble of looking it up, say some $60,009 at a venture. The debentures for the year 1890 were about $56,000.

Whether President McKinley was historically correct in his Fish and Game League address in which he made Vermonters "Puritans," had best be referred to divinity students.[86]

It seems several learned newspaper editors have already locked horns in regard to the matter, but one thing is tolerably plain according to the records: the Vermont legislature of 1834 resolved to have no more Election Sermons with accompanying expenses unless it should be otherwise ordered in the future. The Reverend Warren Skinner seems to have been the last to officiate, his immediate predecessor having been Reverend Tobias Spicer, with whose ministrations in this area former generations were happily familiar.

The legislature of 1872 empowered

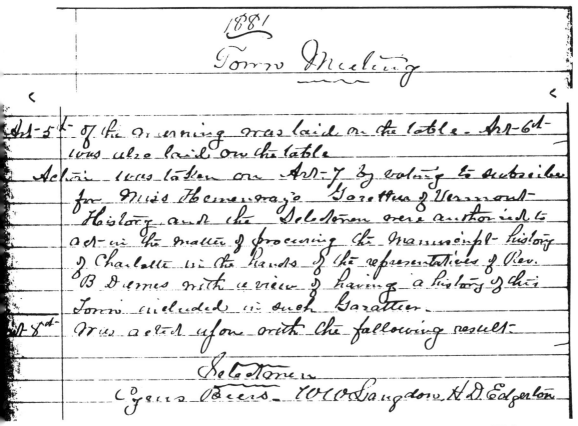

The town was interested in its history in 1881. The above record written by Higbee as town clerk shows that it was voted to subscribe to "Miss Hemenway's Gazetteer of Vermont History." The Reverend Ames's article is in Hemenway's publication, but his manuscript is not to be found.

the governor to appoint some suitable person to edit and publish the journals of the Council of Safety and the early journals of the governor and council to such an extent as seemed necessary to preserve the history of the state. Such records were to be printed, one volume in each year. The Honorable E. P. Walton of Montpelier was so designated by Governor Julius Converse, and the volumes so far completed can probably be found and used in the town clerks' offices in many of our Vermont towns.

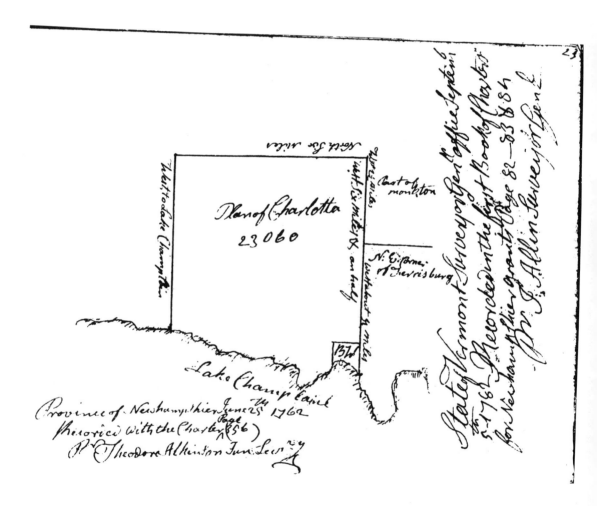

The survey map of Charlotte by Benjamin Ferris, Jr. The lot on the lake marked "BW" is the share that Benning Wentworth got for his trouble in chartering the town. His 500 acres in Ferrisburgh adjoined his Charlotte holding. Town boundaries have not been changed since this survey. From "Book A", Charlotte town records.

XXXI

East Charlotte and Ox Drawings

17 December 1897

East Charlotte was settled about the same time the early pioneers commenced their clearing along the lake. It was generally the case that settlers located first along the lake shore, but Daniel Hosford, surveyor and proprietors' clerk, varied from the rule, build-

Myron Hinsdale Horsford (1821-1890) and his wife Sarah. He was the son of Oran and the grandson of Daniel, the surveyor. A descendant says Sarah "was always photographed with a cat." The cat clearly shown and the names on the case make this daguerreotype even more distinctive. Courtesy of the Horsford family.

ing his log house east of the stone house on the Myron Horsford farm. It is said the uplands in that locality in an early day had an immense growth of sugar maple timber and the pioneers used to seek "maplelands," concluding that it had the best of soil.

The Dr. Strong mill, already spoken of [Chapter XXII], has been located for the writer by Ezra Hosford, whose memory has been called upon for numerous facts regarding the days long gone. Mr. Hosford is among our oldest citizens and his personal recollections coupled with what he may have learned from the generation preceding him have large historical value. The Strong mill for sawing marble stood on the east side of the stream below the bridge near the Abel Leavenworth place which is now owned by Mrs. Jennie Leavenworth Fonda. Dr. Strong was a dealer in gravestones and the marble was cut and dressed in this mill. Above the bridge an immense pine log was placed diagonally across the stream and water near the lower end was conducted into a canal that furnished power for the mill. There was a dam ten or a dozen rods above the bridge

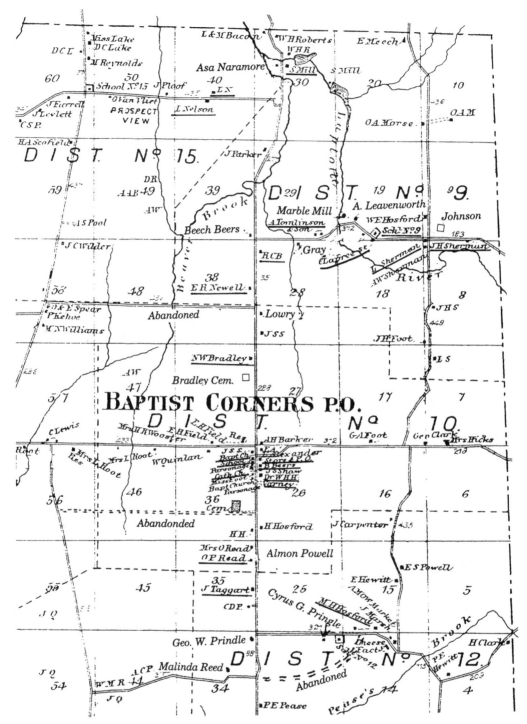

Baptist Corners area from the Beers map with additions for following Higbee in Chapters XXXI, XXXII and XXXIII.

and about seventy-five years ago there was a saw mill on the west bank run by a man named Gow. He had a chair factory on the east bank. At the top of the hill, a little west of the old house now standing, Amos Tomlinson had a blacksmith shop. Near here John Sears had a shop and there is an old cellar on the north side of the road where a man named Pulford used to live. This was a busy place in the early times and no doubt threatened to become a manufacturing center of considerable importance. Amos Hickok built the Abel Leavenworth house and Jarvis Hickok built the old Clafore Laprese house.

The old schoolhouse has stood on the present site many years, one-quarter of it in the highway, to say the least. The Sherman holdings commenced with the buying together of brothers Leverette and William Sherman of a large tract of land em-bracing the farm now in the name and the Peter Stacy farm on the road to Hinesburgh. Leverette bought William's interest and he purchased of Mr. Foote the farm that was known as the John H. Sherman place. Williams put up the buildings on this holding. Greene Tripp used to live in a house between William Sherman's and the Hinesburgh line. A house used to stand in the northeast corner of the crossing of roads, north of Leverette Sherman's where a colored man named Johnson lived. Going north, the house owned by Mr. Robinson, where George Geron now lives, was built by John Mosier. Abel Leavenworth built a house between Mosier's and the Sanford place. The house on the farm now owned by Ella V. H. Bradford was built by Clark Sanford.

The Carpenter school, Dist. # 9, east of the LaPlatte river on the north side of Carpenter Rd. at the top of the hill. The school is now a home on the south side of the road. Undated photo the gift of Hazel Hoskam. Charlotte Memorial Museum Collection.

Is this Mr. Strong's marble mill? On the back of the original photo: "The place where the marble mill burned down." Courtesy of the Root family.

There used to be a house across the road from the Sanford place. Elwood Irish lived on the Hungerford place, now owned by Luther Pierce and his sister Samanda. The farm now occupied by Chester Smith and sold to Mrs. Maeck by Ezra Hosford used to be known as the Elijah and Burr Gray place. The original Elijah Gray house stood on the north side of the road, some twenty rods west of the Tomlinson place. The house was afterwards drawn to the farm now owned by R. C. Beers.

In those days oxen were as often used in farm work as horses, perhaps more frequently, and a "drawing" was nothing out of the ordinary. A half day's ride would engage fifteen or more yoke of "cattle," according to the wants of the occasion, and when these were attached to the monster cable chain, with links of inch-round iron, something had to come. It was generally the building. The oxen were used to logging and all other kinds of heavy hauling and it was magnificent to see those massive shoulders all lifting together. A thirty-by-forty foot barn would slide along like a boy's hand sled, provided things were favorable and nobody got "stuck."

It was not always clear sailing and the way log chains snapped was a caution. But the man who made the "bee" generally mended up the chains and so shortly after some blacksmith prospered. It required a pretty good head for contrivances, withal, to boss the job, so as to steer clear of certain difficulties that always accompanied such undertakings and he who was cut out for it was pretty sure of an engagement. The late Alanson Edgerton had a marked capacity in this direction. Chiefest among his qualifications was a voice that could be heard any required distance and even the oxen came to know that "Are you all ready," meant business for them and everybody and no shirking, until Edgerton's "whoa" fairly shook the ground.

Our Lady of Mount Carmel Catholic church in East Charlotte. During the winter of 1858-1859 it was moved from Starksboro to Charlotte, a distance of ten miles. It had been a Quaker Meeting House. Hemenway's "Vermont Historical Gazetteer," Vol. 1, p. 744 reports that the building was "drawn" to its present site, so it probably came in one piece by the process Higbee describes. Gift of John Holmes. Charlotte Mem. Museum Collection.

XXXII

Baptist Corners and More, a Lime Kiln, Down-Country Horse Buyers, an Up-And-Down Saw Mill, a Stage Road that Never Came

24 December 1897

A few rods west of the Gray house was a brickyard--and the bricks in the house where E. Beech Beers lives were made by Dyer Gillette, who built the house. North of the Beers house and near the top of the hill, Oran Newell had a lime-kiln. A little north and west of this kiln, a man named Andrew Chatfield committed suicide by hanging. He lived a little north of the ledge in a house owned by a Mr. Meeker. Farther north on the hill south of John Patterson's and about the center of the highway where the road runs westerly to the Lewis Nelson place, was and perhaps still is an old well. A workman on the highway was once prodding around with his iron bar, looking not so much for a hole as for stones, when the bar suddenly broke through the crust, slipped out of his hands, and disappeared. Whether it went into this well or dropped into some mysterious cavern, the writer cannot say.

The house owned by John Paterson was originally built for a tavern by Asa Naramore, who also owned a sawmill on the falls above the bridge. The theory of a tavern at certain distances along this north and south road was based on the assumption that this was to be a stage line from Winooski Falls southward to Middlebury; indeed, the early survey, according to Charlotte land records, speaks of it as a "stage road." In point of fact, it is one of the longest and most direct of the north and south roads, through Shelburne, Charlotte, Monkton, New Haven, and perhaps to Mason and Dixon's Line. But somehow the stages shunned this route and tavern builders were doomed to a mild disappointment. John Naramore built the house near the north end of the bridge.

South of the Beech Beers' on the east side stood a house owned and perhaps built by Moses Leonard, who was a long-ago chorister in the Baptist church. Oran Newell lived where his son, the late Edwin Newell lived and died. The present R. C. Beers farm was owned by Nehemiah Lowry, who probably put up some of the original buildings. Ancestors of Dr. Taggert, a well-known old time practitioner, lived south of the Beers place, and

189

still further south on the same side of the road stood a house built by Johnathan Gillette; nothing but a half-filled cellar remains. The W. I. Bradley place was owned by Elisha Newell and Elisha Newell, Jr. occupied it.

South of Mr. Bradley's is an ancient burying ground, under the supervision of the town; according to Mr. Ezra Hosford's recollections, many of the headstones came from the stone mill of Dr. John Strong standing on the creek near Leavenworth's. This is one of the oldest burial yards in town perhaps antedating the one in the west part near the Lewis Barber place. Its use was discontinued on account of frequently striking large unmovable boulders beneath the surface.

Calvin Powell built the house where J. A. Harris lives, but after-wards sold out to William O. Barker. The road, instead of turning south from the west, continued easterly near the house and so on up the hill towards Hinesburgh. Near where the spring is, across from Harris's, stood a building used as a dwelling, shoe shop and tannery by Reuben Martin.

Mr. Martin built the house now owned by Mrs. Henry Claxton and this also was destined for a tavern. William O. Barker bought it in an unfinished condition and after completion ran a public house here for some years.

It was at one time headquarters for down-country horse buyers, as has already been noted in these papers.[Chapter XIV] South of Barker's, James Bennett had a wheelwright shop. Across the road was a blacksmith shop owned by a man

Part of the Bradley cemetery on the west side of Spear St. Ext. north of the Hinesburgh Rd. intersection and south of the Bradley/Eno/Carpenter house. An epitaph on one tombstone here, "Why lovely friend indulge that tear / Why trembling view my dank abode / Though you with me must molder here / Yet Faith can wing thy soul to God. / Sabrina Niles - 1810." Photo taken in 1979.

190

named Prentice. At a later day, the shop came into the possession of Oran Read and about this time the road was changed to its present course easterly. Part of the building now used as a store was put up by William Baldwin for a shoe shop. William Niles had a queer, half-story building west of the road from the present store, extending over a run and in the basement he had a brandy still. North of this and in the same little run, Shivereek Eldridge had a tannery, owned by Nathaniel Newell. Mr. Newell also owned a house that stood about where the Allen creamery is and Eldridge lived there. What with both Martin and Eldridge in the tanning business, the citizens of the Baptist Corners ought not to have suffered for leather in the early days.

The old and probably original Baptist church stood about one hundred feet north of where the present building now stands, whose chaste adornments bespeak the liberality of its friends and members. The house south of the store, owned by Cyrus Beers, was built by William Baldwin. The old and perhaps the first house

An East Charlotte Baptist meeting at the Eno cottage at Thompson's Point in 1909. Front from left: Ralph Clark, Edith Reed [Read ?] Johns, Charlie Johns, Evelyn Hazard, Rene Holmes, Robert Holmes. Center: Guy Baldwin, Ina Reed [Read ?], Alfred Paine[?], Stella Foote Payne[?]. Back: Albert Gove, William Kellogg, Leon Prindle, Sarah Eno, Margaret (Baldwin) Prindle, Jessie (Prindle) Baldwin, Gay Baldwin, Ruby Hazard, George Hazard. Gift of Hazel Gove Hoskam. Charlotte Memorial Museum Collection.

The former Lyceum Hall Association building, next south of the Baptist Church in East Charlotte. The Charlotte Grange #398 purchased it in 1958. Gift of John Holmes. Charlotte Memorial Museum Collection.

that stood on the Curtis L. Van Vliet farm, where the late Joseph Shaw died, was built by John Wescott. A district school used to stand nearly across the road from the Read house where the Catholic parsonage now is.

The Frank Colt house was built by Dr. Isaac Foote. William Powell built the house since owned and improved by Dr. W. H. H. Varney. Isaac Foote also built a house near where John R. Taggart lives. Roger Hosford, grandfather of Ezra Hosford, built the house on that farm something over one hundred years ago. Many of the original door latches are still in use on the venerable and well-preserved old homestead. Deforest Hyde built the O. P. Read house, though changes and additions have been made. Almon Powell once lived nearly across the way in a house built by Mr. Lockwood. Grove Hosford built the old steep-roofed, one story dwelling that still clings to its life, where Oran Read lived and died.

Mr. Read and Herman Horsford built a sawmill west of the road on what was called the Hoag lot. Ezra Hosford, then a young man, helped hew the timber for the frame. The lumber that went into the Alpheus Williams brick house, now owned by the Wilbur Foote estate, was sawed in this mill and the old up-and-down saw no doubt rasped out a good many other bills for lumber for the architectural doings of a previous generation. Doubtless many a lad in days long gone took his side on the "carriage" that hitched along, cog at a time, until the board dropped off and the saw

The up-and-down saw in the mill at the Shelburne Museum. The log carriage and the wheel with ratchet to move the log along as it was cut by the blade can be seen in the background. Photo taken in 1990.

seemed to stop for breath, while the sawyer reversed things, sending the carriage and log and boy back again with many a jot and jolt and rumble.

John Taggart lives on the old Norman Atwood place and Buel Atwood lived in a plank house near where George W. Prindle's tenement now stands. Perhaps this was in whole or in part the original Atwood domicile. Solomon Johnson built a plastered house standing where the brick house of George W. Prindle now is or nearly on the present site. The house owned by Andrew Franklin was built by Ezra Dorrman; here was another tavern, whose proprietor dreamed of both riches and renown from feeding the passengers on the proposed "stage route" that seemed to be ever coming, but failed to arrive.

The road leading easterly used to be some hundred rods to the south and was a continuation of the highway easterly from the Malinda Read place bearing to the north and coming into the present route near the Myron H. Horsford stone house.

Mt. Philo from the entrance to Morningside Cemetery. This road once continued on to Guinea Rd. The intersection of One Mile Rd., Guinea Rd. and Bingham Brook Rd. can be seen over the roofs in the left center of this photo taken in April, 1990.

XXXIII

Cyrus Pringle: World-Famous Botanist, Apple Orchards, Temperance and Apple Bees

31 December 1897

Cyrus Guernsey Pringle, the botanist. He preferred this spelling of the name, the rest of the family used the other version. Courtesy of Elinor (Prindle) Benning.

Gideon Prindle built a house on the old road leading eastward, but after it was changed to the present line it was torn down and some of it went into the house now owned by

Cyrus G. Pringle, the famous botanist and explorer of the Mexican wilds. Perhaps few men bear their heaped-up honors with the modesty of this citizen of ours who had rather discover a new plant than rule a kingdom. His assistance, botanical and horticultural lore are eagerly sought in both hemispheres.

Oran, son of Daniel Hosford, built the Myron Horsford house, and some seventy-five rods easterly is the old cellar where Daniel Hosford's house stood. As has before been stated, Daniel Hosford was a surveyor, and he laid out most of the old highways in town. An east and west road used to run nearly on the line of the driveway to the cemetery south of the Baptist Corners, and continued to the north and south road through Guinea. Ira Lowry used to have a house south of the road, a little west of the cemetery--still westward, a man named Keeler used to live. Near the southeast corner of the burying ground was a brick yard run by Roger Hosford. Isbon Prindle had a yard near George W. Prindle's and in these yards, bricks were made for most of

195

"Cyrus Pringle. Lost on the desert," the title given by the donor, his niece Carrie Prindle. *Charlotte Memorial Museum Collection.*

the brick houses in the eastern section of the town.

Scattered through fields and in unexpected places, one comes upon old apple trees or decaying stumps of trees that blossomed and bore fruit more than a century ago, and the curious often wonder how it came to be. Look a little closer and you find a grassy knoll which covers the foundation of a chimney stack--its volume of smoke drifted over the tree tops of the virgin forests amid whose clearings the forefathers planted seeds.

In those days the owner of "grafted fruit" took the highest seats in the realm, and barreling apples was an unknown industry. About the only market was the cider mill owner and brandy distiller, who converted the common fruit, "sour enough to make a pig squeal," into the wherewithal to do

a "haying" or hospitably entertain the "Elder" as he made his saddle bag rounds of the "circuit." Reference to such things is in no sense a disparagement, for custom made a law for itself, and the consciences and the morals were perhaps as keen and high as the

The home of Cyrus G. Pringle on Prindle Rd. when is was being renovated by new owners in 1980.

196

like commodities of today. Years have passed since the "Washingtonians"[87] sang their songs and circulated their pledges. Legislatures have grappled with the subject and passed laws enough to fill Noah's Ark. Prohibitive statutes have endeavored to prohibit-- perhaps with some degrees of success; and after all this upward climbing, both Maine and Vermont find unlimited opportunities for official "raids" on rum-holes, and prosecuting officers grow rich with a term or two of occupying this office.

It is asserted as a fact that in many of the counties the income of the State's Attorneyship makes it a more desirable office than any other in the State. It is also claimed the liquor law has been so "fixed" that stopping the traffic and shutting up the saloons would be an unprovided-for calamity to the prosecutors.

And all the while we make finger boards of ourselves pointing backward to the "drinking days" of the fathers-- when, population considered, they could discount us two to one as a temperate people. In view of the weakness of our law or the knock-kneed rate with which it is executed, scores, if not hundreds are discussing the trial on something else, and scores if not hundreds are asking the question if they are not somewhat in the right. Bangor, Maine, the fountain-head of radical legislation on temperance, is asking herself how she is to shut up her saloons.

Burlington, Vermont, with 90 to 100 "resorts," and one man says 190, offers perhaps the best paying berth for a "prosecuting attorney" in the State; and still the "resorts" flourish like a green bay tree in the desert, and in due season the "prosecuting attorney" regales himself with an elegant mansion on the "Hill". There the wise and good and learned are supposedly associated in their own good company.

This is not a treatise of temperance, only the question has arisen incidentally, growing out of an unfortunate reference to the old apple trees of the fathers; and it affords striking examples of the proneness of mortal man to fall into moralizing when he ought to have spoken of the apple bees and fun and frolics those trees were instrumental in bringing about, when the laughing girl whirled an unbroken paring three times around her head to see it fall upon the floor as the initial letter of the name she was to bear after wedlock; and the boys helped along a certain game of "string", wherein a thousand dollars would have been no inducement to cease striking at a certain hand until the hand was hit and the forfeit blushingly paid and taken.

There was a practical side to it in the meantime, for ten or a dozen bushels of apples were quartered and cored and strung that would weigh some six pounds to the bushel when properly dried, and at six cents a pound, this meant a modest income to the madam. True enough a dozen pumpkin pies had to be made and a ten-quart panful of doughnuts was none too lavish a provision. But neighborhood matters were talked over, and

Cyrus Pringle (left) on Prindle Rd. east of his house. The other man is unidentified. Some of Pringle's orchards are in the distance in this rare photograph of a winter scene. Gift of Carrie Prindle. Charlotte Memorial Museum Collection.

Whatever the use of the apples Charlotte's large and beautiful orchards flourished. Pictured, the Holmes Orchard on the west side of Lake Rd. south of the Holmes Bridge. Charlotte Memorial Museum Collection.

Bar bills from an 1810 account book. A glass of rum and a half mug of flip were popular drinks. Flip was a sweetened mixture of beer and spirits warmed by a hot iron. Charlotte Memorial Museum Collection.

the spinning of so many knots of yarn or the weaving of flannel for winter wear was canvassed and considered with professional pride.

It was a hearty, homely way of helping each other. It was the shortest road to an evening of useful pleasure. It brought the neighbors together without the flummery of kids[88] and the fifteen-minute social call of fashion; and in the glorious moonlight on the homeward way more than one compact was entered into respecting the rest of the journey of life.

HENRY CLAY
ADDRESSING THE SENATE.

"Perley's Reminiscences" by Perley Poore. A. W. Mills, Tecumseh, Mich. 1886.

XXXIV

Preservation of the Union and Our Democracy

7 January 1898

Evidently the politician was active in the early days, perhaps fully as much so as in this generation. Issues growing out of the formation of new states and the ever-present question of slavery and the aggressions on free territory by the slave oligarchy kept party lines closely drawn. "Abolition" became prominent at a comparatively later date, but all through the years the dominating character of the Southern slave owner was constantly felt, and constantly a source of irritation. Questions of such vital interest to humanity would not down or would not stay down, and states even so far removed as Vermont from the scene of action, as the national capital has ever been, felt the thrill of controversy in every vein.

Comparatively a short period elapsed between the surrender at Yorktown and the exasperating assumption of Great Britain in her asserted right to stop American ships on the high seas and impress into her navy whomever she claimed as a British subject, but it had been long enough to build up a nation that dared grapple again with its old antagonist-- a nation that had perhaps inherited

enough of the instincts of the sea to man and sail and fight its ironsides to the dismay of presuming England, and with courage enough to whip the best troops the world ever saw.

It was only thirty-six years from 1776 to 1812, but a development unexpected, unprecedented in wealth, in enterprise, in men, attended this "experiment in government," and a

WEBSTER'S REPLY TO HAYNE

"Perley's Reminiscences" by Perley Poore. A. W. Mills, Tecumseh, Mich. 1886.

Union, unique as it was grand, was flying its thoroughly respected flag in the winds of every sea. Menacing as had been a foreign foe, prompt as had been our people in "millions for defense, but not one penny for tribute," the danger to our institution, and danger there was, was found at home. The alluring metaphysics of Calhoun, the bold and brilliant attacks of Hayne, required the marvelous oratory of Clay and the magnificent eloquence of Webster to nullify and refute their eloquence and even then it postponed the inevitable only for a season, and it built up in the hearts of men in the North and East and West so fiery a love for the Union and the Constitution of the fathers that the blood of a terrible war could not suppress or extinguish it.

Do the dwellers around the mountains sufficiently comprehend the magnitude of the service such as Daniel Webster and Henry Clay rendered their country? (Not that other names are to be disregarded or the orators and statesmen of a later date overlooked.) But these two men came to the front at a period in our history when the great argumentative questions of Constitutionality or harmonizing by pacific means by compromises, were to be met and adjusted. If there is not a "Divinity that shapes our ends," how comes it that the generations provide men for each emergency, from the Father of his Country, sleeping at Mount Vernon, to the liberator of a race sleeping among the friends and scenes of his youth? We shall not speak too highly of such men while they live; we cannot be too reverent at their tombs.

We say an "experiment in government" and perhaps from its inception to this hour no nation has ever been so complete a study to an astounded world. There had been republics, it is true, and the men of '76 had traditions from which to model a state. But in South America, in Europe, in Mexico, nowhere had there ever been a self-governing people but in whose recurring change of political organizations, bloodshed and assassination were predominating features, and disintegration a perpetual menace.

And now came the United States of America, opening its doors to the universe, providing even in its Constitution for an entire change of government, in an administrative way, every four years, granting the greatest liberty to tongue and press and pen, adjusting in reality all matters of state and national policy by the ballot, coercing no man, appealing perpetually to the people, abiding the verdict of the people. No wonder we were pronounced "a failure" at the outset. Kings said the people cannot be trusted. They underestimated the men of New England from the start.

They are coming to comprehend them. The secret of it is and was: it is your government and mine. You and I and every other citizen are responsible for what we have, for what we do. I belong to one party, you to another, and each watches and criticizes the other, as a check upon the other, and herein is safety. Parties are a political necessity; they are the ma-

The sinking of the ALABAMA.

From "The Youths' History of the United States." Vol. 3, p. 268. Cassell Publishing Co. New York. 1887.

chinery of government. When rebellion to Constitutional law raised its bloody hand in 1860, some of the nation cried, "Behold, the time has come." The "experiment" has failed, and shame to our race, those of our own speech and lineage were the most indifferent to our necessities, nay, more, they opened their shipyards to the building of ALABAMAS[89] and their harbors to the sheltering of vessels that dared not carry a flag.

The English-speaking race is yet to dominate the world, and it is hoped the time will never come when its two mightiest representatives array themselves in opposing battle line. But if it ever does, the memory of things that occurred when we were struggling for constitutional government will sever the arm of a million men. Even now, those of the South in their secret heart despise a foreign power that sought to strengthen themselves by weakening us in our hour of sorest need.

One thing we should teach our children, and it should go into our literature to latest time. The mighty empire of northern Europe, representing perhaps the most enlightened absolutism of modern times, recognized the justness of our cause, the benefit to mankind of our continued existence, and in the darkest hour of the struggle, when the intervention of England seemed most imminent, the ominous gathering of the black war ships of Russia along our coasts served notice that the United States would have one ally in her extremity that had better not be defied.

Is it any wonder that we took official action a little time ago in sending food to her famine-stricken people? Very few doubt the assumption that the controlling motive actuating English sympathizers and abettors was not love for the South. They cared no more for them, only as a means for certain accomplishments, than for the Feegees [Fijians] or the Greenlanders. They saw an opportunity for the long wished for disintegration. Civil war carefully nursed and covertly assisted might do what they had ever failed in doing. It was a thrust in the dark, a stab in the back, when the nation was facing a foe.

But the flag still floats and only one flag--its stars increased. The brave men of the South who fought against it then are today protected at home and abroad by its folds. The cause for which they took arms may always seem somehow a righteous one to them, and their sons and daughters may inherit the father's devotion, but they are American citizens all, and if the day ever dawns when it becomes necessary to take up arms in defense of national life, the North and South will march in the same battle front. The men of the North slower in action, perhaps like their climate cold blooded, but with the given persistency of the bulldog; the men of the South fierce as tigers in the whirlwind rush of battle; both of them intelligent, liberty-loving, proud of their nation, unconquerable. [See *Charlotte in the Civil War*, Chapter XLII.]

William Wallace Higbee, 1842-1911, Charlotte's preeminent town official: Town Clerk from 1873 to 1911, one term each as Town Representative and County Senator, student of town records and author of essays on town history. Courtesy of Nancy Sabin.

"The 1850 Charlotte Town Meeting House."
From a 1975 watercolor by Richard Alther.
Courtesy of the Charlotte Historical Society

XXXV

Town Officers
and the 1850 Town Meeting Hall

14 January 1898

It will be recalled that John McNeil was the first town clerk of Charlotte. Benjamin Ferris, Jr., and Daniel Hosford had each served in turn as proprietors' clerk. The difference was this: the township was originally granted to seventy proprietors, and without coming to the territory they perfected a regular organization, elected a moderator and clerk, assessed taxes; in fact, did all necessary business such as was afterwards done in town meeting. Most of these early meetings were held in Dutchess County, New York. Later, and when sufficient settlements had been made, the town organized and entered upon its official career. When John McNeil was elected clerk, he probably lived near the original ferry in Cedar Beach Bay.

It seems that in 1849, at a town meeting held according to call, "at the Congregational meeting house," the third article in the warning was "to see if the town will raise money to build a town house," and a committee consisting of Luther Stone, William E. Sherman, Leonard Sherman, Abner Squier and George Pease was appointed to investigate the matter and report at a subsequent meeting. It was also voted "that the town pay to the Congregational society five dollars for the purpose of cleaning the church that they have met in for the past forty years."

At a special meeting held April 26, 1849, it was voted "that the town build a town house, to be situated on

A Charlotte official, our representative in the state legislature in 1836-37, Pitt E. Hewitt. The carte-de-visite was taken not long before he died in 1875. Courtesy of Elinor (Prindle) Benning.

land owned by the town which lies near the town pound," and that the building was to be of brick, and in size thirty by forty feet. A building committee was appointed, consisting of Chauncey Shelden, Leverette Sherman, and D. C. Lake. The committee was authorized to "move the site of the house ten or twelve rods either way, as they thought best."

At an adjourned meeting held May 12, the committee reported they had inspected the town house in Hinesburgh and Williston; that the Hinesburgh town house suited them as to size, and the Williston town house as to inside arrangement. As to location, they had "affixed upon a site for the location of said town house, between Hyson Rich's dwelling house and O. J. Baldwin's barn; that said site can be bought for $25." The town then voted to rescind all previous votes on town house matters and to build on grounds selected by the committee, to cost about one thousand dollars. It was also voted to "hold town meetings in the Baptist church, until said house is completed."

The Freemens' meeting of 1849 was held in the Baptist church, and at this election John Sherman had 135 votes for town representative to 132 for E. H. Wheeler, the latter being defeated for the second term, or "dying a yearling," as it was called. The reason for this was purely political and not of a personal nature. Mr. Wheeler sympathized with the "Free Soldiers," afterwards merged into the Republican party, losing his election by a narrow margin of only three votes. He was afterwards elected to the senate for Chittenden County and thus matters were evened up.

In the meantime, it seems "town house" matters were again unsettled, for November 2, 1849, the selectmen were petitioned "to call a town meeting as soon as may be, for the purpose of taking into consideration the locations of a town house."

Probably the old, uneasy feeling between "east" and "west," that before occasioned as much trouble in "sticking the stake for the meeting house" so many years ago, had crept to the surface again. In accordance with this petition, a meeting was called at the Baptist church for November 14, "for the purpose of taking into consideration the locations of a town house and see if the town will change the same." Peter V. Higbee, Herman H. Newell, and Charles B. Cook were the selectmen. The town meeting opened

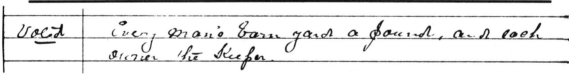

One piece of business that was voted on in the 1881 town meeting: "Every man's barn a pound and each owner its keeper." This saved transporting lost or strayed animals to the town pound, but assured that the owner would pay a fee for recovering his stock.

Town Clerks of Charlotte

Benjamin Ferris, Jr.	1783-1785 (Prop. clerk)
Daniel Horsford	1785-1787 (Prop. clerk)
John McNeil	1787-1790
Isabel Strong	1790-1799
David Hubbell	1799-1801
Medad Lyman	1801-1802
Isaac Webb	1802-1804
Jeremiah Barton	1804-1813
Zaddock Wheeler	1813-1823
George Newell	1823-1827
Noble Lovely	1827-1834
Samuel H. Barnes	1834-1847
A. H. Lyon	1847-1853
D. C. Gillette	1853 (March-Aug.)
William A. Sherman	1853-1855
Ezra Alexander	1855-1872 (Res. 10/72)
E. H. Wheeler	1872-1873
W. W. Higbee	1873-1911 (Died in office)
May Higbee	1911-1920 (Died in office)
Anna L. Byington	1920-1937
G. L. Root	1937-1941
Mae M. Foote	1941-1947
Murchison L. Williams	1947-1953
Kenneth Taggart	1953-1954
Frank Potter	1954-1959
Mary Waller	1959-1966
Priscilla L. Spear	1966-1974
Hazel W. Prindle	1974-1988
Terry B. Silva	1988-

This list of the town clerks who have served Charlotte was compiled by Priscilla Spear and updated in August 1990 by Hazel Prindle. Both had served as Town Clerk.

agreeably to the warning, and A. L. Beach was chosen moderator. "The meeting then adjourned to a schoolhouse near William S. Baldwin's shoe shop," and it was "voted not to change the location of the town house." Thus the matter came to an amicable adjustment, the present building was erected, and the election of 1850 was held in it.[90] Not to be partial in such matters, the town voted to pay the Baptist society five dollars for the use of their church the same as they had paid the Congregational society.

A tintype of the town house though at the time the child and horse were perhaps the important subjects. Tintypes are backwards--the hill is not on the right when viewing the front of the building--and this kind was made from 1856 to around 1870. Voters approved building this town house in 1849. Charlotte Memorial Museum Collection.

XXXVI

Indians and Early Settlements, the Hollow and Industries

9 June 1899

Possibly it may be concluded by a continuation of these "mountain" papers that the writer holds an unappeased grudge against the public, hoping in this way to settle the score. Assuming that the expressions of commendation, coming from various points of the compass and from those whose judgments are of no small value, indicate that these sketches have been somewhat of interest and worth the trouble of perusing, we may again follow along some of the highways where the fathers and the mothers walked long ago.

The newspaper goes everywhere. Through the west, the south, in the great cities, *The Vermonter* finds weekly readers in faraway Vermonters, and names and places are familiar to them as to us. They hear familiar names, imagination takes in familiar scenes--the pleasures and the pains of old days return and in an hour a score, perhaps two score years are lived over again.

But alas, too often we "listen for a voice that is stilled"--we wait in vain "for the touch of a vanished hand"[91]. But this is life, and the world rolls round, daylight comes and goes,

Ad for the "Vergennes Vermonter" from the Child Gazetteer, 1881-82. Most of Higbee's essays were published in this paper.

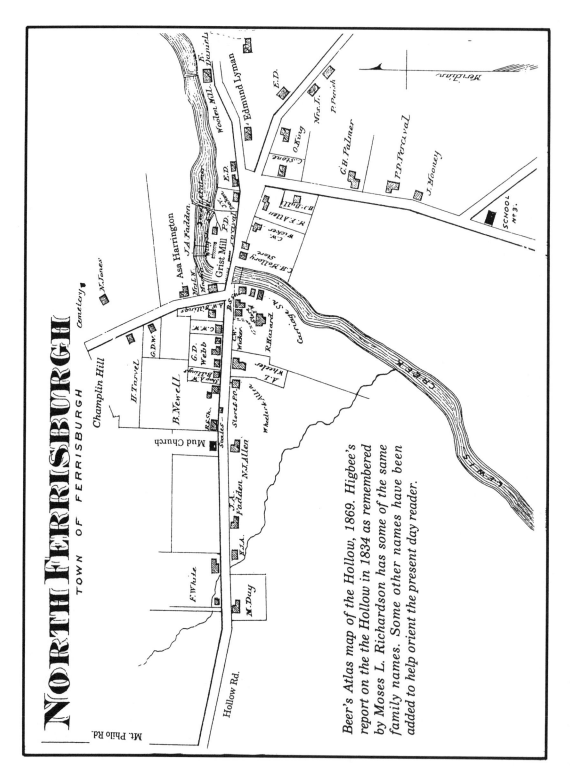

NORTH FERRISBURGH
TOWN OF FERRISBURGH

Beer's Atlas map of the Hollow, 1869. Higbee's
report on the the Hollow in 1834 as remembered
by Moses L. Richardson has some of the same
family names. Some other names have been
added to help orient the present day reader.

From "Barber's History and Antiquities for the Northern States," by John Warner Barber. 1842.

winter, summer, seedtime, harvest-- and it seems to matter little whether you and I are here to help or hinder. Mortal man is prone to magnify his own importance, and many a one has tickled his fancy with thinking of the great part he plays in the drama--how is it in fact? Some day his title span, too, is run.

This beautiful lake of ours, this magnificent valley, have been high- ways along which the nations have been putting up historical mileposts ever since the romantic soul of de Champlain dilated on his discovery. Long before the French and English chased each other back and forth from Crown Point to Quebec, others less powerful in numbers, but compensat- ing for this perhaps in fierceness, ranged these woodlands or skimmed along these waters--when Rock Dunder formed the boundary line of the implacable Iroquois, and the Mohican warrior was numerous as the leaves of the forest.

As King Philip[92], looking from the summit of Mt. Holyoke or Mt. Tom, mourned the decadence of his race and vowed eternal enmity to the desecrators of his fathers' graves, so, no doubt, some other desperate war- rior chieftain has contemplated from our mountains the oncoming ex- termination of tribes and people. Is there anywhere in the American In- dian history a chapter that is not pathetic? The logic of events was against him. The inexorable law of civilized progress embraced his extinc- tion and he was to disappear. But this was his land. The pilgrim built his fires upon the cold ashes of his deserted wigwam. But what are homes and native land and the graves of kindred before the hand of might? Tears may intervene, blood flow in streams, eloquence rend the skies, but the strong hand is withheld not.

Probably some of the most stirring incidents of early Vermont history are connected with the settlement of the lake towns in what is now Addison

The Champlin cemetery, North Ferrisburgh, with Mt. Philo in the background. Sarah Champlin's tombstone is in the foreground, Thomas Champlin's stone behind it, Phoebe Champlin's is the larger stone on the right. Photo taken in April, 1990.

County. For a long time this entire section was included in Rutland County, if indeed it did not extend to the Canada line. Settlers sought the lake as a means of communication as it was easier to carry goods by boats than pack it overland along lines of marked trees. These very conveniences had their drawbacks in the case of Indian incursions, but it was all taken into consideration and the risk accepted, for no finer lands had yet been seen in New England than were found in the Champlain Valley. Then, as now, the uplands of Massachusetts were inferior to us in quality, and the lake towns were settled directly after the granting of charters around 1762.

Shelburne, Charlotte, Ferrisburgh, Panton, Addison, and Monkton[93] came into political existence about the same time under the administration of Benning Wentworth, Governor of the Province of New Hampshire, who seemed to have been an important personage in the councils of King George. If Governor Wentworth lived long enough to get the "rise" on the corner lots that somehow fell to him under the various charters, he must have had a good bank account. But New England land was longer incubating, so to speak, than our western possessions, and a good many acres may have represented only a modest number of dollars lost here.

The late Moses L. Richardson of North Ferrisburgh at the time of his death was the oldest citizen of that locality and he was probably the oldest

212

living link that connected the present with the past. Mr. Richardson came to the Hollow in 1834, when a boy. The old "Wicker Store," as it was called, then stood next west of the bridge. A plank house stood where Mrs. Keeler now lives, and Asa Harrington lived there and ran the grist mill. Harrington built the Keeler house that burned down several years ago. The present Rufus Hazard place was occupied by William Hazard. The Champlin house on the hill was occupied by Benjamin Champlin; the Billings place by George Meigs. Part of the house now owned by Michael Flemming, in 1834 stood a little east of John S. Wheeler's and was bought and moved by Mr. Flemming to the ten acres which he had originally bought of John Hazard.

Michael Flemming and his wife came from Ireland and Flemming worked a good many years for the late Judge Meech of Shelburne, whose magnificent real estate holdings have already been spoken of in these papers. Mrs. Flemming is a sister of the late John Farrell who lived on the stage road south of S. A. Williams, and who was the enthusiastic Irish hunter whose "whist there, will yem moind the yowl of 'im," seemed to do him more good than to catch the fox the dog was chasing.

David White lived in the house that stands west of the Dr. Collins' place. A barn standing north of David Ploof's present barbershop, and the dwellings spoken of, embraced the buildings west of the bridge in 1834, as recalled by Mr. Richardson. At that time a travelled road ran over the hill past the Champlin house, coming into the present highway near where Edward Lacoy's house stands. It was a terribly steep and slippery place both summer and winter and tested the skill of the drivers and the muscles of the oxen both going and coming. Old residents say that patrons of the saw and grist mills used to count on "doubling up" as a matter of course, and "Champlin Hill" was always reckoned in as an important factor in estimating their return with a load of mill stuff.

George Meigs built the old Methodist church standing nearby on the present site in 1840. Previous to this, meetings were held in schoolhouses and private dwellings, but they were well attended and the circuit preacher found a congregation of intelligent and attentive audiences.

In 1834 there was no regular post office. Phil Millard, who lived in the Collins neighborhood, was employed to go once a week to Vergennes to get the mail. He generally made his rounds on horseback and carried a full-grown dinner horn with which to summon his patrons. Letter writing being somewhat expensive in those days, when it took six to twenty-five cents to transport a letter, and not ten newspapers where there are now a hundred, it is probable Mr. Millard was not overburdened. The first post office was established at "Martin's," with Stoddard Martin postmaster.

The site of Mrs. Tabor's house was occupied by a blacksmith shop owned by Frank Tandaw. This shop burned down and Tandaw built a shop in the

Hollow west of Mrs. Esther Newell's, previously spoken of by the writer. A popular landlord and successful horse trader in his day was Nicholas Tandaw, known also as "Uncle Nick Guindon", was brother of Frank.[94] We have previously written about his tavern located where the late George W. Palmer lived.

After Asa Harrington, the grist mill in the "Hollow" came into the possession of George Hagan who, at his death, was buried in the Friends' yard, near H. R. Baldwin's in Monkton. In 1834 the house now owned by George King was occupied by James Barton, a blacksmith, who had a shop where George Armbor's house stands. Where John V. Dakin lives was a blacksmith shop run by Frederick Fuller. Edmund Lyman had a small country store on the bank north of Martin F. Allen's. The road then ran where the footpath now is and was another steep grade up and down which the fathers used to scramble and slide with infinite patience. The "Wicker" house stood there then, with its shingled sides, but without its present modern additions. The house now owned by

Allen Hall (former Wheeler and Allen Store), dated on the roof 1884 from an early 1900's postcard.

Same view, April 1990. Both photographs taken from Champlin Hill.

The home of Norman J. Allen in the Hollow circa 1910. Fire destroyed some of the house and additions have changed its looks but the house is still there. Courtesy of the Wheeler/Kingsland Collection.

The Wheeler home in the Hollow. Porches and dormers have been added but this house is also still in use. Photo circa 1880. Courtesy of the Wheeler/Kingsland Collection.

Lyman woolen mill in the Hollow with Champlin Hill on the right, the Methodist church on the horizon on the left. Courtesy of Bixby Free Memorial Library.

Martin F. Allen was built by John Van Vliet about 1836 but of course subsequent owners have enlarged and improved it up to the present time.

Edmund Lyman lived in the red house standing on the point of land between the Monkton road and the road leading to the woolen factory of Theodore Lyman. Theodore Lyman lived in the house that was burned several years ago under the ownership of Mr. Daniels. Jonathan Lyman, his father, lived between this house and the factory. Jonathan Lyman once had a woolen mill on the water power near Russell Miller's or at least he carded wool and made rolls there. The house now occupied by Joseph Laquire stood there then and was occupied by the Lymans for their workmen. A bee keeper named Beady lived in the John P. Kenyon house but the building was owned by Joseph Rogers.

With the exception of the old red store on the site of C. H. Mallory's east of the bridge, the buildings mentioned in this connection were the only ones within half a mile of the bridge when Mr. Richardson first came to the Hollow.

216

About the time Norman J. Allen built the store occupied so long and successfully by Allen & Wheeler, Aaron B. Webb established his tannery after learning the business with Sheldon Wheeler of Charlotte, whose daughter he married. Theodore Lyman manufactured full cloth, all wool cassimeres, satinets[95] and flannels. He made yarn besides rolls enough to have reached around the world several times had they been spun into a single yarn. Lyman's full cloth was a standard for estimating the wearing and staying qualities of almost all commodities, and he was justly proud of his reputation, too.

The wool came in the fleece, was sorted, cleansed, carded, spun, colored in the various departments, and came out cloth. The coloring house stood a little below the factory near the bank of the creek and contained more villainous smells than a common nose could ordinarily put up with. Then the dyes, or most of them, came in the wood or bark, and the operator had to boil out the color in kettles. These kettles were set in arches and held from five to six barrels each, and the cloth was colored in them, being drawn out and in the fluid by a reed so as to insure an even color.

It was particular business, and a careless hand could easily ruin a fine piece of goods. Lyman employed twelve to fifteen hands. The late Moses L. Richardson worked for several years in that dye house. After coloring, the cloth was boiled to take out superfluous matter, and then hung on tenter bars to dry. Those tenter bars had some fifteen or twenty yards capacity on which all cloth was hung after fulling or shrinking. From the bars it went through the knapping and shearing process and was then pressed and called ready for market, generally twenty five yards in all.[96]

It was an awe inspiring time when the small boy was permitted to go to the Hollow with his daddy and take a turn through the grist mill and the saw mill and listen to the clatter of shuttles up at Lyman's. Zounds, it did not seem possible that the world could be so large, and what a tumultuous world, too. A visit at the blacksmith's opened up a vista of dirty hands and face that was appalling to the boy who was always being impressed with the idea that he must keep those portions of his anatomy spick and span.

Outside of a pair of new cowhide boots, all for himself, that the shoemaker over at Webb's had been pegging away at for an interminable length of time, to the boy's idea, the choicest spot of all was the store where the boy's round eyes saw raisins and sugar, always just out of reach, and jars of striped candy--and candy balls and lemon drops--and in the showcase--jack knives. It fairly took the boy's breath away to look things over, and if it happened that anybody, no matter who, was thoughtful enough to give the boy a stick of striped candy or a handful of raisins, the day for him was rounded out to completeness. Ten to one a nibble or two at the candy satisfied all present wants, for the boy instinctively thought of the mother at home, who must enjoy the sweet surprise of seeing him unroll his wonderful gift.

It is said that before the building of the woolen factory, this site was occupied by Robert and William Hazard in the manufacture of iron, the ore probably coming from New York. The coal used in the business was burned in the vicinity and coal burning was a regular industry[97]. The writer recalls when Joseph Allen burned a coalpit on the stage road in front of his blacksmith shop, near where William Noonan's house stands. I think Harmon Ball used to make a business of burning coal to supply blacksmiths. Then land had to be cleared, and coal brought money along with a lot of hard work too.

A nineteenth-century shoemaker illustrating a story in a contemporary scrapbook. "The boy's" bootmaker in the Hollow may have looked a bit like this. The Charlotte Memorial Museum Collection.

The burying ground on the hill east of the Champlin house is largely a private yard though there are a number of unmarked graves. Mr. Richardson thought that several members of a family named Borden were buried there. The headstones of the Champlin family indicate: Thomas Champlin, 1835, aged 75 years; Sarah, wife of Thomas Champlin, 1842, aged 83; Elisha P. Champlin, 25 years old; B. W. Champlin, 1864, 61 years old; Phoebe, wife of B. W. Champlin, 1844, aged 43; George W. Champlin, 1860, 31 years old. The grounds are nicely fenced and indicate care, though the Champlin family long since ceased to occupy the old homestead. Ezra Champlin, a former schoolmate of the writer, went to Minnesota and became one of the foremost farmers and citizens of Blue Earth County.[98] Roxana Champlin, who was for a long time a successful teacher, is also a resident of Minnesota. Thus the years bring changes, and it may be well to recall the names of those who in their way and time were busy workers in the human hive.

Reuben Martin, who died September 30, 1838, aged 92 years and three months, was the first one buried in the cemetery near the Methodist church, North Ferrisburgh. There are now some seven hundred graves in that cemetery. Both Reuben Martin and his wife Sarah lived to remarkable age--Sarah Martin died March 23, 1845, aged 90 years and six months. Reuben Martin was the father of Stoddard Martin, or "Squire" Martin, as everybody knew him for miles around. He was the principal trial justice in his day for North Ferrisburgh. But perhaps as remarkable an inscription as is often found on a tombstone is the record of the death of Mary Griffin Champlin, wife of Benedict Champlin, born July 20, 1796, died 27 March 1896, lacking only a few months of living one hundred years. Up to a short time preceding her death she was active in mind and body. What a thought to talk of the happenings of eighty, ninety years ago, and be yourself a party to them.

"Mary G. Champlin. July 20, 1796 - March 27, 1896." is written on the back of this photo. Please note how much labelling means nearly one hundred years later. Courtesy of the Frost family.

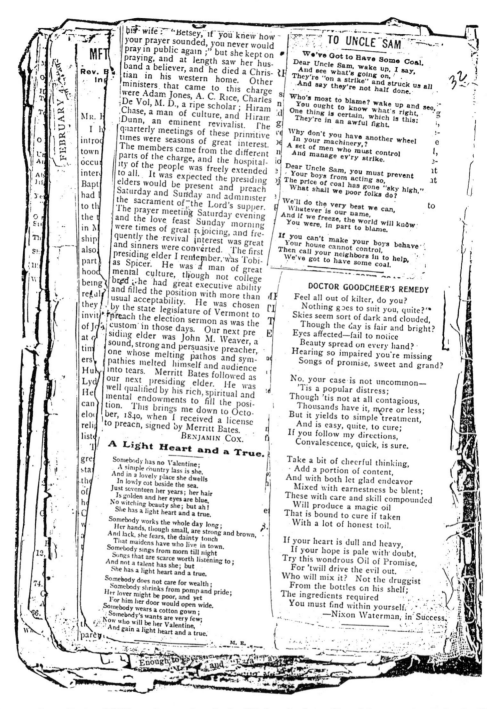

A page from Daisy Williams' scrapbook. As Higbee had predicted (see next page), she "had pasted in these papers...." The scrapbook helped in collecting his papers for this book. Copy courtesy of Roy Thorp.

XXXVII

Otter Creek: an Old Indian Trail, Yorker Claims and the Westminster Declaration of Independence

7 July 1899

Concede that our original intention was simply to chronicle some of the most accessible items of local history that future generations, perhaps stumbling upon some old scrap book, where lovers of the curious had pasted in these papers with recipes for herb teas and cough remedies and choice methods of pickling hams, might know who lived here, or whose house stood over yonder ruined cellar wall.[99] The idea was to take in a few highways around Mt. Philo and Pease Hill--but other roads were found leading hither and yon, and the temptation to become prolix and tiresome grows with what it feeds upon.

Although several of the towns along the lines of Addison and Chittenden Counties, as they now are, were chartered in 1762-3, it is doubtful if they contributed much in population for some time after that. True, the names of original grantees appear upon the records of these towns, and transfers of real estate were recorded by the "Prospectors' Oath." But to sell land was one thing, to live on it quite another, especially as New York was then grasping for all the land to the Connecticut River. All parties well understood that the contest over rival claims had only commenced. The hotbed of Green Mountain politics was in the south of the state, and about 1770 the old Catamount Tavern in Bennington, built by Captain Steven Fay, became the gathering place for those who shaped the destiny of this new people.

Immigrants found the only two accessible routes either from Albany way or New Hampshire--one by way of Bennington, the other down the Otter Creek Valley, crossing the mountains, practically along the present line of the Rutland Railroad. This route along the Otter Creek was the old Indian trail from the Connecticut to the lake, as tradition has it.[100] But the Bennington route was probably the most used as the most direct road to the lake and the easiest to travel.

About 1770 it was uncertain what political power would dominate the settlers here, outside of themselves. In fact, Congress was then appointing commissioners to interview the Green Mountain Boys and find out the ways and the means for quieting the clamor between the Yorkers and the Grants. It is quite evident that the money and the diplomacy of the New York claimants were having an effect on Congress, for the tendency seemed in their direction, not so much by open decisions as by suggestions and recommendations for settlements that recognized New Yorkers more than was agreeable to Chittenden, Allen, Baker, Warner, Fay, and others who were not only firm believers in the "beech seal,"[101] but stood ready to lend a hand as occasion required. It is not to be understood for a moment that these rugged early settlers were lacking in loyalty to the national course, for whoever inhabited Charlotte or Ferrisburgh or Monkton were certainly part of the group of men who fourteen years before Vermont was admitted into the Union pledged "5000 soldiers, capable of bearing arms in defense of American liberty."

In addition, they offered to "clothe, quarter and feed them" at the expense of Vermont. Actions that speak louder than words thus testify to the invincible courage of these highlanders, who were driven by the force of circumstances to defy the world in defense of their own.

Certainly no state in American history ever occupied so unique a position as Vermont when, at Westminster, January 15, 1777, she made her "Declaration of Independence." Through the influence of counter claims to the territory, she was held at arm's length by Congress and it became a question of going it alone or not going at all.

A Continental Congress resolution of May 15, 1776 recommended:

To the respective assemblies and conventions of the United Colonies, where no government sufficient for the exigencies of their affairs hath been hitherto established, to adopt such government as shall, in the option of the representatives of the people, best conduce to the happiness and safety of their constituents in particular and America in general.

It will be readily seen that this action of the Grants at Westminster was no defiance to Congress, was no act of disloyalty to other states then engaged in the Revolutionary struggles, but was the outcome of a magnificent self-reliance in the justice of their course. It was not the hardihood of desperation; it was the courage that comes from being in the right and maintaining it. Let us quote from this Westminster Convention of 1777:

Whereas, the Honorable the Continental Congress did, on the 4th day of July last declare the United Colonies in America to be free and independent of the Crown of Great Britain, which declaration we most cordially acquiesce in, and whereas, by said declaration the arbitrary acts of the Crown are null and void in America, consequently the jurisdiction by said Crown granted to New York government over the New Hampshire Grants is totally dissolved. We therefore, the inhabitants of said tract of land, are at present without law or government, and may be truly said to be in a state of nature, consequently a right remains to the people of said Grants to form a government best suited to their prosperity, well being and happiness: We, the delegates from the several counties and towns, do make and publish the following declaration: That we will at all times hereafter consider ourselves as a free and independent state, capable of regulating our internal police in all and every respect whatsoever; That the people of said Grants have the sole and exclusive right and inherent right of ruling and governing themselves in such manner and form as in their own wisdom they shall think proper, not inconsistent or repugnant to any resolve of the Continental Congress. That we will firmly stand by and support one another in this our declaration of a state, and endeavoring, as much as in us lies, to suppress all unlawful riots and disturbances whatever. Also we will endeavor to secure to every individual his life, peace, and prosperity against all unlawful invaders of the same. We hereby declare that we are at all times ready in conjunction with our brethren in the United States of America to do our full proportion in maintaining and supporting the just war against the tyrannical invasions of the ministerial fleets and armies, as well as any other foreign enemies, sent with express purpose to murder our fellow brethren and with fire and sword ravage our defenseless country.

Thus Vermont became an independent republic.

A panther which shows the wildness of our area when settled by the pioneer fathers and mothers. "Harper's New Monthly Magazine," p. 739, May, 1855.

Country life as illustrated in the famous "McGuffey's Revised Primer and Readers," 1886 edition. Courtesy of Katherine Teetor.

XXXVIII

Vermont Before Statehood, a Generation of Heroes and Brave Mothers

14 July 1899

As the scattered settlers in those towns met each other a little over a century ago, let us imagine the themes that engaged them the most. Our forefathers, as they gathered about the great fireplaces of their log cabins, listening to the winds moaning through a trackless wilderness--ready at any moment of the day or night to grapple with a wily foe--is it any wonder that they were brave? Is it any wonder that mothers, living in such an atmosphere, feeling the terrible pressure of such times, brought into the world a generation of heroes? While we honor the fathers and commemorate their deeds in song, story and granite, always with them let us place the heroism, the Roman courage of the mothers. With the fathers was the physical facing of known dangers, the madness of actual battle, the proud reliance on brawn and muscle, the daring and the doing. With the mothers was the consciousness of weakness, the stillness of the cabin home, the helplessness of infancy, the agony of anxiety. Let us never underestimate the mothers of Vermont.

The convention at Westminster gave the state the name of New Connecticut, but at an adjourned meeting held in Windsor, June 1777, it was "Resolved unanimously that the said district described in the preamble to the declaration at Westminster shall hereafter be called and known by the name of Vermont." And in this convention the delegates, seventy-two in number, after voting such a change in names, again pledged themselves unanimously to stand by each other and "their brethren in the United States, to contribute their full proportion towards maintaining the present just war against the fleet and armies of Great Britain." Whether they contributed their just proportion let Bennington and Ticonderoga answer.

The citizens of these towns, surrounded as we are today with the comforts and elegancies of modern ingenuity and enterprise, can hardly realize the rugged road over which the generations have passed to attain these things. From Connecticut to Vergennes on a vestibuled train is quite another thing to a horseback ride for days in the shadows of the densest woodland, guided only by a line of blazed trees, admonished by the howl of the wolf or the scream of the panther. If nature was rugged, government was perhaps equally as much so. But as the soil possessed the elements of boundless future productiveness, so these hardy forefathers of ours evinced that genius of adaptability that built up a state and a nation.

It may not be time lost to examine some of the early foundations. The "beech seal" days were stirring times, and doubtless now and then some luckless seeker of New York land titles felt, in his bones, that the inhabitants of the Grants were strikingly vigorous if not lawless. But the fathers were law abiding men, even though it may have been said of them that, like Cromwell's Roundheads, they were saints in prayer but devils in a fight. Under the early charters, each town in the New Hampshire Grants possessed the right of self government in March meetings, the election of its own officers, and management of internal affairs. But in 1770 the New York courts repudiated these charters in towns west of the Connecticut River and the inhabitants found themselves liable to arrest and eviction at the hands of New York sheriffs for lands they had already paid for in good faith.

Here was something not denominated in the bond, and to meet the exigencies of the occasion "Town Committees of Safety" were appointed; their business was to attend to these New York claimants as questions arose. A common disaster threatened the Grants, and they decided that no one man should stand persecution alone, but the interest of each one made the interest of all. As necessity arose these town committees met and adopted measures for general protection; but the war of the Revolution increased our responsibilities and it became necessary to be represented by agents in the Congress, to guard against land-grabbing legislators who were blocking our admission into the Union. In December 1775, a warrant was issued calling for a "General convention of delegates from each town." And this convention was assembled January 16, 1776.

XXXIX

A Network of Highways and the Road from the Hollow to Monkton

21 July 1899

In times past the Monkton Road from North Ferrisburgh or the Hollow, as everybody called it, ran north of its present location, through the "Priest lot" past the house where Elder Dodge lived following as it now does in front of the old Warren Partch place, where Daniel Bull lives, to the red schoolhouse on the corner. From the schoolhouse it runs easterly over the hill by the Rotax farm, the present farm homes of Henry R. Baldwin, John A. Palmer and Albert Baldwin, intersecting the north and south roads near the house of Harry Walston.

This was probably the main thoroughfare to the "Ridge" and the "Boro," but either the perversity of human nature, the increasing demands of business, or the outgrowth of modern enterprise necessitated a change and the traveler finds himself now confronted with a network of highways absolutely bewildering and all bringing him to the same restful haven. There is the old road, then another not quite so old, then the new road--and the future only knows how many more remain to be developed. Sometimes these parallel lines are half a mile or so apart, and again twenty or thirty rods, and where the public has worn one of them down too thin it shifts to the other. Another wise precaution: nobody seemed left out in the cold as few of the old roads were discontinued when the new ones were laid, and so every house is thoroughly accommodated, and you always "get there" no matter which road you take.

In politics and everything else, Monkton never does things "to the halves"--it is either well done or not at all. It seems that several years ago somebody conceived the idea of shunning the sharp hill near the Rotax place and the red schoolhouse by running a south-easterly course, coming into the north and south roads southerly of Elijah Carl's. The idea seemed consistent, and the visions of a road over which you could "trot right along to the Hollow," gave promise of realization. But somehow there was a hitch and the road question leaped into huge proportions in a twinkle. The petition was refused by the town authority, and county commissioners were called out: the late C. W. Reed of Addison, George Hammond of Mid-

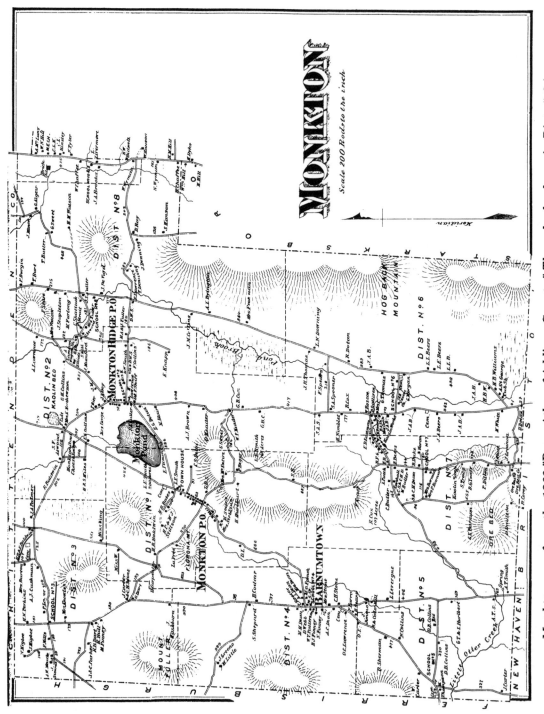

Monkton map from the 1869 "Beers Atlas of Addison County." The red school was in Dist. # 3 in the northwest corner as were several of the farms mentioned in this chapter and the next one. Higbee's network of bewildering highways is apparent.

dlebury, and the late Carlton Stevens of Vergennes. The commissioners interviewed the territory in question. After listening to suggestions of excited taxpayers, gathering wisdom from The Reverend John H. Stewart of Middlebury and W. W. Rider of Bristol, representing the town of Monkton; the late Honorable George W. Grandey of Vergennes and Judge James M. Slade of Middlebury for the petitioners, the commissioners decided to lay the road as called for.

By this time the "dander of everybody has riz." If a mile of new road was good, of course several miles were better and for about six months the air was full of roads.

It seemed an electrical storm of highways, zigzagging in every direction, and as for thunder--well, it was a tearing time, and so much electricity evolved that surveyors had to go off by themselves down into the cedar swamp to get their compasses pointing anywhere. The question seemed to be how many roads could be crowded into a given space, and would the Boro hold them when they arrived there.

It was a success. The Boro has never yet gone back on its record and if crowded a little too hard there was the "Ridge" to take some of the overflow. There is no danger of highway robbery of the mails or anybody else in this section, for the highwayman cannot have the least idea which road the traveler will take. There are so many roads that there is no room for fences and the drifting snows of winter are largely avoided. All the while the people are certainly to be congratulated for their success.

If you wish a carriage drive affording a variety of mountain and valley views, take the road northerly from H. R. Baldwin's towards "Leavenworth's mills" on Lewis Creek--though the busy mills have fallen to decay years ago--even as those who toiled in them have returned to the dust from whence they came. On your right is Douglas hill, with a full New England variety of verdure, and here and there a rugged face of red rock projecting from among the trees. On this hill is the cave already spoken of and the "oven" that continues to excite the interest of the scientist. Why this section has not become a Mecca for those who love to hold communion with nature in unexplainable.

There is beauty everywhere. The woods are all quivering with bird songs and springs offer their gifts to the thirsty and contribute sparkling streams to the little valleys. Stretched at length upon carpets of moss and pine, indulging day dreams to the music of wind and leaves, the poet or painter finds here fit subject for his best endeavors. The Green Mountains are not far away; he is among their foothills. The Adirondacks form a distant junction with his western sky--and if it is sunset--a thousand artists could hardly catch and hold the gorgeous beauties that the God of nature reveals with omnipotent lavishness. Mile upon mile of crimson and gold and blue--cloud outlines that picture airy continents with island and mountains and seas--and who knows but millions of fairy inhabitants. But the sunset fades, this cloud-land world grows dim and disappears as often

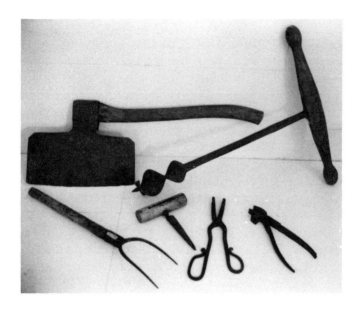

Early 19th century tools such as were made by blacksmiths. Top: a barking ax which might have been as pleasant to use as Higbee's hoe; a drill bit. Bottom: a two-tine fork; "D. W. Hazard's" reamer--the name is burned into the handle with a branding iron; primitive tongs; cobbler's tool (combined hammer and pliers). Charlotte Memorial Museum Collection.

dims and disappears some fondly cherished hope of the human heart.

Northward from Baldwin's the road winds in beauty under overhanging birches, beeches, maple, butternut, tremulous poplar and broad-leaved bass woods--a paradise for chipmunks and squirrels and the lumbering woodchuck who squares himself upon his haunches and looks at you with astonishing solemnity as though a study of human nature was his most pleasing pastime. But he is more active than he seems and while looking you over he is generally seated in close proximity to his hole into which he suddenly dives with a sharp whistle. If you have a little spare time, and have not disconcerted him in particular, wait a few minutes and observe first the tip of a brown nose sticking out the hole-- then a little further development of nose, every individual smeller doing duty, twitching to detect all possible

danger. A short period of meditation is followed by the head and shoulders, and if the world seems suitably peaceable, the "chuck" suddenly darts to an upright position on his doorstep and resumes his judicial attitude.

As for coons, the surrounding ledges and great hollow basswoods have been pre-empted by them long ago, as outlaying cornfields testify by bushels of half-eaten roasting ears lying on the ground or hanging to the riven stalks. At such times the owner of a good coon dog is the most popular boy in the community, and has plenty of volunteers whenever it is announced that a certain night is to be devoted to "cooning." It not unfrequently happens, however, that the hunters, in the boundlessness of their enthusiasm and appetite for roasted coon, do more damage than the coons, and the owners of melon patches and the best of the early apples have been known

Steps of the Quaker (Baldwin) school on the south side of Lewis Creek Road at the inter-section with Roscoe Road. The foundation wall can still be found surrounding the birch trees. The school building is now a storage shed on the farm north of this intersection on the east side of Roscoe Road. The Quaker meeting house from Monkton, opposite the school on the north side of Lewis Creek Road, was finally torn down about 1970. It was last used as a shed on the farm north of this site and on the west side of Roscoe Road. Photo taken in the spring of 1989.

Monkton views circa 1910. Two of the Boro. Courtesy of Doris Agan. The main street at the Ridge, looking north. Courtesy of Elinor (Prindle) Benning.

232

to insinuate that they had more melons and apples the night before the hunt than the morning after.

Just around the turn, where W. H. Steady lives, Alpheus Varney built his stone blacksmith shop [see Chapter XXI] where is inscribed on a great flat stone set into the wall, "A. Varney's Shop, 1833," and over the door is painted a hammer, an adz, a chisel, a draw shave and an axe, indicating that A. Varney was ready to turn out any kind of tool the public might choose to call for--as in fact he could and did. There are in existence today numerous tools that he forged and tempered, and his ingenuity was equal to almost any demand. All you had to do was to tell "Uncle Alpheus" as near as you could what sort of a thing you wanted, and he would hammer and grind and file and twist and bend until he got it. Whether he made his own gun or not, he was fond of rifle shooting, and Thanksgiving turkey shoots were apt to find him "squinting along a clouded barrel" and he generally got his money's worth.

If the curve is the line of beauty, no wonder this north and south highway is attractive, for until it reaches the creek there are hardly ten consecutive rods that run in a straight line. North of the old Varney shop, and on the western side, close by a beautiful grove of maples, stands the cozy little schoolhouse that used to be known as District No. 11 in the days before the legislature blotted the time-honored district schools from the map of the state. Were the question submitted to the people without prejudice from anybody, it is doubtful if they would pronounce our schools one whit better than under the old system. While so far as concerns expense, it costs the state thousands of dollars more than formerly. But this is a restless age; the "shrine" of the new influenced us, driving us away from the old.

About 1861 the Quaker church that stood near the Friends' burying ground in Monkton was taken down and moved to the corner north of the Varney place, and at one time a numerous congregation of Friends held regular services here. But death and removals resulted in diminishing these quiet worshipers until the building was sold and it has taken another removal, going to the north side of the east and west road, where George M. Hazard has made it into a friendly dwelling house.

In the Quaker Cemetery in Monkton west of Roscoe Rd. and north of Rotax Rd. The gravestones of the Wings: Phebe, Abbie and Mary. The Quaker meeting house was near this cemetery. Six acres were allowed by the Friends Society for their meeting house, the cemetery, the preacher's house and land enough for a garden, cow and horse. This was near the Hoag farm (see Chapter XX). Photo taken April, 1990.

XL

The Friends' Cemetery In Monkton and Moving To The West

28 July 1899

It may not be generally known but it is an historical fact that credit for the first anti-slavery movement in Vermont is due to the Society of Friends who petitioned the legislature in 1835 for the passage of a resolution to Congress asking for the abolition of slavery in the District of Columbia. This petition sent shivers up and down the backbone of the politician, no doubt, and it was dismissed by yeas, 86; nays, 34. Notwithstanding this the sentiment of Vermont was then and always was on the side of liberty. This state was never a safe place for the slave owner to bring his "property." It was a Vermont judge who demanded "a bill of sale from the Almighty" as evidence in his court.

Speaking of the Friends Church in Charlotte and their burying ground in Monkton, it carries the man of today a long way into the past to walk among the old graves, many of them unmarked, and read the names of those whose families are now perhaps extinct. It was not the custom of the society in those days to do much adorning, either in life or death, and there are numerous graves that are marked with simply rough stone slabs, with perhaps initial letters cut into the face and nothing more. Still, their dead sleep well, and the grandest "monumental pile" after all, is the memory of good deeds done, of kind words fitly spoken.

Some of the headstones show simply the age, others the date of death and the ages. The Alpheus Varney stone, and that of Phila, his wife, indicate their ages as 75 and 80. A dark-colored undressed stone reads--M. Seiple, 1848, aged 88. The grave of George Hagen, aged 66, 1852, marks the resting place of the previously mentioned English miller. The headstones of the Miles family read: Henry Miles, born in England 12 March, 1795, died 1885. Mary Hagen Miles, born in England 1793, died in 1885.

This yard contains the remains of many very old people. Henry Miles was 90 and Mary Miles 92. Rachel Cronkhite who died in 1859 was 91. Nabby Bates who died in 1840 was in her 94th year. Mary Wing died in 1897, aged 88. Abbie Wing, 1891, aged 91. Phebe Wing, 1881, aged 72. Phebe Holmes, wife of Gideon Wing, 84. Gideon Wing, 1836, aged 76. A row of snow white marble headstones mark the graves of Phebe, Abbie, and Mary Wing, the free-will offering of a kind lady in Ferrisburgh, whose numerous and unostentatious charities mark her indeed "a friend of her race." Plain stones are marked,"L. C. B., 1839.", and another, "C. B.," with no date. The stone of Stephen Haight gives his death as May 20, 1825, aged 87 years. Benjamin H. Haight, March 10, 1821, aged 62. Bridget, his wife, died March 5, 1856, aged 96 years. A single stone is marked, "M. C.,1822." There are probably those who can give information as to graves marked with only the year and initial letters.

William G. Noonan died in 1852, aged 54 years. Alice G. Noonan, his wife, died in 1891, aged 91 years. John W. Noonan died Sept. 13, 1862, aged 25 years, and his headstone reads, "A soldier of the Vermont Cavalry, Co. A." John Knowles, who lived on the Elijah Carl place, died in 1859, aged 69. Sarah, his wife, died in 1873, 73 years old. William Dean, father of Joshua M. Dean, was buried here in 1874, aged 78. Here lies J. Richard Dean, who died in 1893, aged 34 years--in the prime of life's usefulness. A single headstone is marked, Sarah Stevens, 1842, aged 47. The late Joshua M. Dean of Ferrisburgh is buried here among his kindred. Here is found the grave of Andrew Holmes, who died in 1865, aged 55 years--and Ruth Gary, wife of Andrew Holmes, 1896, aged 80 years. James Baron, who formerly lived in Charlotte, died in Ferrisburgh in 1893, and was born in 1812. Elijah Baron died in 1874, aged 79. Betsey J., wife of Solomon Q. Barton, died in 1887, aged 74 years.

Horace Palmer of Charlotte, whose death occurred recently at 95 was the oldest citizen in town. He was born in a house that stood in the meadow west of the Nathan Perkins place in 1804. His father, Joseph Palmer, who lived to be 93, used to live north of the Norman Wells place and the foundations of the house can be seen today. Horace Palmer was bright and active and his recollections of the past were well worth hearing. A generation and more had come and gone within his memory, and most of those who were in active business when he built his first house down the creek from his home, as it now stands, are sleeping the sleep of death. So go the years, and very few remember them to this extent--but now and then, old Father Time forgets his business and a son or daughter slips by the allotted space in wonderful degree.

These are among the many who quietly repose beneath the flowers and verdure of summer or the snows of winter, but no more to them are sunshine and storm. High hopes and fond anticipations stirred the hearts of these who listen no longer to the tread of human feet. Ambitions, hopes, fears, loves--what are they now--useless for us to peer into the beyond--but somehow, sometimes the feeling comes that the loved and lost are speaking to us again out of that mysterious world whose paths no living foot hath trod--out of that wonderful brightness upon which no human eye ever yet has gazed. Among all peoples, there has always been, there always will be, a reverence for graves. He who wantonly desecrates one is an outcast, condemned and shunned. Mankind finds here its final resting place. The quietness and the decorum of the living, passing from mound to mound evinces a desire to disturb not their dreamless sleep.

The farm that Henry R. Baldwin owns and lives on used to be owned by Jonathan Holmes; Nicholas Holmes owned the present John A. Palmer farm and built the old farm house, but he sold out to Joseph Hurlburt and moved to Charlotte, where he died. Medal Hurlburt lived on this farm at the time he went west. Mr. Hurlburt and his wife, Thala Dean, a sister of Mrs. Charles D. Prindle of Charlotte, and Almon Atwood and wife, who lived on the Guy Willoughby farm in Charlotte, started together for the west in 1856. They went in two teams, Mr. Hurlburt taking a fine pair of Morgan horses that he intended selling before his return. While crossing Lake Michigan, the steamboat burned and both Mr. Hurlburt and wife and Mr. Atwood and wife were drowned. The bodies of Mr. and Mrs. Hurlburt were

THE EMIGRANTS' HALT.

Henry Baldwin's ash poles held up the cover of a wagon like this for the Hardy families to use in their westward trek. From "Harper's New Monthly Magazine," p. 159. 1856.

237

never found but the remains of Almon Atwood and wife were recovered, brought back and they were buried near Monkton Ridge. This sudden and shocking calamity cast a great gloom over the entire community, as both families were much thought of by all their fellow townsmen.

William Noonan lived in a house that stood on the corner west of H. R. Baldwin's. A house used to stand between J. A. Palmer's and Albert Baldwin's where Lyman Hurlburt lived. The Wing family lived a great many years on the homestead now owned by Antwine Wisenback. On the road south of the Wing place, a ruined cellar wall marks the site of a farmhouse where Swift Chamblin once lived with his family of thirteen children, and it is said that of these children six became preachers. One of the sons, Hiram Chamblin, graduated from Middlebury College and died while pastor of a Congregational church in Texas. Henry Chamblin, another son, was a Methodist minister who preached in Pennsylvania. Swift Chamblin was an uncle of the late Roderick Baldwin of Monkton. Possibly this sketch may come to the attention of those who can recall still further particulars about this corner of Monkton.

Two brothers, Nathan and Truman Hardy, held and built their homes on the farms now owned by Harry Waltson and Albert Russell. The Hardys sold out and went to Illinois with their families, where they became wealthy holders of great prairie farms. A trip to Illinois now would not be much of an affair, even with an entire farming outfit, but it was another thing altogether when, as a boy, Henry R. Baldwin remembers their going down into his father's ash swamp for light poles. These were afterwards shaved on one side and then bent over the double wagon box as a framework for a heavy cotton cloth covering. Into those wagon boxes were packed the family belongings of Nathan and Truman Hardy, and this was the vestibule train with which they traveled to Illinois. It took them a good share of the summer to make the journey but doubtless they found plenty of company along the road, for this was the only way in which the western pioneer reached his new home thirty-five or forty years ago.

XLI

Thompson's Point Illustrated
Connection with Early Events--Romance and History--
Most Beautiful Resort along Champlain

25 August, 1899

Four generations and more ago[102] Thompson's Point first saw the face of a white man. This white man was Samuel de Champlain. On the 6th of July, 1609, he entered upon the waters that were ever after to bear his name. This new world, with its wonderful possibilities of romance and realities, somewhere might contain mountains of gold, somewhere might gush that magical spring whose quaffing returned again the vigor of youth.

As the representative of a great nation and as a loyal subject of his king, he would plant the lily flag on this incomparable domain. Spain had already

Champlain's Battle with the Iroquois, drawn by Champlain in his diary.

146

Personally appeared Nelson Hickok the Signee and Sealer of the above written instrument, and acknowledged the same to be his free voluntary act and deed Before me Clauson H Wheeler, Justice Peace

Rec'd for record 14th July 1840 at 11 OClock A.M.

and recorded from the original Attest Jam'H Barnes, Town Clk

H & N Barnes
To
Town of Charlotte

Know all men by these presents that we Hyder and Naaman Barnes of Addison in the County of Addison & State of Vermont for and in consideration of the sum of Forty two Hundred dollars current money of the United States, received in full to our satisfaction of the Inhabitants of the Town of Charlotte in the County of Chittenden & State aforsd the receipt whereof we do hereby acknowledge, have given, granted, bargained and Sold and by these presents do give, grant, bargain, Sell, alien, convey and confirm unto the said Inhabitants of Charlotte aforesaid, the following described land in said Charlotte call'd and known by the name of Thompson's point, bounded East by Anthony Field's, north west & South by the Lake Shore Containing two hundred & thirty acres, more or less,

To have and to hold the above granted and bargained premises with all the privileges and appurtenances thereof and thereto belonging, to the said town of Charlotte to their own proper use, benefit and behoof, forever

And we the said Hyder & Naaman Barnes do for ourselves our heirs executors and administrators, covenant to and with the said town of Charlotte and their assigns, that at and until the ensealing of these presents we are well seized of the premises, in fee Simple; that we have good right and lawful authority to bargain and sell the Same, in manner and form as is above written; that they are free and clear of all incumbrance; and that we will warrant and defend the same against all lawful claims and demands of any person or persons whomsoever. In Witness Whereof we have hereunto set our hands & seals this eleventh day of April &c

Signed Sealed and delivered
in presence of Ezra Holt   Hyder Barnes   /Seal/
            Luther Stone Jr   Naaman Barnes   /Seal/

State of Vermont
Chittenden County ss   Charlotte April 11th 1839
        Personally appeared Hyder & Naaman Barnes the Signers and Sealers of the above written instrument and acknowledged the same to be their free voluntary act & deed Before me
            Ezra Holt Justice Peace

Rec'd for record at 1 OClock P.M. July 14th
1840 and recorded from the original
        Attest J H Barnes, Town Clerk

The 1839 deed wherein Hyder and Naaman Barnes conveyed Thompson's Point to the Town of Charlotte. The conveyance for two hundred and thirty acres was in fee simple.

a foothold in North America. England had a colony of nearly five hundred in Virginia. France was sweeping down from the north. These old antagonists were to grapple again for supremacy under the somber shadow of the great American forests.

Champlain was enchanted with the scene on that July day. He came up the lake with the northern Indians or Algonquins, who were advancing upon the territory of that powerful confederation, the Iroquois. The latter were the "Romans of the New World," the eastern door of whose "long house" was tended by the Mohawks and the western by the Senecas on the Great Lakes. The council fire was kept burning by the Onondagas of central New York. This wonderful confederation of the "six nations" has been deemed a model of government and Indian tradition ascribes its origin to the wisdom of Hiawatha, who, in the fifteenth century dwelt among his people on Onondaga Lake.

Perhaps on that fateful July voyage the canoes of Champlain's party were drawn up on the south shores of Thompson's Point. Champlain may have landed here to counsel with his warriors for they had now crossed Iroquois territory. Split Rock, or Regioch-ne directly opposite Thompson's Point, on the New York shore, was the boundary line between the Iroquois and the northern tribes. To cross this line was invasion and that was war.

While Champlain was deliberating here in council, the swift canoes of his Algonquin scouts shot off to more southerly points. The fierce Iroquois, knowing of their approach, had already assembled on the plain and head lands of what is now Crown Point. Champlain, in his diary, says they arrived in front of this point just at nightfall when the Iroquois were engaged in the war dance. The tribes, by mutual agreement, delayed the battle until the next day. In that next day's fight, so disastrous to the Iroquois, these mountains echoed for the first time to the sound of firearms. All this was over a hundred and fifty years before Thompson's Point had an English name.

Lake Champlain was called by the Iroquois, Caniadare Guarante--the door of the country--and perhaps we can conceive of nothing more appropriate when it is understood that up and down these waters and along these shores floated and marched the soldiers and Indian warriors of six decisive wars. It is not an assumption to say that this valley has seen the making of as much American history as any other territory on this continent, if it does not lead them all. Was this nation to be English or French? It was decided along the shores of Lake Champlain nearly twenty years before the battle of Lexington. Was this nation to be English or American? It was largely decided along Lake Champlain when Ethan Allen and his eighty Green Mountain boys captured Ticonderoga, when Burgoyne and his seven thousand soldiers and two thousand red warriors marched through it to the surrender of Saratoga, when McDonough sailed from the mouth of the Otter Creek to Cumberland head and in Plattsburg Bay showed English sailors what American sailors could do for home and kindred; for since that day a hostile cannon has never yet sent its sullen boom among these mountains.

The question has often been asked where Thompson's Point derived its name and it is difficult to give a definite reply. The town records do not show that any one of that name ever had a deed of this land or ever gave a deed of it.

I have consulted with Rowland E. Robinson of Ferrisburgh in regard to this and there is perhaps no better authority in the state. Mr. Robinson is inclined to coincide with the theory that this point, and possibly the one in Colchester, received their names from some hunter or trapper who camped along the shores long enough to associate himself with the localities and thus give them a local name. Perhaps the Colchester land records may show how their "Point" originated. Ours has a green old age for it was so recognized over one hundred years ago.

The only instance in which a Thompson did any conveying is in vol. 4, page 111, when Abel Thompson and Jonathan Sexton, both of Ferrisburgh, and Stephen Pearl of Burlington, joined in two deeds to John McNeil and Charles McNeil. It seems the McNeils owned a large tract in common and they deeded it to Thompson, Sexton and Pearl as arbitrators, and it was then re-deeded to them in severalty. The land so conveyed embraced the present McNeil ferry farm, and that south of it, taking in a part, at least, of McNeil's point or lots No. 120 and 114 drawn to the original

right of John Brownson and Isaac Corsa. These conveyances were made and recorded in 1804.

In 1762 Joseph Ferris, Jr., became the owner of lot No. 122, as one of the original grantees. October 8th, 1787, Joseph Ferris, Jr. deeded an equal one-half of this lot to Samuel Scovil and described it as "lying on the south side of Thompson's Point, joining on the great bay." This traces the land to the original grantee, and we find that in 1787 Thompson's Point was known, and so designated in the first conveyance from the original holder.

In 1809 Stukely Wescott, grandfather of Mrs. Henry Field of Ferrisburgh, bought 146 acres, part of the present Town Farm,[103] of William C. Harrington of Burlington. The description begins "at a dry cedar tree on the south side of a point of land called Thompson Point." Harrington sets up his title as coming from the "legatees of John Thorp, who owned the farm in his life time." The singular feature is that other "Thompson's Point" north in Colchester.

The lake south of Split Rock is called "The Narrows." Split Rock, by the Iroquois, was called Re-gioch-ne. It is said this name came from a Mohawk warrior who was drowned there. But as to Thompson's Point: the London map of 1779 gives the point of land on the east side of the lake and opposite Split Rock as "Point Regiocine."[104] The question is, is this identical with the Iroquois name given to Split Rock: were the makers of this map at fault, placing the name on the wrong side of the lake? Let us assume

242

The Town Poor Farm's house and barn on Thompson's Point Road. The farm buildings burned in 1964. Photo, taken circa 1935, was given to the Charlotte Memorial Museum by Albert R. Hawley.

that everybody was right--that the unfortunate Mohawk gave his name to Split Rock, and the "Regiocine" was the name of the Indian maiden whose lover went to his death beneath the dark waters. In this we shall harm no one, and perhaps perpetuate an old and pleasing tradition.

This portrait of William Gilliland (1734-1796) by noted artist Ralph Earl was done when the wealthy New York landowner was 55 years old. An ardent supporter of the American Revolution, he held 30,000 acres on the west side of the lake at the end of the war. Courtesy of New York Historical Society, New York City.

Nonetheless, we are indebted to the French and Indians for most of the early names that appear on that early map of 1779. The large bay southeast of Thompson's Point, that we call Ball's and Thorp's bay, was called "Bay of the Vessels." It is conjectured this commodious harbor may have been a rendezvous for early fleets. Garden Island, off the mouth of the Lewis and Little Otter Creeks, was "Red Island." Westport Bay as we know it, is designated Bay des Rocher Fendus, or "Bay of the Broken Rocks." It is claimed that this should apply to Whallon's Bay north of Split Rock, but it does not so appear on the map.

Thompson's Point had early names: May 10, 1765, William Gilliland embarked from New York with goods and chattels and a large number of employees to ascend the Hudson, and by this route, Lakes George and Champlain. He would thus reach a magnificent territory he held by purchase and grant on the western shore of the lake, from Split Rock to Willsboro Point or Bouquet River, going inland approximately three or four miles.

The writer may have more to say of this gifted and enterprising pioneer in a paper to be entitled *Along the Shores*.[105] Mr. Gilliland kept a diary that was compiled and published with other valuable historical matter by Winslow C. Watson of Port Kent, New York, under the head of *History of Champlain Valley*.

Under the date of July 10, 1765, Mr. Gilliland says:

Our four carpenters began to cut and square timber for the mill, the other hands being employed cutting wood for coal, clearing land, etc. All the cattle having been brought safe from Crown Point some time ago by four of our people, who having swam them across the lake at Crown Point, drove them through the woods on the east side of the Cloven Foot, from thence we ferried them to the Cloven Rock in a scow hired from some New England men, and drove them from thence through the woods to Milltown, having now given that name to the land at the Falls. James Stocker, John McAuley, Moses Dickson and myself having brought four bateaux deeply loaded with boards and provisions from Crown Point, whilst the others were driving the cattle.

The Cloven Rock was Split Rock and the Cloven Foot was a name Gilliland gave to Thompson's Point. This name was doubtless suggested by the gulf or gorge in the face of the cliff, just north of the end of the Point (as looking at the end of this point from the lake, in crossing to Split Rock, the shape of a moccasined foot "clove" between the heel and the ball is not entirely imaginary). Here then we have two names that have plenty of antiquity to recommend them, one in 1765; the other in 1779.

According to the "Documentary History of New York" it is not improbable that "Point Regiocine" or Thompson's Point figured still further in the French and Indian Wars as they were called. Robert Rogers, the daring scout who was connected with Israel Putnam in their Indian campaigns, reported to Sir William Johnson, the English commander, July 7, 1756, that they passed Crown Point and landed at the point about 25 miles north on the east side of the lake. At this place they intercepted some boats loaded with grain, flour and brandy. Rogers says they hailed the boats as they were passing and ordered a surrender. But this not coming promptly enough they fired into them, captured the boats and twelve men. Three of the men were killed and two wounded. Rogers naively reports that one of the wounded could not march, therefore put an end to him. They "destroyed the cargo," but with rare presence of mind, "excepting some few cases of brandy and wine which we hid in a very secure place." Probably none of the company forgot where that "secure place" was.

From Rogers' report it is not straining things to assume that Thompson's Point was the place. Here was the narrowest spot in the lake north of Crown Point--the only place where boats could be hailed and fired upon from the shore successfully--and it is about the distance indicated. It seems entirely reasonable to assume that Rogers and his men and perhaps Israel Putnam laid in ambush on Thompson's Point in 1756.

The century of existence since the Scovil deed has done little to efface or change the Point's rugged outlines. Forests have been felled and grown again. Generations have tilled its acres, and one by one gone to their long home. But its miles of rocky

One side of the gorge near the end of the Point, with a view of the Charles Barton camp. Gilliland called this gulf in the cliffs "Cloven Foot." Photo taken in April, 1990.

shore still meet the water's soft caress or thundering crash with unresponsive indifference. It has seen strange sights. It has heard strange sounds, but the secret of every sight and sound is locked safe in its stony heart, and no one can find it out.

It was always a great fishing ground where pike and bass and perch responded readily to the enticements of the angler; and an old-time famous hunter named Hough used to say that many a deer has he chased from Mount Philo to the Point from whence the deer swam to the New York shore to escape the dogs who were after them. But for years no one

A hard-sided tent, used by the Stowell/Carroll family and still in their possession. As a boy, Henry Stowell camped with his father and brothers in 1850 at the Point. As a Civil War veteran, Captain Stowell and his family tented at McNeil's Bay, the Jolly Club and Deer Point. After renting Ovette Stone's house at the Point they built the present house in 1890. Courtesy of William V. N. and Laura Carroll.

A well-dressed assemblage in front of a very high tent. The congratulatory pose may have been part of a Sunday School recognition gathering, probably in 1876. Note bulletin boards mounted on trees to the extreme left and right. Courtesy of the Wheeler/Kingsland Collection.

Successor to the original Camp Pleasant and a variety of other later arrangements the Thompson's Point Country Club was organized in 1921. There are two clay and one all-weather courts. Courtesy of the Vermont Division of Historic Preservation.

thought of camping here, except now and then an old Indian trapper who used to set up his wigwam under the cedars of the little south bay. Perhaps he was an Algonquin, revisiting the scenes of his father's exploits, thirsting for the departed glory of his race. But certain it is, in place of scalp locks at the entrance of his lodge, were numerous muskrat skins stretched on bent willows, and instead of the perfume of Jockey Club or musk was the all-pervading aroma of the skunk--very nearly taking the place of the musk, however.

Now and then a party of men and boys "after haying" would bring down a wagon box of straw, buffaloes[106] and

blankets and risk a night of it. But there was generally more light than darkness, for the dead cedars made handy wood, and they would have been called a party of genuine fire worshipers by the way they piled on the brush and encouraged the flames.

Gradually it began to creep into the minds of men that here was a spot of sport and recreation, and in 1870 James Squier, Carlos C. Martin, Lewis B. Fuller, Henry C. Leavenworth, Dennis W. Hazard, Ovette E. Stone,

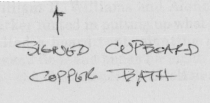

The lake steamboat CHATEAUGAY, pictured with two less distinguished lake vessels. Along with the TICONDEROGA, this steamer made regularly scheduled stops at the Point. Courtesy of the Wheeler/Kingsland Collection.

the old Indian trapper days.

In 1872 the company was increased by the addition of John H. Thorp, Ira Russell, T. D. Chapman, A. P. Kennedy, M. F. Allen, Joseph Barton, Luther D. Stone, Harvey C. Martin, Henry C. Root, William M. Read and Chauncey Pease. A club house was built near the end of the Point, replacing the board tent with quite a pretentious affair for those days.

Things moved on as usual with clubs and club houses for several years, the late Dennis W. Hazard acting as secretary. The last entry appeared in 1879 when the club probably ceased to exist.[107]

The first private cottage on the Point was built by John H. Thorp in 1874 and is the one he now occupies. I understand this to have been the first one built on the lake shore between Burlington and Basin Harbor.

To one who compares the Point as it was 30 years ago with it today, the contrast is immense. In addition to as fine a location as can be found on the lake, Thompson's Point is fortunate in possessing a first-class citizenship. Every cottager seems proud of his cottage and surroundings as nice lawns, green vines, quaint nooks with inviting hammocks are in evidence everywhere. Not only the comforts but the elegancies of summer home life surround you at the Point.[108]

Night and morning the steamship CHATEAUGAY of the Champlain Transportation line enters the broad bay and in a magnificent half circle swings up to the commodious dock, taking you to Burlington or down the lake as far as "the islands" to the north or, on her return trip, to Westport on the south. These daily arrivals of the steamer interest everybody and she is greeted by children on the dock, many a flag and pleasant salute, almost always responded to by the captain and pilot with a sounding whistle and courteous lifting of the cap.

A little more than two miles away is the Charlotte station on the Rutland railroad, and near the highway leading to the Point direct, is a flag station on the Rutland road, where travelers can take all regular passenger trains.[109]

Either by rail or by boat, Thompson's Point people have unusual facilities for communication, and many of the business men in Burlington who have cottages here go back and forth every day. "Glenwood Inn" offers its broad piazzas and magnificent outlook to the tourist who feasts his eye on the finest lake and mountain views in New England. All that while mine host Williams and his

The Point's Glenwood Inn, also known at the Hotel Charlotte, served steamboat tourists and Pointers alike. A corner room held a candy show case and the post office where mail arrived twice a day, carried from the Thompson's Point railroad station. (See Chapter XXII.) Meals and overnight accommodations were offered. Courtesy of William V. N. and Laura Carroll.

The old Glenwood Inn, now a summer home. About 1920 the then owner removed the porches and moved the building northwards. Though steamboat service continued at the Dock, the days of an available hotel were ended. Photo taken in April, 1990.

A winterscape at the base of the North Shore's high cliffs. Charlotte's late Jim McDurfee, veteran outdoorsman, tows his fishing shanty to a favorite spot to be joined by dozens of others whose "winter houses" dot the frozen lake. Photo published in 1967. Courtesy of the National Geographic Society.

Leonard Andrews of Hinesburgh, after a period of "tenting out," built his "Point of Oaks" camp on the third of the three points. Later, his widow, "Grandma Andrews," gathered family and friends here for many summers. Courtesy of William V. N. and Laura Carroll.

Three generations at the Stowell camp in 1907. Seated: Grandmother Stowell holding infant Bill Carroll alongside brother Stowell. Standing: Julia (Stowell) Carroll and brother William. Courtesy of William V. N. and Laura Carroll.

U.S. Supreme Court Justice David J. Brewer and his wife in front of "Liberty Hall." Photo taken in 1906. Courtesy of William Mott Hall.

excellent wife are preparing another feast that perhaps is equally satisfying to a hungry man.

And the summer traveler seems to appreciate it too, for he lingers along these shores as though loath to depart.. There is a comforting sound in the old English word "Inn" that smacks of home ways and home-like cooking, delightful restfulness and a hearty welcome. He finally departs with a firm resolve to come again some day.

As to fishing, there is no end to sport in that line: all kinds of it, from the boy with a pin hook to a hundred feet of line and a sinker that weighs a pound. But Carl and Fred and Herbe and Jim and Brooks, who have been conversant with the habits of fish for centuries, use some thirty feet of line, more or less, and they know all about the "north reef" and the "south reef" and where to anchor in order to get into the "run" of the pike, somewhere down among the rocks at the bottom.

It is not rulable for one fisherman to "cut off" another, and in order to get first place each has to rise a little earlier than the other of a morning. So much so that not infrequently one of the company anchors on the reef all night and literally rocks in the cradle of the deep, while dreaming of pike that weigh a ton.

This reef runs southwest from the end of the point about half a mile, with a depth of water of from 20 to 40 feet, sloping eastward and an abrupt drop-off on the west. Anchored just right, one end of the boat will need 30 feet of line; the other end perhaps a hundred or more.

Off the mouth of big Otter Creek there are about 75 acres of shallows, if water can be estimated in that way, where it is claimed a man can wade around and pull his boat along after him with a rope, in case of a storm and he not much of an oarsman. But he must be careful of going too far west or down he goes, with a plunge into 75 feet of water. The place is not crowded with pedestrians, however.

Some of the finest sites for cottages, and room enough for a village, remain untaken along the "Flat Rocks" on the southeast shore. There is plenty of water for another steamboat landing and one of these days, when the town opens up a road through the beautiful cedar woods to the eastward, the delighted cottagers will build another dock and the CHATEAUGAY will take a wider sweep in the "Bay of the Vessels" and respond to another series of enthusiastic flag wavings.

The western end of the Flat Rocks is known as "Cedar Point" and Robert Cartmell of Middlebury displayed artistic taste by building a cottage here. Not far from his door the waves tumble in from the south over jagged rocks and Mr. Cartmell has appropriately called his summer home "The Breakers." Farther north and following the broken shore to a secluded little bay and safest of harbors, M. F. Gove of Charlotte has built "Cedarena," and the place is as pretty as its name. Near neighbor to him is a new cottage built by the late S. J. Davis of Lincoln but now owned by Wallace Farr of the same town. Not far from the eastern end of what may be termed Thompson's Point bay is

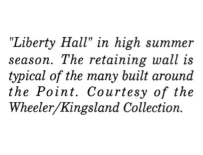

"Liberty Hall" in high summer season. The retaining wall is typical of the many built around the Point. Courtesy of the Wheeler/Kingsland Collection.

"Point of Oaks," the summer home of Leonard Andrews of Hinesburgh. They first camped here but later on erected the cottage in which they have spent each summer for the last ten or fifteen years. "Maplewood," owned by Eno and Wooster of Charlotte, stands on a knoll back from the shore, almost hidden in the dense foliage. With its nice lawn in front, fine cedars, singly or in groups and wide verandas, inviting one to easy chairs, "Whileaway" is the home of Capt. Henry Stowell of Troy, New York. The late Prof. C. E. Colby of Columbia college, New York, who was a gentleman of fine culture, found no place that seemed more restful to him than "Bonnyview," with its shrubs and trees and quietness.

The witchery of the place pursues one all the way along the winding path by the lake shore, and others must have felt it too, for here is "Waterwitch," the home of Clarence Hicks of Burlington.

The "Pioneer," true to its name, is the oldest cottage on the Point, one of the most retired but sightly of locations. The proprietor, John H. Thorp, sits in his front yard and salutes the CHATEAUGAY as she passes morning and night within a hundred feet of his door. "Idlewild" of A. D. Gibbs, Burlington, is no less beautiful upon Champlain than it would have been upon the Hudson. "Restabit" of Mrs. M. K. Payne of Windsor; "Edgewood" of Arthur Crane, Burlington; "Welikeit," E. B. Bailey, Burlington; "Auldwood," Rev. W. S. Roberts of Burlington; "Dudropin," of Read and Sawyer, Essex Junction; "Crowsnest," Clarkson and Fuller of Burlington; "Bungalow," Geo. L. Pease of Williston, all front on a nicely graveled, curving

CAMPS IN PLACE AT THOMPSON'S POINT
At Time of W. W. Higbee's Manuscript

Code	Date	Original Builder	Owner (1899)	Name	Present Owner (1990)
A	1870	Eight sportsmen at Camp Pleasant	Clarkson and Fuller	Crows Nest	(empty lot)
B	1874	John Thorpe	John Thorpe	Pioneer	Allmons
C	1880	Ovette Stone	Charles Colby	Bonnyview	Colbys
D	1883	Mr. Hubbell	Edward Irving	Rocky Comfort	Hodges
E	1887	T. P. Fuller	Henry Green and T. P. Fuller		Moore/Booth/Rixford
F	1887	M. F. Allen	M. F. Allen	Twilight Lodge (burned in 1907)	Lot to Currier
G	1887	M. F. Allen	Sarah Allen	Sunset Lodge	Reid
H	1887	A. D. Gibbs	A. D. Gibbs	Idlewild	Gibbs
I	1887	Seven Families from Essex Junction	Read and Sawyer	Dudropin	VanZandt
J	1887	Leonard Andrews	L. Andrews	Point of Oaks	Simpson/Brown
K	1890	Henry Stowell	Henry Stowell	Whileaway	Carroll
L	1891	E. B. Bailey	E. B. Bailey	Welikeit	Paul
M	1891	Frank Manchester	Justice Brewer	Liberty Hall	Currier
N	1894	Clarence Hicks	Clarence Hicks	Waterwitch	Rowe
O	1894	M. F. Gove	M. F. Gove	Cedarena	Price/Bloch
P	1896	Arthur Hosford	Arthur Hosford	Glenwood Inn	Bartons
Q	1896	George Foote	George Foote	Rockcliff	Barton
R	1896	Willard Greene	Willard Greene	Cozynook	Moore/Booth/Rixford
S	1896	Eno and Wooster	Eno and Wooster	Maplewood	Kuenne
T	1896	E. E. Clarkson	Mrs. M. K. Payne	Restabit	Crane
U	1896	Robert Cartmell	Robert Cartmell	The Breakers	Lutz
V	1897	George Pease	George Pease	Bungalow	Openshaw
W	1897	S. J. Davis	Wallace Farr		Trainer
X	1899	Arthur Crane	Arthur Crane	Edgewood	(site) Hicks
Y	1899	W. S. Roberts	W. S. Roberts	Auldwood	Ward/Gilroy
Z	1899	C. L. Atwood	C. L. Atwood	Bluff Lodge	Illick

N↑

44° 16' 00" N

73° 18' 00" W

Two bathing beauties at the Point. This 1893 pose well illustrates swim attire that was suitable. The viewer can also note the stony/pebbly nature of the shore which, however, never impeded dedicated swimmers. Courtesy of the Vermont Historical Society.

path from which you look down upon the water and are sheltered by tall pines and cedars. A railing along the pathway holds quantities of torches that are made abundant use of at nightfall. "Rocky Comfort" has been lately purchased by Edward Irving of Burlington. David J. Brewer of Washington, D. C., associate justice of the United States Supreme Court, has an elaborately finished cottage nearest the end of the Point that he has named "Liberty Hall." Judge Brewer is enthusiastic over the beauties of this portion of Lake Champlain. "Twilight Lodge" of M. F. Allen and "Sunset Lodge" of Sarah F. Allen of Ferrisburgh; "Rockcliff," of George A. Foote of Charlotte; "Glenwood Inn," Arthur H. Horsford of Lowell, Mass.; "Bluff Lodge" of C. L. Atwood, Starksboro, are situated along the abrupt western shore, where the outlook to the Adirondacks and up and down the lake is unsurpassed. Towards the eastern end and on the north side is a beautiful and secluded spot called "Deer Point," where H. M. Hull of Hinesburgh has a cottage.[110]

Thompson's Point has between

Stone pier, one of three that supported an iron water tank. A windmill, erected in 1896 by 14 families in the Thompson's Point Water Association, supplied power for the pump. The pier nearest the lakeside fell into the lake when the cliff crumbled. A new tank was built in 1923 and an electrically powered system serves the camps of the Thompson's Point Association. Photo taken in April, 1990.

four and five miles of water line, with dense evergreens, poplars, birches and maples shadowing the whole. There are beautiful sand beaches, where bathing is safe as though one were in a tub; pebbly shores, flat rocks, rugged and grizzly fronts, from which you look down into the black water, forty feet below.

Near the south end are several large boulders of rose granite that, according to the regular order of things, are as much out of place here as the same number of sperm whales. The learned in such matters claim that the proper home for these boulders is Nova Scotia. Doubtless they had a "pass" on some iceberg in a very early day, that expired at Thompson's Point.

The town grants leases that run for fifteen years, at an annual rental of ten dollars. It appoints in town meeting an agent who has charge of this

The "Ti Dock" in its heyday. Many residents used the steamers to commute to work in Burlington and waterways were the main commercial routes. Live chickens and cows, too, came on the lake boats to spend the summer at the Point, providing valuable table supplies. Courtesy of the Charlotte Memorial Museum.

property, issues the leases, and to whom the cottagers can apply. Its present efficient agent is George A. Foote. It has been the policy of the town to co-operate with the cottagers in making this place attractive for summer homes, where people can come with their families, feeling that good order and good morals are necessary requisites. Leases will not be granted to undesirable individuals.

The growth of the Point in public favor has taken the town by surprise, and certain reservations, such as alleyways and a public water front, would probably have been made had the magnitude of things been comprehended at the outset.

It is desirable, not only for the town but for its welcomed summer citizens as well, that such things be looked after in the future. The town will probably retain certain lots so that those who do not care for lake fronts can have full right to boats and boat houses. It has already a good carriage road the whole length of the Point to the dock, and it is safe to assume that newer territory will be well cared for in the future. The water supply is excellent and unfailing, provided by a "water company" of the cottagers, who put up a wind mill and a large reservoir, conveying the water in surface pipes to each cottage, the intake pipe extending into the deep water of the broad lake. The town and the cottagers united in building the steamboat dock.

The lake here is about a mile wide, and a delightful row or sail takes you to a place of general interest on the

View of Split Rock and the lighthouse on its adjacent mountain, the only one to rise up at the lake's edge. New York State's Adirondacks in the distance. Photo taken in April, 1990 from the gorge at the Point.

New York shore--Split Rock and its light house, known to local mariners.

Take a row or a sail around the north side of Split Rock and see the petrified snakes and judge for yourself how they came there. Up in the face of the cliff, three or four great fellows that look black and ugly. Nearer the water it seems several rattlers had their last wriggle about the commencement of the Stone Age. The Lake Champlain sea serpent cannot be depended upon with any degree of certainty and it will not do to count

The Sea-serpent, Lake Champlain

From "A Family Canoe Trip," by Florence Watters Snedeker, Harper & Brothers, New York. 1892. Courtesy of Phyllis Deming, The Village Bookshop, Shelburne.

upon him as an attraction, but these of Split Rock were there when Champlain and his Algonquins crept up the lake in 1609.

The deepest water is off this shore and steamboats run so close to the land in places that one can toss a pebble to the rocks from the saloon deck of the VERMONT. The lighthouse keeper makes a daily record of the passing of all steamers and tug boats, their names and the hour, the direction of winds but not the force.

The Vermont shore from Split Rock is a magnificent picture. The Green mountains are from fifteen to twenty miles inland, and the country slopes gradually towards them with its foot hills, orchards, woodlands, finely cultivated farms, flocks and herds,

ancestral homes; and only a little while ago, on the dial of the ages, the silence of a wilderness, no commerce, no industry, no hearthstone, a dark and bloody ground where the Iroquois glutted his thirst for blood and feasted his fierce heart on the agonies of torture. It is not a dream. The scene is as real to us this day as was the other to that white man, four generations ago.

Moonlight excursions always take a turn this way, for the Point people outdo the Aurora Borealis in the line of illumination on occasions. A good many years ago a mosquito was seen flying south-easterly, a long way from shore, but he was drowned and was the last of his race in this vicinity. Charlotte merchants take orders and deliver them at the cottage doors. Daily mails reach them from the post office. A regular "accommodation line" meets all trains, and tourists walk only when they insist upon it.

As for boating, there are sail and steam yachts; naphtha and gasoline launches; row boats; canoes; miles of beautiful bay, "moonlight and star- light, tenderly streaming." Why not music and singing and happy hearts, why not the old, old story, until one by one the boats are moored? Strollers under the shadowy trees are called home by Curfew bell and Thompson's Point is aleep.

A well-dressed camper on the South shore walk. In the earliest days, each camp had lanterns and reflector lights on poles near the path. In 1906, the Association voted for Dietz lamps. In 1919 electric lights replaced oil lamps. Courtesy of William V. N. and Laura Carroll.

Memorial Day celebrations were widespread after the Civil War and Higbee highly commended such patriotic activities. From "The Youths' History of the United States," by Edward S. Ellia, Vol. 4, facing p. 220. Cassell Publishing, N. Y. 1887.

XLII

Charlotte in the Civil War

Names of the Men Who Filled the Town's Quotas of Soldiers
The Town Paid a Total of $24,915.71
For War Purposes -- Stirring History
of a Time When War Was the
Paramount Interest.

21 January 1901

Nearly forty years ago the booming of that signal gun across Charleston Harbor inaugurated the most stupendous conflict of modern times. Those who were middle-aged at that time are long since dead. Men now sixty were then hardly old enough to vote. The middle-aged of today know nothing of the great rebellion except from history; and to the school children it is as remote as the Revolution. But there are remaining those who participated in it--in the trenches, on the battle fields, in the hospitals and in the horrible prison pens. War has many phases. It is not alone at "the front" that patriotism develops. The army without guns and ammunition is a mob. Banners may wave, bugles blow, but without the "sinews of war" banners lead a forlorn hope, and bugles will sound only a retreat. Those in the field must be clothed and armed and fed by those at home. One is the heart, the other the blood. The heart ceases to beat, the blood no

longer circulates; draw away the blood, the heart is useless. Together they represent life, strength, intellect. The

An unidentified Civil War sergeant probably photographed in his new militia uniform before he went to war. Charlotte Memorial Museum Collection.

261

man with the gun, the sword, the cannon, must be more than duplicated by the man with the hoe, the axe, the chisel, the loom, or the plow.

April 12th, 1861, electrified the nation. The storm had been gathering for a generation but thus far its fearful whirl had not commenced to devastate. Suddenly it was war or disunion. On April 15, 1861, the day after the surrender of Fort Sumpter, came President Lincoln's first call for seventy-five thousand volunteers. Vermont, among the States of the North, answered him from her hills. The tramp, tramp, tramp of her soldiers was heard on almost every battle field until exactly four years from the day of surrender at Sumpter, the stars and stripes again floated above the ruins of the fort. The war was over, but the cost of it--not so much the hundreds of millions of money--but the dead, the maimed, the invalids. The price was fearful, but the nation lived. Self-government by the American people was established for all time. Vermont, in war as in peace, was what the towns made her. The towns filled her quotas and her treasury. The towns maintained unblemished the reputation of her heroic dead, our forefathers, who were ready, if need be, "to retire into the defiles of her inaccessible mountains and defy the world." Charlotte was one of those towns and the part she took in the rebellion is obtained from records and reports of committees under instructions from town meetings.

The first mention of the Rebellion in our town records is a petition to the selectmen requesting them to call a special town meeting May 14, 1861, "To see if the town will raise money to defray the expenses of the families of the volunteers from said town who may enlist in the service of the United States."[111] Peter V. Higbee was moderator of this first war meeting. The records state that the matter was debated and finally the article was laid on the table, certain resolutions were adopted and the meeting adjourned. Unfortunately, there is no record of these resolutions. It will be remembered that the first call from the President was for three months' men, and as it was the general opinion that the war would be a short affair, the action of the town is probably accounted for in this way. But August 20, 1862, the selectmen were again petitioned to call a special town meeting "to raise the money offered to volunteers as bounty for services for nine months in the present war for the Union." The signers of the petition were George R. Pease, Benjamin Beers, John Hazard, J. G. Thorp. The selectmen were D. L. Spear, L. D. Stone, H. C. Leavenworth. This meeting was called for September 2, 1862. After the introduction of several resolutions and debate upon them, the meeting adjourned to Dec. 2, when on motion of E. H. Wheeler the town voted "to raise a tax of 35 cents on the dollar of the grand list to pay the bounty money to four sharpshooters and eighteen nine-months' men promised them by the selectmen." It seems the money had already been raised by advances, for the meeting voted "to pay back to certain individuals that money they have advanced for the above purpose."

A yea-and-nay vote was called for on the motion to raise money, and 91 voted yes; 12, no. Evidently Charlotters were for sustaining the Union.

The third war meeting was called by the selectmen, without petition, for December 14th, 1863. According to articles 2nd and 3rd in this call, it had come to be understood that war meant business for the town was called on to make good its part of the quota of the 300,000 men and to provide ways and means for bounties and advancements to volunteers. It was voted to pay each volunteer $300. The selectmen were authorized to make a temporary loan for the purpose of paying the bounties and to assess a tax of one hundred cents on the dollar of the grand list of 1863 for war purposes.

About the darkest days for the North were in 1864 when it became necessary to draft men into the army. The first mention of the "draft" is found in the call for the town meeting of March, 1864, wherein the 4th article is "To see if the town will vote a bounty to volunteers in case the town is called upon for more men by draft." The records say "the 4th article was dismissed." Evidently the people only let go to get a new hold, for a special town meeting was held April 23rd following "To see if the town will vote a tax sufficient to cover all the expenses already incurred by the selectmen in raising three men to fill the quota of the town under the last call for 200,000 volunteers--also to authorize the selectmen to raise men and pay bounties for volunteers against future calls." Evidently Charlotte was still for sustaining the Union, for the town

meeting of 1864 authorized the selectmen to raise men and money without limit for present and future calls. No wonder Gov. Smith assured President Lincoln that "Vermont was in the fight to a finish."

Another town meeting August 16th, 1864, was "To see if the town approves of the plan of paying bounties to drafted men who shall put an acceptable substitute into the army and also vote additional tax to that voted April 23rd, 1864." This meeting voted to authorize the selectmen to fill the quota of the town under the existing call for 500,000 men and also to raise a tax of one hundred and fifty cents on the dollar in addition to the tax voted in April of that year.

On January 7th, 1865, the town meeting was grappling with the question of paying bounties to those who had already put substitutes into the army or who should do so in the future; and it seems this matter was not settled when another meeting was called for January 28th, 1865, "To see if the town will raise money to make the necessary arrangement for filling the quota of the town under the call of the President for three hundred thousand men." The town authorized the selectmen to fill the quota under this call and to raise an additional tax of one hundred cents on the dollar of the grand list of 1864, if necessary. Charlotte was still in favor of sustaining the Union.

The magnitude of the struggle can be better comprehended by this generation when it is recalled that in the space of four years from 1861 to 1865, President Lincoln called for seventy

"The Battle of Antietam," from an 1887 color print by Prang & Co., Boston. Courtesy of Paul R. Teetor

"The Battle of Cedar Creek," painted in 1871 by Julian Scott of Johnson, Vt. The original is in the Vermont State House.

five thousand men, then three hundred thousand, then two hundred thousand, then five hundred thousand and finally "three hundred thousand more." Such massing armies had never been known since gun powder played its part in war. The important battles of the Revolution, decisive as they were for this nation, were skirmishes in comparison with Gettysburg, Antietam and Shiloh. At Waterloo, something like 70,000 men on a side contended in a battle line of about a mile in length from ten o'clock in the forenoon until five in the afternoon. At Gettysburg, from ninety to one hundred thousand on a side surged back and forth for three days until Lee's sullen retreat, leaving over 20,000 dead, wounded and prisoners. The loss in Meade's army was about 23,000. It is claimed that for magnitude, generalship, stubborn courage, the Wilderness campaign between Grant and Lee outranks anything in modern history. Vermont was in the Wilderness fight. Vermont men held the line at Cedar Creek for Sheridan. Stannard and his Vermonters plunged headlong into Pickett's flank at Gettysburg, rolled up the charging line and, when Pickett failed, Gettysburg was won. Who sent these Vermont men to the front? Back here the towns all through the war were filling their quotas, raising money; the towns all through the war were the mighty "reserve" of the nation. Never a day so dark, a crisis so imminent but Lincoln's call for help met full response. When we consider the sources from whence all these sup-

John H. Thorp as he posed with a group of Masons circa 1906. He furnished a substitute in the Civil War, was keeper of the flag of the Scott Guard, had the oldest camp at Thompson's Point and had the diary of his grandfather, Ezra Holt. Charlotte Memorial Museum Collection.

plies came, the insignificance of the single town, geographically speaking, ceases.

We were not only sending men and money, but were training them. A military company called Scott Guard met one day a week for drill. The late Heman H. Newell of Chicago was captain, and to an intense love of military life he united such glowing patriotism and tireless energy that drilling was anything but a picnic to the citizen soldiers. The ladies presented the company with a fine silk flag that is now in the custody of John H. Thorp. Music was furnished by a drum corps; Calvin Stebbins with his fife and Lewis Barber with his drum stirred the emotions, while Hiram Bishop pounded out the time on the bass drum. Joseph Harrington of North Ferrisburgh was a good snare drummer and often drilled with the company. The Four Corners and the green near the Congregational church were favorite drilling grounds though the guard generally deployed in skirmish line in the meadows east of what was then Alexander's store and many an imaginary confederate was forced to retreat into the woods and bushes of Pease Mountain before the advancing skirmishers of the Scott Guard. On one occasion the Hinesburgh company under Capt. John H. Allen united with the Guard at the Baptist Corners and it was a day long remembered for military evolutions. The "Guard" wore blue flannel shirts, dark trousers and gray caps. The late Noah Allen of Burlington furnished the headgear and each member as his name was called advanced from the ranks to receive his gray cap with "S. G." in gilt letters above the forepiece. This ceremony took place in the yard of the late Joseph S. Shaw.

Not infrequently the ladies spread a table of doughnuts, biscuits and coffee for the hungry warriors, and this part of campaigning had nothing about it that was disagreeable. Meetings of the women were held in different parts of the town, but generally in the Congregational vestry to prepare lint and bandages for the front and army hospitals. This was terribly suggestive work to those whose loved ones were perhaps at the moment in the battle line.

During the enlistment of Berden's sharpshooters, the late Charles Seaton had charge of target practice here for a time, and the firing stand was from the grounds opposite and back of the Congregational church to an object at the base of the hill, north of the parsonage, where many a minnie bullet is today buried in the gravel bank.

The first cavalry regiment of which our present townsmen, Michael Quinlan, Frank Guyette, the Juniper Island lighthouse keeper, and the late George Sherman, were members, was hurried to the front by way of the Rutland and Burlington railroad and the boys were evidently not luxuriating in palace cars as they went thundering by on special trains.

Facilities for news getting in 1864 were slim in comparison with today's telegraphs and telephones and daily papers; the weekly and semiweekly Tribunes, that almost everybody subscribed for, seldom lacked for interested readers. The only postoffice in town was at "Alexander's" and his large store was often crowded with listeners while someone read aloud from the single daily paper. Saturday night was always sure of a full house, for vast interests were at stake. While men were talking quietly with one another here cannon and rifle were perhaps flashing death and mutilation at the front. Occasionally some living skeleton from Andersonville or Libby

Prison, as Truman Naramore when he returned, reminded us of the horror of war through which men lived. The burial in one day of two soldier boys, Cassius Newell and Alonzo Root, in the west [Barber] cemetery reminded us of the horrors of war in which men died. Christian VanVliet, now living in Essex Junction, was one of the selectmen during part of the war. Henry C. Leavenworth, now living in town, was one of the selectmen in 1861. He was continued on the board during the entire war.

At one time the selectmen were enlisting officers. But at all times they

Henry C. Leavenworth as he posed with a group of Masons circa 1906, long after his duties as selectman in filling draft and volunteer quotas in the Civil War and his charter membership in the first Thompson's Point campers group. Charlotte Memorial Museum Collection.

were the executive officers of the town and requisitions for men were made through them. They were responsible for the filling of quotas. The enormous calls up to 1864 were telling on the visible supply and a "corner" on men was imminent. The general government passed what was called the "Commutation Act", enabling those who were drafted to pay $300 to the government in lieu of personal service, but before this there was often a lively scramble for substitutes and quotations ran high. Henry C. Leavenworth, as selectman, participated in the filling of all quotas either by draft or volunteering, and doing this called him from Canada line to Brattleboro, according to circumstance. The quota had to be filled and enlisting officers did not always confine themselves to the handsomest man in the community, or the most polite. Bounty jumpers were not hard to find and when once engaged, it was frequently a question of wit whether the selectman turned his recruit over to the officer or he turned the selectman down, money and all.

But all this time, money was plenty. Taxes were high and so was everything else. Cows sold from $75 to $100 each, dressed pork $20 a hundred, corn $2.00 a bushel, butter 50 cents a pound, wool 90 cents to a dollar a pound, tea $2.00 per pound, three pounds of granulated sugar for a dollar. Cotton cloth was out of sight. Farms sold readily from $75 to $100 per acre. Everything was inflated. At one time it took $2.50 in green backs to buy a dollar in gold. Hard money

"Amos N. Bennett, born Dec. 4, 1831, died May 3, 1863. Mrs. Hunt's uncle, her mother's brother" is the caption inside the case of this tintype. He enlisted from Montpelier and was killed in action. Gift of the Hunt family. Charlotte Memorial Museum Collection.

"Archibald Poole, husband of Mary Kehoe Poole taken on return from Civil War," is the caption in the tintype case. This Archibald Poole was the grandfather of Peg MacDonough and Florence Horsford and of the "Archie" Poole remembered by older local citizens. Courtesy of Peg MacDonough.

such as silver and gold was not in circulation at all.

The government issued "script" for small change; five, ten, twenty-five and fifty cents. In many instances before these government issues were made, merchants issued printed due bills that passed current in business and were redeemed on presentation.

Outside of town meetings, called by the authorities for business purposes, war meetings were held in the town house and churches. Patriotic addresses were made by enlisting officers sent out by the government.

Perhaps 1864 witnessed the most intense strain upon the entire North.

Draft riots in New York and other large cities menaced public safety and it became necessary to withdraw the "commutation" clause, making it obligatory upon every drafted man who passed examination to go into the army. This made it easier for the selectmen, but the "substitute" market was correspondingly buoyant and "$1000 paid for substitutes" was the familiar legend at more than one enlisting station. Burlington was headquarters for this section and it was no country convention crowd that thronged the north side of the public square where the United States marshal's office had an ominous look and

270

the "examining board" passed sentence on "eligibility." Candidates for examination from this section recall how the sight of sick and maimed soldiers at the hospital, where the Home for the Destitute now stands, had anything but an enlivening influence being too suggestive of war's sternest realities.

At one time there was a call for men and a war meeting was held at the Baptist church at East Charlotte. About midnight the quota was filled by volunteers. It was proposed to join with men from Hinesburgh, but the call proved to have been made by mistake and the men were released.

The fall of Vicksburg and the placing of Grant at the head of the army marked the most exciting period of the war. The present generation has no conception of public feeling at that time. Farming and business, important and necessary as they were, seemed secondary matters. The all-engrossing theme was the war and the news from the front. Everybody felt that the crisis had come, and the nerves were tingling at the possibilities of the future. General after general had failed to force the Southern line. But with the hour came the men. Grant, Sherman, Sheridan, Thomas, Howard, Hooker, Stannard and the march to the sea, Chicamauga, the Wilderness, Appomattox.

Years of peace have healed sectional animosities. The old North and the old South exist no longer. A common interest and a single flag characterizes the American people. The recent flash of a foreign sword, the boom of a foreign gun caused the men of the North and the men of the South to stand side by side, and who could bid them stay. But we cannot, we must not, forget those perilous days. We must not fail to teach our children that the patriotism counting most for humans stands first and foremost and always for its country's flag, that its country's laws must be respected and obeyed, that in union alone there is strength and life.

At the town meeting in March, 1866, a committee consisting of Ezra Hosford, E. H. Wheeler and D. L. Spear was appointed to ascertain the amount of money raised by the town for war purposes, the names of those who were credited to the quotas of the town whether by draft or enlistment, those who procured substitutes and those who paid commutation money, also the amounts paid as bounties and to whom paid. This report was presented to the town at the annual March meeting in 1867 and was accepted and adopted. Being so near the close of the war when things were fresh in minds it is no doubt substantially correct. The whole amount paid out for war purposes was $24,915.71. The whole amount raised and paid into the treasury in 1863 was $2,077.10. In 1864, $23,378.65. According to the report, the collections for war purposes seem mostly to have been made in 1864 except the amount paid in 1862.

The committee gave the following names of eighteen nine-months' men who enlisted in the fall of 1862 and who each received $90 bounty: J. Gilbert Barton, William P. Barton, Joseph Besette, Hiram Bishop, George A. Clark, Horace N. Delmeater, Henry Drum, Joseph Guillette, Frank R. Hill, Heman A. Hyde, William Lincoln, Samuel S. Page, Gideon D. Prindle, Alonzo E. Root, Benjamin H. Taggart, James Washburn, Milo A. Williams, Myron M. Williams.

Sharpshooters who enlisted in 1863: George W. Spear, James M. Ball, Alfred S. Burnham, William Quinlan, Jacob Lacoy. They all received $100 each except for Jacob Lacoy who, by the report, received no bounty.

The three-years' men who enlisted in December, 1863, and received a bounty of $300 each are reported as follows: Galord B. Smith, Lewis C. Prindle, James Deraur, William C. Powell, Thomas Young, Benjamin McCandish, John Larama, James Little, John Coleman, Eliphalet Culver, Moody Haskell, George H. Hoyt, Delinus L. Melvin, Joseph W. Townson, Joseph Besette, John Whitney, Edward L. Hibbard, Alonzo H. Danforth, William Dunn, Horace H. Preston.

In April, 1864, three men enlisted who received $150 each: George W. York, George W. Hewitt and Frank Baslaw. But in the fall of 1864, seventeen men were enlisted and at that time bounties had climbed to the top shelf. These men enlisted for one and three years: Edward Corbit, one year, $550; Alexander Besette, one year, $500; Abe Pulsifer, one year $700; Peter Cross, one year $550; Alfred Parkhurst, one year $650; Alpheus George, one year, $700; Adam Smith, three years, $1000; Freeman Mason, three years $1000; James German, three years, $1000, David Patterson, one year, $600; David Robertson, one year, $700; William Kinsley, three years, $1000; Lucius L. Clark, one year, $700; James B. Williams, one year, $700; Edward C. Scott, one year, $700; Joseph Fonda, one year, $600, colored man obtained South, three years, $400. Expenses for raising these men, outside of the bounties, $517.20

The following six were enlisted in spring of 1865: William Essor, three years, $600; Joseph Burbo, one year, $550; James Stone, one year, $500; George W. James, one year, $550.

The enrolled men who furnished substitutes were D. L. Spear, paying $187; John H. Thorp, $550;[112] Christian VanVliet, $900.

Those who paid commutation: Spicer T. Jones, Levi Meader, Henry W. Prindle, William B. Thorp.

Those who entered the service by draft: Isaac Prince, Jr., Cyrus G. Prindle [Pringle].

Those who received bounties by special vote of the town: Alpheus Tatro, $150 and Abner J. Fonda, $300.

The committee reports that Joseph Kehoe stands accredited to the town and re-enlisted after October 17, 1863 with no town bounty.

They report the following 20 names who enlisted for the town and received no bounty from the town previous to October 17, 1863: Daniel B. Ball, Rollin W. Barton, John Besette,

John Coleman, John Daniels, James H. Davis, Abner J. Fonda, Joseph Gravel, Henry Hough, Truman C. Naramore, Joseph Kehoe, Jacob Lacoy, Cassium F. Newell, Clark L. Parks, John Quinlan, Charles Seaton, George D. Sherman, Alonzo B. Stearns, Henry B. Wilder.

The committee reports that the above 20 men enlisted wherever they pleased but were accredited to the town. Of course the entire quotas were not filled by home men and several names are not familiar to any one in town, except perhaps as the selectmen at the time may recall them. This is doubtful, for recruits came from elsewhere and frequently regiments that had a temporary over-supply filled the bill for a liberal "consideration" to somebody.

The object of this paper is to preserve in print the findings of the committee, and the action of the town during the war. As time passes, the record of these things will increase in worth and interest. What an immense service could have been rendered to the people of this town had someone compiled the names of those who served from here in any part of the Revolutionary struggle or during the war of 1812. Charlotte commenced her political existence in 1762, early enough to have had some of her sons among the Green Mountain Boys who entered Ticonderoga with Ethan Allen. How much satisfaction it would be to know who they were. We are apt to overlook the fact that what is actual participation to us will some time be history to others. Not many years hence things now familiar will be forgotten. It will be doing posterity a kindness to record them.

"Swords into ploughshares" were the words in Charlotte after the war, though perhaps Higbee would have preferred the ploughshares being on sulky plows. (See Chap. XIX.) From "The Youths' History of the United States," Vol. 3, p. 380.

273

Mt. Philo from Bixby Island (now Dean Island). Photo by H. Custer Ingham (1863-1931). Courtesy of Bixby Free Memorial Library.

XLIII

Beautiful View from Mt. Philo

20 July 1903

"Welcome to Mt. Philo" is the hospitable legend that greets one at the entrance to a mile of perfect highway, winding up the southern slope of this magnificent outlook. Mr. James H. Humphreys of Dorchester, Mass., and his wife, Frances W., fortunately indeed for the public, have fallen in love with this portion of the Champlain valley and Mt. Philo in particular and wonderful things are revealed for the artist's eye and the poetic soul in consequence.[113]

Do you want an unobstructed view of the Green Mountains from north to south, as far as the eye can distinguish, taking in the spires of Montreal, so they say? Do you want to follow the windings of the lordly Adirondacks until the unaided eye distinguishes nothing but blue sky, merging into mountain top? Do you want an unbroken view of 75 miles of Lake Champlain, lessening to a seeming river far away to the south, and widening to the north into the expansive Plattsburgh bay and rough waters of old Cumberland Head? Do you want to look down upon the hundreds of farms in Chittenden and Addison counties that have the appearance of beautiful parks and lawns-- for you are not so high up but everything is distinct? Do you want to see Burlington, the Queen City of Vermont, and how appropriately she is named? Do you want to see Vergennnes, the oldest city in the State but sprightly as a maiden despite her years? Do you want to see Hinesburgh and Monkton Boro and Monkton Ridge and the Center and by all means the Hollow and "Martinville"--not forgetting Hotel Champlain and Willsboro and Essex, Thompson's

An early 1900's photo of the road up Mt. Philo soon after it was built by the Humphreys. Pease Mt. is in the middle background. Courtesy of the Wheeler/Kingsland Collection.

The high rock of Mt. Philo from a postcard circa 1915 showing the iron rails that protected visitors from the vertical drop. Courtesy of the Bixby Free Memorial Library.

Mt. Philo showing the roofs of the Mt. Philo Inn. The early Humphreys' road crossed the open field to the left of the buildings on the hillside. The Humphreys' home is below this road and shows between some trees. Charlotte Memorial Museum Collection.

A summer house and the farm buildings at the Mt. Philo Inn from a 1910 post card. Charlotte Memorial Museum Collection.

The view from a summer house from a post card around 1910. Thompson's Point is seen beyond the building on the right. Charlotte Memorial Museum Collection.

The tent colony for campers at the Mt. Philo Inn during the early 1900s, Courtesy of the Wheeler/Kingsland Collection.

State Park Rd. from Rt. 7 to Mt Philo. In 1888 it replaced Old Town Trail to the north and Claflin Rd. to the south of it. Courtesy of the Wheeler/Kingsland Collection.

Point, Cedar Beach, Long Point--in fact all creation? Then climb the winding stairs in Mr. Humphrey's 50 foot tower and there you are.

And all this time, while driving up the mountain on as perfect a highway as any city street, you have been treated to perpetual surprises in new outlooks at each recurring curve in the winding road. Part of the way goes through "Partridge Glen," where tall pines soothed in rugged rocks, mossy logs and rich underbrush tell why the glen is so inhabited, for our partridge is a tidy bird and loves nice housekeeping. Are you a climber, not afraid of a bit of personal effort, then leave the wagon road near the pine grove where 25 or 30 great boulders, some of them weighing a hundred tons each, called a halt a hundred years ago to their headlong rush from the summit. Rest a bit under the pines that have grown up among these foot-balls of nature, and among them follow the windings of the "Mountain spring path" along the mountain's western and northern face. Go past the ice-cold spring, all the time in the dense shade of evergreen woods with here and there an inviting seat and where an opening has been cut for an outlook to the bold and rugged western front. Here a substantial iron railing set into the rock guards you from a plunge of a hundred feet of precipitous descent.

Mr. Humphreys is a lover of nature and has profited by his study of it and has caught the poetry of the wild woods in the names of the many cozy nooks scattered along the drive and paths. The sunrise often finds him on the summit. He not only enjoys his mountain, but he enjoys the enjoyment of the public. The people are welcome, but he asks them to respect his confidence and refrain from marking trees, pulling up shrubbery or in any way unnecessarily defacing the grounds or buildings. People will go hundreds of miles to see the beautiful or grand in nature; let them not forget this most magnificent outlook in New England; let them accept the hospitable invitation of Mr. Humphreys' "Welcome to Mt. Philo."

279

Lake Champlain.
1835.

The Steam-Boats Franklin & Phoenix

have been put in perfect order for business, and will run the ensuing season in the following order—leaving each place at ONE o'clock, P. M. until further notice.

FRANKLIN
Capt. R. W. SHERMAN,

Will leave **Whitehall** every.................. and **St. Johns** every.............................

TUESDAY, THURSDAY & SATURDAY,	MONDAY, WEDNESDAY & FRIDAY.

PHOENIX
Capt. DAN LYON;

Will leave **Whitehall** every.............. and **St. Johns** every.......................

MONDAY, WEDNESDAY & FRIDAY,	TUESDAY, THURSDAY, & SATURDAY

Freight will be received on board either Boat, and discharged at the usual landings on the Lake.

BURLINGTON, April, 1835.

PRINTED AT THE FREE PRESS OFFICE, BURLINGTON.

XLIV

McNeil's Ferry: Past and Present

19 October 1903

Speaking of the recent purchase of the McNeil Ferry property by Mrs. Joseph Winterbotham, the *Free Press* referred to it as an "old landmark." How much of a "landmark" it really is, or how important to business relations it was in an earlier day hardly one in ten of the present readers of the *Free Press* has the remotest idea. Now and then one of the older residents of Charlotte and adjoining towns knows something about it from observation; but the middle-aged business men of today depend upon tradition if they wish to know anything about the "ferry" as it was and even tradition, in this age of newspapers and books, grows dim and uncertain over the events of sixty or seventy years ago. Perhaps the public will forgive me for attempting to detain them a little and for putting into print the facts and recollections, some of them from the land records of Charlotte.

In 1792 Charles McNeil of Litchfield, Conn., obtained on tax sale, lot No. 120 embracing the whole of McNeil's Point, then called "Allen's Point", where Cedar Beach is now located. The first ferry ran from Cedar Beach bay to Essex, N. Y., and only a few years ago the old dock timbers

were in existence and could easily be seen. Near the point was a home that accommodated the traveling public and probably Charles McNeil owned the ferry. At that time, a highway ran partly along the line of present travel on the Cedar Beach road past the head of Converse bay meeting the present road a few rods south of where it now does and near where James B. McNeil's house once stood; the building being at present on

A sail ferry. From "A Family Canoe Trip," by Florence Watters Snedeker, Harper & Brothers, N.Y. 1892. Courtesy of Phyllis Deming, The Village Bookshop, Shelburne.

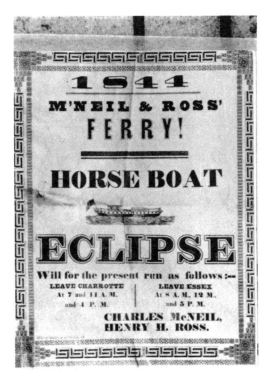

A horse boat, the ECLIPSE, *as shown on a broadside. Courtesy of the Lake Champlain Transportation Company.*

Dennis Toner's farm, moved there by Mr. McNeil. This early ferry did business for a number of years--how long, it seems difficult to ascertain--but later on another was established that came to be known far and near as "McNeil's Ferry." It was established where the wharf now is on the Winterbotham purchase.

In 1784 Ethan Allen of Bennington sold to John McNeil, the father of Charles McNeil 2nd, the north half of lot No. 119, and in 1792 John McNeil bought on tax sale the north half of lot 120 and the south half of lot No. 119. This gave John McNeil 300 acres embracing the "ferry farm." Whatever the business rivalries that tradition says existed between the two brothers on

account of their ferries, the one on the John McNeil purchase survived, and in time an immense traffic was done at this point

The first ferry was of course a sail boat, but as business increased, more certain means for regular communication were adopted. About seventy years ago, a horse boat was built for the purpose at Shelburne harbor. The boat was owned by McNeil and Ross; Charles McNeil, who was the father of William McNeil of Shelburne, living on this side of the lake and Henry H. Ross of Essex, New York.

Present readers may not understand the methods of horse boating. The boat was a side wheeler, and power was conveyed from an immense wheel lying horizontal with the deck or a little below it, connecting by cogs with the side wheel shaft. This horizontal wheel was propelled by six horses, three on a side, walking on lags or tread power on the principal of horse power now used. The horses were tandem rigged and hitched back by side tugs to whiffletrees or hooks. The pull of the horses conveyed the power to the wheel underfoot. It was a hard place for horses, and an occasional break in the planks or lags meant a broken leg every time. The captain, Harvey Hinckley, was engineer-in-chief, and the fuel was a whip and an increased demand for speed meant more energetic application of rawhide.

The captain took turns in living, one season in Essex and another on the Charlotte side. When here, McNeil kept the horses on hay and

The second VERMONT coming into the dock at Thompson's Point. Courtesy of the Root Family.

On Deck of the "Vermont"

grain and Ross did the same in return. The small red house on the easterly lake road was the captain's home when here.

The building now standing east of the homestead was the ferry "tavern" and it had a great run of custom, for

From "A Family Canoe Trip," by Snedeker.

1844 CHARLOTTE HORSE FERRY

"The Charlotte News" presented its version of the horse boat on Oct. 12, 1989 after the "National Geographic" article was published. Courtesy of Charlie Lotz.

283

1849.
LAKE CHAMPLAIN.

EVENING LINE.

THE STEAMER	THE STEAMER
BURLINGTON,	**WHITEHALL,**
Capt. William Anderson,	**Capt. Gideon Lathrop,**

Leaves Whitehall,   and Saint Johns,   Leaves Whitehall,   and Saint Johns,
MONDAY,   TUESDAY,   TUESDAY,   MONDAY,
WEDNESDAY and   THURSDAY and   THURSDAY and   WEDNESDAY and
FRIDAY, at 12 M.   SATURDAY, at 2½ P. M.   SATURDAY, at 12 M.   FRIDAY, at 2½ P. M.

MORNING LINE.

The Steamers **United States** and **Francis Saltus**, will soon commence a **Day Line**.

THE STEAMER	THE STEAMER
UNITED STATES,	**FRANCIS SALTUS,**
Capt. P. T. Davis,	**Capt. T. D. Chapman,**

Leaving Whitehall   and Saint Johns   Leaving Whitehall   and Saint Johns
TUESDAY,   MONDAY,   MONDAY,   TUESDAY,
THURSDAY, and   WEDNESDAY, and   WEDNESDAY, and   THURSDAY, and
SATURDAY, at 4 a. M.   FRIDAY, at 2½ A. M.   FRIDAY, at 4 a. M.   SATURDAY, at 2½ A.M.

The Boats of the Day Line will leave St. Johns either in the evening (after the arrival of the last train of Cars from Montreal) or as early as 2½ o'clock, A. M. of the above mentioned days, as their convenience may require or weather permit. Passengers intending to take the Day Boats at either end of the Lake can lodge on board,—at St. Johns it will be necessary for them to do so.

The Day Boats will arrive at St. Johns in time for the Cars to Montreal same evening, and at Whitehall at half past 2 o'clock, P. M., in time to arrive at Troy by the Rail Road Cars for the evening boat to New York.

Every attention will be paid to the comfort and convenience of passengers

Passage Through $2---Meals Extra. No charge for berths in the Cabin on the Night Boats—When passengers lodge on board the day Boats and the passage does not amount to 50 cents, 25 cents will be charged for berths. Berths in State Rooms 50 cents each in all cases.

☞ This arrangement to continue until further notice. ☜

The Captains and Officers of the Boats are strictly prohibited from taking in charge in any manner whatever, any letters containing Money or any Bank Bills, Jewelry or other light and valuable articles. The Champlain Transportation Company will not undertake to transport any of the above mentioned articles, nor will they hold themselves responsible therefor. Neither will they hold themselves responsible for letters containing Money or any Bank Bills, Bills of Exchange, Jewelry, or any other light and valuable articles which may be put in charge of any Express man, or the Agent of any Express line, who may be on board ; nor for any other goods or property in such charge unless specifically reported to the Captain.

Merchandise deemed extra hazardous on account of fire, and green Hides, will not be taken on board nor transported at any price.

BURLINGTON, APRIL, 1849.

there was not only ferrying, but a great many back country people came to McNeil's to meet the line steamboats that stopped here regularly twice a day in their trips from Whitehall to St. Johns. People from Hinesburgh, Huntington and Starksboro came to this point to ship their produce and get their Troy and Albany freights.

In addition to the line boats, a fleet of sloop-rigged canal boats were constantly going and coming, loaded with all kinds of commodities. They would sail up the lake to Whitehall where "Billy Kane, the rigger," as he was called, would take down the mast and sails so the boats could go through the Champlain canal to Troy and from there by tug boats to New York or elsewhere. On the return trip, Kane would replace mast and sails and the voyage northward would be resumed. There was then little or no "towing" on Lake Champlain. Each boat went alone, and a strong south wind was pretty sure to bring a dozen to twenty white-winged freights around the headland of Split Rock. The "ferry" was generally sure of a liberal consignment of heavy merchandise: salt, sugar, molasses, now and then possibly a quart bottle of "Old Holland," besides dry goods and notions, for country merchants did not order goods by telephone those days, and "going to market" was a long-looked-for and momentous occasion.

The horse boat was a money-making venture for her owners and it is exceedingly unfortunate that her name remains unattainable. It is hoped some one can supply the missing link.[114] She was scheduled for three trips a day, morning, noon and night, but stood ready for more than this on call. Her capacity was by no means inconsiderable, and she needed it all to accommodate the cattle traffic between Essex and McNeils.

In those days Jack Simonds did an immense business butchering cattle in Shoreham, Addison county, and great droves of beeves were picked up in northern New York, largely in St. Lawrence county, driven to the vicinity of Essex and there held on adjoining farms until ferried across, seventy-five to one hundred at a time. On this side, the bunches were held until the entire drove was over when the drive would be resumed to Simond's slaughter yards. It was no uncommon thing to see McNeil's pastures and meadows crowded with cattle after haying and harvesting when the handling was the liveliest. At that time the Society of Friends was strong in this section and their yearly, or more frequent meetings, took them in great numbers to the York State side and

Landing

The CHATEAUGAY from "A Family Canoe Trip" by Snedeker.

Claremont, 1808

The CLAREMONT [sic] from a commemorative post card. Courtesy of Mary Lighthall.

the "ferry" was their objective, coming and going. In the old horse boat days, St. Lawrence county was "West," and Ohio was "Way West." Probably many a St. Lawrence community can to-day trace its ancestry back to Vermonters for scores of them went there, and "McNeil's" was a household word, long to be remembered. Many a longing eye looked back over the three miles of blue water to catch a last glimpse of its rocky shore, for over there were the migrants' parents and friends, old homes and tender memories.

There was a store and storehouse on the wharf and at one time Horace Lovely did a great business in the wholesale and retail line, supplying this and adjoining towns with everything kept in the country stores of those days. He bought large quantities of produce and other dealers had shipping deliveries made here, so that canal boats frequently tied up to the dock for days loading produce. The present small inlet a little east of the wharf was deep and free from obstructions. Capt. Caleb E. Barton, who ran

a canal boat on the lake, frequently wintered his boat there.

Morning and night the line steamers swing up to the dock and WHITEHALL, SARANAC, PHOENIX, CHAMPLAIN, WASHINGTON, UNITED STATES, and SALTUS were familiar names a generation or so ago. At one time a fierce steamboat war broke out and rival boats tried to outsail each other. I think the SALTUS figured largely in the maritime disturbance and during one season at least the public had cheap rides galore. One could ride from the "ferry" to Whitehall for twenty-five cents, possibly this was for the round trip, and it looked at one time as though the public would be actually paid a liberal compensation for taking a trip.

Before the opening of the Champlain canal in 1823, the trade in iron, manufactured on the west side of the lake, and lumber, from this side, was confined largely to Canada as transportation from Whitehall to Troy was made by teams. The "ferry" had its share of lumber shipments and great rafts of logs were frequently windbound in the bay. Rafts were frequently made up in the cove at the mouth of the Thorp brook from the immense growth of pine and other valuable trees in the "greenbush" area.

The first boat through the Champlain canal was from Vermont-- the GLEANER, owned by St. Albans parties, loaded with wheat and potash. There were several asheries in this town, potash was almost legal tender and was an important item in the ferry shipping trade.

For a long time there was more or less trans-shipment of produce at Whitehall, regular canal boats not being built to stand the lake winds and waves; but dealers in butter and cheese, particularly, protested against the damage to goods by over-handling and delay, and in 1841 the "Merchants' Line" was established, using boats built for both lake and canal, and so rigged that the masts and sails could be removed and replaced in Whitehall, or as before described. Large quantities of butter and cheese came from Charlotte and several eastern towns, always famous dairy sections; and nearly every pound of it was shipped at this "ferry." During the best days of this line as many as 40 boats were thus employed.

The horse boat continued for many years to cover herself with glory and also proved a wealth producer to her owners, but finally fell a victim to the infirmities of age and one day, when loaded with cattle from the Essex side, she gave such unmistakable evidences of a collapse before reaching shore, that the horses were taken out of their merry-go-rounds, the deck sides knocked off, and horses and cattle unceremoniously plunged into the lake. The old horse boat was floated over the bay where for many moons the mermaids sported in the water-logged cabin. Anticipating some such event, the owners had provided a small steamboat christened the BOUQUET, and two days after the shipwreck she made her first trip on the "ferry" route. But during all those years other agencies had been at work, other avenues of trade and commerce had come into competition.

The whistle of the first locomotive of the Rutland and Burlington railroad, about 1849, signaled the commencement of the end of certain kinds of lake traffic. The competition of the Vermont Central, about 1854, opened still another way to Boston, and quantities of business that had formerly gone to Troy, Albany and New York went elsewhere. Railroads running into northern New York from this section and into central New York from the south stopped the travel by stage and private conveyance. Gradually, but surely, the business of the "ferry" grew less and less. Human ingenuity or enterprise were powerless to prevent it. Railroad transportation acted like a tonic on humanity and everybody was all at once in a hurry. Merchants could hardly stand the delays in the old ways of obtaining foods, for customers pushed them to expedition and the public is inclined to be inexorable.

Citizens of Charlotte who witnessed from the "ferry" the passage of the first steamboat on Lake Champlain, the VERMONT, in 1808 saw the second steamboat in the world, the first being the CLERMONT, built by Fulton on the Hudson.[115] The VERMONT was built like a large canal boat only longer and wider, quite in contrast with her namesake of to-day. The eternal fitness of things calls for the continuation of that name so long as a steamboat is run on Lake Champlain. Her machinery was rude

The first VERMONT from a 1909 postcard. Courtesy of the Wheeler/Kingsland Collection.

This is a picture of the first Steamboat on Lake Champlain (and the second in the World.) It was built and launched at Burlington, Vermont, in 1808 and completed at Basin Harbor, Vt. It commenced navigating on the lake in 1809, just 200 years after Champlain had entered its waters in a birch bark canoe.

The owners and builders were two brothers, John and James Winans; it was called the "Vermont;" and was 120 feet long, 20 feet beam, 167 tons measurement; with an engine of 20 horse power, and commanded by Capt. John Winans.

On June 4th 1810 Charles McNeil received credit of $2 for taking ten oxen "acroast" the lake according to this account book. Charlotte Memorial Museum Collection.

288

of course, the application of steam power having to be learned by experience and many of the sail boats on the lake could probably have out-speeded her, but it was a new era in the worlds history and Vermont was in the van.

The charter for a ferry between Charlotte and Essex was granted to Charles McNeil of the former and H. H. Ross of the latter in October, 1821. These were the horse boat days, but in 1827 they built the steamboat WASHINGTON, intending it for the ferry business. She was too expensive for the work and was sold in 1827, probably being replaced by horse power again until 1848 when the BOUQUET was built.

This paper is not intended for a history of navigation on the lake or an approximation thereto. In point of fact it is doubtless a presumption to characterize it as historical at all. But how are those who come after us to know what had happened here and there along the avenues of life unless some one takes time to make a record.

The present owner of "McNeil's" has reason to congratulate herself upon her acquisition. No finer spot can be found along the shores of Lake Champlain. From the bluff head land of her western lawn she looks out upon a water highway traversed by the fleets and armies of England and France when those two great nations were in a death grapple for the ownership of a continent. Past her door, for nearly a century, marched the crowded ranks of trade and commerce. But the departure of the old has not lessened the beauties of the new. The same eternal hills mirror themselves in the waters of this magnificent lake. Sunrise and sunset paint the same glorious tints on sky and cloud.

A present-day ferry in McNeil's cove. Illustration from the masthead of the "Charlotte News," September 14, 1989. Courtesy of Charlie Lotz.

The Charlotte Methodist church which became the Breezy Point library. It was located on Greenbush Rd. south of the Four Corners. According to the Beer's map the parsonage was between the Seminary building on the north and the church on the south. Charlotte Memorial Museum Collection.

Mutton Hill from Barber Hill. On the right: Church Hill Rd., Congregational church, Spear's Garage; foreground: Greenbush Rd. The west village is hidden by trees on the left. Route 7 shows on left (north) end of Mutton Hill. Photo taken in 1980.

XLV

The Breezy Point Library Association, the Methodist Church History and Good Influences

14 January 1904.

In August, 1899, thirteen young ladies of Charlotte, Miss May Cook, Miss Pearl Cook, Miss Maude Russell, Miss Mary Russell, Mrs. W. V. Beach, Miss Josephine Williams, Miss Carolyn Williams, Miss Sophia Williams, Miss Belle Owen, Miss Emma Leavenworth, Miss Elizabeth Holmes, Miss Mabel Higbee and Miss Mary Yale gave a play called *Breezy Point* in the former Methodist Church.[116] This entertainment was a success, netting over $60 to its promoters at its two presentations, proving the old superstition of 13 as an unlucky number to be without foundation in fact. At the outset nothing positive had been decided as to how this money should be used, but feminine wisdom that seldom goes far wrong if left to its own devices settled the question. It was decided to form the "Breezy Point Library Association" which was incorporated under the laws of the State of Vermont, Sept. 18, 1902, and whose charter for maintaining a free public library recorded at the town clerk's office of Charlotte enables the corporation and their successors to take and hold real and personal estate, either by gift or purchase, to sue and be sued, as set forth in the quaint language of the old common law. The town clerk's office has thus far had the honor of affording shelf room for this library that by purchase and gift now numbers nearly 700 volumes. It

Miss Pearl Cook one of the cast in "Breezy Point." She later married John Spear and with him, May Foote and Daisy Williams founded the Charlotte Memorial Museum. She also wrote and published poetry. Charlotte Memorial Museum Collection.

291

The playbill for "Breezy Point," the play that gave its name to Charlotte's library that was in the old Methodist church at the Four-Corners. Charlotte Memorial Museum Collection.

has been a pleasure to the custodian to note the interest taken by our people and he takes this opportunity to congratulate the Association on the evident appreciation of its efforts by the general public.

As soon as it can conveniently be brought about the books will be placed in the room designed for their use on the first floor of the building and access to them will be had at certain times as will be designated and published by those who are in charge of all these matters.

Unlike most or many of the rural towns in Vermont, Charlotte has no trade center to whose stores, mills, shops and churches population naturally gravitates. George the 3rd kindly undertook to arrange matters for us in this respect. When in his charter of 1762, he laid out a village plot of 200 acres in the supposed geographical center of town, being lot No. 54, and as near as can now be figured out, is on the road leading north through "Guinea" and embracing property owned by the Mary Fletcher hospital or Joseph L. Quinlan or both of them. It may be said that there is nothing particularly tropical, or never was, about the location in question suggested by the name except the three or four colored families who settled there in the days long gone and the whimsical conceit of our fathers established a local application that will probably follow on to the end of time.

There has always been an "east" and "west" side as regards the State and nothing but the Green mountains are to blame for it. Nobody has yet been able to point out that Vermont has suffered from it in the least. There has always been an "east" and "west" in Charlotte, and where can you find a town but has some "Over the Pond," or "Over the Creek," or "South of the River" made so in the natural divisions of land and water? Nobody has yet been able to point out that Charlotte has suffered from this in the least. There has rarely, if ever, been a question involving the general interest of this town that has not been discussed and settled on broad grounds. I believe there never will be.

The town has always been foremost in education and general culture. Some of its citizens have been leaders as teachers, professional men and statesmen. On moral and society questions it has always stood in the front ranks and close by the flag. It stands there to-day. In the great Civil War, in the days of the immortal Abraham Lincoln, this town was always ready with its money. Its sons were found in the ranks of the nation's fighting men. Some of them are living today and will bear me witness on this statement. Some of them were brought here from hospitals and battlegrounds in caskets draped with their country's flag sleeping their dreamless sleep.

According to the best obtainable information, there was a "Charlotte Social Library" in existence in 1826 that was kept in the law office of William Noble. Mrs. Jane Hibbard of Chicago, a daughter of Mr. Noble, writes: "My memory goes no further back than 1835 or thereabouts. The library was then kept in my father's law office which was the southwest upper room in the house of E. H. Fields. That small library had much to do with making Charlotte, which was said to be at that time, a town of more general intelligence than any other one in that part of the State." Let it be said that Mrs. Hibbard's loyalty to Charlotte was augmented by a gift of some two hundred volumes of general literature and reference books that will be on the Breezy Point library shelves.

No one knows how many books the "Charlotte Social Library" contained, but one stray volume on exhibit here is No. 331. The association was a careful and economical organization as evidenced by the rules and regulations bound on the inside of the front cover of each book.

On September 14, 1842, an organization known as the "Charlotte Young Men's Literary Club consisting of 73 charter members was perfected in East Charlotte for the purpose of cultivating the habit and art of public speaking as set forth in their constitution. The first officers elected were: president, Ezra Alexander; vice president, C. M. Cady; secretary, J. N. Root; treasurer, Reuben Pease.

Their records fail to state where the first meeting was held, but it is a remarkable fact that for more than fifty years this society held to its organization, that here were intelligently discussed questions affecting the welfare of the town and State. No matter if their decisions were not heralded abroad--its work was worth the effort. The debating societies and the town meetings of New England may not have their exact counterparts anywhere, but they have been moderately educational, both as to matters legislative and self-governing.

Aided by the kind patronage of the public, the Breezy Point association accumulated from plays and ice cream sales a little over $60. To this amount Miss Jeanette B. Bouton of Charlotte added $300, John H. Converse of Philadelphia $100, Fred S. Pease of Burlington $25, Mrs. Joseph Winterbottom $25. Besides, numerous entertainments realized handsome amounts. George A. Foote handed the treasurer $30 obtained by personal solicitation and $10 for himself and

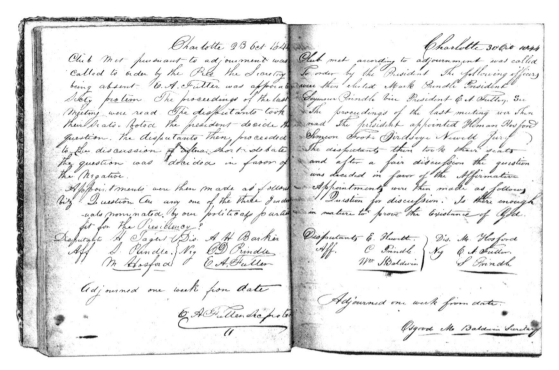

Pages from the record books of the Charlotte Young Men's Literary Club for October 23 and 30, 1844. The first page set the subject of the next week's debate, viz.: Are any of the three individuals nominated by our political parties fit for the Presidency? The debate was decided in favor of the affirmative.

sister, Miss Flora Jane Foote. Miss Caroline A. Yale gave $5.

Of the books now in the library the association has bought and paid for about 350 volumes. The two largest donations of bound books were made by Mrs. Jane J. Pope of Chicago. These books have not all been shelved for want of room.

On May 11, 1903 William V. Beach and Edna S. Beach deeded to the "Breezy Point Library Association" a lot of land 86 x 120 feet, on which the building stands. The association has slated the roof and remodeled the interior giving them what you may see there: a spacious dining hall, a kitchen

and the library room which when properly shelved will contain more than two thousand volumes. They hope eventually to connect with this library a reading room that shall be warmed and lighted at proper and stated periods, and in which will be found as many papers and periodicals of the day as their finances will admit of furnishing. In addition are an auditorium with substantial and finely decorated stage, pronounced by experts the finest to be found in any country town in the whole state.

This building and lot cost the association $500. They have expended in repairs about $500. They have in the

bank, as a fund for the monthly purchase of books, about $34. They are in
debt $250 of borrowed money to com-
plete their repairs and decorations .

This is the financial condition of
the association. According to the
terms of their incorporation they can
legally hold either personal property
or real estate, given or bequeathed. It
seems that the association has commended itself to the continued consideration of the public.

In 1822 Ammi Fuller, a wealthy
citizen of Charlotte, made provisions
in his last will "for the support and
payment of the constant preaching of
the Gospel in Charlotte by the minister of the Methodist Church or
society." Certain real estate was designated in his will, the income from
which should be used for the purpose.
A portion of that real estate is embraced in the 60 or 70 acres, "more or
less that has been known as the Thorp
or Bradey lot." A section of Mr. Fuller's will says, "And in case the Methodist Church or society, from any
cause, shall become extinct, the interest aforesaid shall be at the disposal of

*The Charlotte Meeting House. After the
Breezy Point Library was damaged and
with no financing available for repairs the
Breezy Point organization donated the
building to the Shelburne Museum. It was
moved and renamed. Photo taken in 1979.*

*In 1950 a storm did ex-
tensive damage in Char-
lotte. The roof at the
back of the library
building was blown out.
S. Russell Williams
photographed the
damage. He donated his
negatives to the Char-
lotte Memorial Museum
Collection.*

the annual conference of Methodists, within whose bounds the said church or society in Charlotte may be." The trustees named in the will were Ithiel Stone, Jonathan Breakenridge, Asa Forbes, Joseph Simonds, Thomas N. Hickok, Jonathan Breakenridge, Jr., and Myron Breakenridge.

The conditions of this will do not effect the real estate embracing the parsonage property and the church property, or the land on which the meeting house stands, and it is discussed in this connection to correct an impression seeming to have prevailed, that the real estate purchased by the Association could not be deeded. It formed no part of Mr. Fuller's estate.

On July 10, 1819 Jonathan Breakenridge of Charlotte deeded to Justus Byington, Joseph Simonds, Asa Forbes, Thomas N. Hickok and Jonathan Breakenridge of Charlotte, Nathan Gage of Shelburne, Daniel Norton of Hinesburgh, trustees of the Methodist Episcopal Church, the land on which the Methodist meeting house now stands. This land was deeded to such trustees, subject to whatever rules or dispositions the conference of the church might see fit to put forth.

The parsonage property was deeded to similar trustees, with similar provisions, by Myron Breakenridge by the deed of May 16, 1836.

The entire property was deeded by Norris R. Miller of Shelburne, under vote of authority of the quarterly conference to William V. and Edna S. Beach of Charlotte, and they deeded the church property, so called, to the Association in May, 1903.

This is the condition of the Association as regards their real estate.

The Charlotte Methodist Episcopal church was organized in 1801 by Reverend Ebenezer Washburn and the building stood nearly on the site of the present library building. The wooden building was started in 1819 and finished in 1833. Connected with it was a parsonage and here lived the presiding Elder of the district. The church and parsonage burned in 1837, after which the present buildings were erected.

The old Seminary building was once the Troy Conference Academy, and great hopes were entertained of building up here an educational and denominational center such as now exists in Poultney.[117] It is said numerous apparatus were removed from here to the Poultney school.

The earliest records to which I have had access in regard to Methodist history are the "minister of the first quarterly conference in Charlotte station, June 30, 1827." Lewis Place was Presiding Elder; Benjamin Griffin, Station preacher. The records show Jonathan Breakenridge, local preacher; Myron Breakenridge, local exhorter. In this meeting Myron Breakenridge was secretary; Myron Breakenridge, Jonathan Breakenridge, and Amos Tomlinson, stewards. Jonathan Breakenridge, John Byington, and Stoddard Martin were public collectors. In 1830 Reverend Tobias Spicer was presiding elder, Jasper Evan, preacher. The quarterly conference seems to have been alternately in Charlotte and Shelburne.

At one time this was the central

296

spot for Methodism in the Champlain valley. The district parsonage was here; Shelburne, Burlington, Ferrisburgh and Vergennes were supply stations. The presiding elder, the Rev. Tobias Spicer, lived here in 1830, when the parsonage burned, and Mr. Spicer lost all his furniture, clothing and papers. I am told that the parsonage was twice destroyed by fire. The first meeting house burned, and the present building erected on its site in 1840.

In 1833 and to 1836, Cyrus Prindle was presiding elder. This Cyrus Prindle afterwards became a foremost leader among the Wesleyan Methodists, who withdrew on the slavery question, and he was ever after a "plumed knight" on the slavery question in theology, so long as it remained an issue. [See Chapter XV.] In 1854 it was voted "to be connected with North Ferrisburgh on conditions of mutual agreement." John J. Boynton was recording secretary from 1843 to 1861.

Some eighty acres of land was left to the Methodist church by the will of Ammi Fuller. A yearly rental was being paid, and this, in connection with local contributions, was used latterly for the support of occasional service by the church. No regular service had been held here for several years.

No one need tell what influences have gone from beneath this roof. The character of our people reveals it. The first care of the generations gone was to establish the church and found the school. The earliest records in your town clerk's office place beyond the possibility of any denial the evidences of that first care.

The Vermont of to-day, with its railroads, its telegraphs and telephones and broader means of culture, has only entered into the reaping of what the fathers sowed. One by one those earlier workmen have disappeared, as we, too, shall disappear in our turn some day.

Thus time works his changes, ceaseless as the cycles of the sun. He is pictured to us as wrinkled, old and gray, but he marches onward with the vigor of eternal youth, with energies as fresh as when the morning stars sank together over the birth of the world. It is for us to face the responsibilities of our day, as the fathers and the mothers faced theirs. We are remembering that the present is all that mortal man can call his own, for tomorrow is something that may never come and nowhere in all the annals of the ages has yesterday been seen again.

A survey made in 1842 of Greenbush Rd. and the Stage Rd. (now Rt. 7) in Charlotte and Ferrisburgh. The survey, even though much later, used the original map with the proprietors' grants and BW (Benning Wentworth) listed in the southwest corner of town. The Thorp store location and the "old still" are on the map. Original map in the John Johnson papers, Special Collections, UVM Libraries. Used with permission.

Appendix I

The Charter of Charlotte, Vermont

Charlotta.

GEORGE THE THIRD, By the Grace of GOD, of Great-Britain, France and Ireland, KING, Defender of the Faith, &c.

To all persons to whom these Presents shall come,

Greeting

Know ye, that We of Our special Grace, certain Knowledge, and meer Motion, for the due Encouragement of settling a New Plantation within our said Province, by and with the Advice of our Trusty and Well-beloved BENNING WENTWORTH, Esq; Our Governor and Commander in Chief of Our said Province of NEW HAMPSHIRE in New-England and our COUNCIL of said Province; HAVE upon the Conditions and Reservations herein after made, given and granted, and by these Presents, for us, our Heirs, and Successors, do give and grant in equal Shares, unto Our loving Subjects, Inhabitants of Our said Province of New-Hampshire, and Our other Governments, and to their Heirs and Assigns for ever, whose Names are entered on this Grant, to be divided to and amongst them into Seventy One equal Shares, all that Tract or Parcel of Land situate, lying and being within our said Province of New-Hampshire, continuing by Admeasurement, Twenty Three Thousand & Sixty Acres, which tract is to contain Six miles square and no more; out of which an Allowance be made for High Way's and unimprovable Lands by Rocks, Ponds, Mountains and Rivers, One Thousand and Forty Acres free, according to a Plan and Survey thereof, made by Our said Governor's Order, and returned into the Secretary's Office, and hereunto annexed, butted and bounded as follows, Viz. Bigining at a Marked Tree standing in the Northerly Side Line of the Township of Monkton thence running West about Two Miles & an Half by Monkton to the North Westerly Corner thereof which is also the North Easterly Corner of Ferrissburg & from thence about Four Miles by Ferrissburg aforesaid to Lake Champlain then bigining again at the first Mentioned Marked Tree & running from thence North Six Miles to A Marked Tree, thence West about Six Miles to Lake Champlain afore Said then as the Said Lake runs Southerly to the North West Corner Bounds of Ferrisburg aforesaid And that the same be, and hereby is Incorporated into a Township by the Name of Charlotta And the Inhabitants that do or shall hereafter inhabit the said Township, are hereby declared to be Enfranchized with and Intitled to all and every the Privileges and Immunities that other Towns within Our Province by Law Exercise and Enjoy: And further, that the said Town as soon as there shall be Fifty Families resident and settled thereon, shall have the Liberty of holding Two Fairs, one of which shall be held on the _____ And the other on the _____ annually, which Fairs are not to continue longer than the respective following the said _____ and that as soon as the said Town shall consist of Fifty Families, a Market may be opened

299

and kept one or more Days in each Week, as may be thought most advantageous to the Inhabitants. Also, that the first Meeting for the Choice of Town Officers, agreeable to the Laws of our said Province, shall be held on the last Thursday in July next which said Meeting shall be Notified by Mr. Benj. Ferriss who is hereby also appointed the Moderator of the said first Meeting, which he is to Notify and Govern agreable to the Laws and Customs of Our said Province; and that the annual Meeting for ever hereafter for the Choice of such Officers for the said Town, shall be on the Second Tuesday of March annually, To Have and to Hold the said Tract of Land as above expressed, together with all Privileges and Appurtenances, to them and their respective Heirs and Assigns forever, upon the following Conditions, viz.

I. That every Grantee, his Heirs or Assigns shall plant and cultivate five Acres of Land within the Term of five Years for every fifty Acres contained in his or their Share or Proportion of Land in said Township, and continue to improve and settle the same by additional Cultivations, on Penalty of the Forfeiture of his Grant or Share in the said Township, and of its reverting to Us, our Heirs and Successors, to be by Us or Them Re-granted to such of Our Subjects as shall effectually settle and cultivate the same.

II. That all white and other Pine Trees within the said Township, fit for Masting Our Royal Navy, be carefully preserved for that Use, and none to be cut or felled without Our special License for so doing first had and obtained, upon the Penalty of the Forfeiture of the Right of such Grantee, his Heirs and Assigns, to Us, our Heirs and Successors, as well as being subject to the Penalty of any Act or Acts of Parliament that now are, or hereafter shall be Enacted.

III. That before any Division of the Land be made to and among the Grantees, a Tract of Land as near the Center of the said Township as the Land will admit of, shall be reserved and marked out for Town Lots, one of which shall be allotted to each Grantee of the Contents of one Acre.

IV. Yielding and paying therefor to Us, our Heirs and Successors for the Space of ten Years, to be computed from the Date hereof, the Rent of one Ear of Indian Corn only, on the twenty-fifth Day of December annually, if lawfully demanded, the first Payment to be made on the twenty-fifth of December, 1763.

V. Every Proprietor, Settler or Inhabitant, shall yield and pay unto Us, our Heirs and Successors yearly, and every Year forever, from and after the Expiration of ten Years from the abovesaid twenty-fifth Day of December, namely on the twenty-fifth day of December, which will be in the year of our lord 1773 One shilling Proclamation Money for every Hundred Acres he so owns, settles or possesses, and so in Proportion for a greater or lesser Tract of the said Land; which Money shall be paid by the respective Persons abovesaid, their Heirs or Assigns, in our Council Chamber in Portsmouth, or to such Officer or Officers as shall be appointed to receive the same; and this to be in Lieu of all other Rents and Services whatsoever.

In Testimony whereof we have caused the Seal of our said Province to be hereunto affixed. Witness BENNING WENTWORTH, Esq; Our Governor and Commander in Chief of our said Province, the 24th Day of June in the Year of our Lord CHRIST, One Thousand Seven Hundred and Sixty Two And in the Second Year of Our Reign.

B. Wentworth
By His Excellency's Command,
With Advice of COUNCIL,
T. Atkinson Junr, Secry
Province of New Hampsr June 24th

Recorded According to the Original Charter Under the Province Seal--

T Atkinson Junr Secry

The Names of the Grantees of Charlotta:

Benja Ferris, Joha Akin, Benja Ferriss Junr, Josiah Akin, Daniel Wing, Elihu Wing, Lott Trip, David Akin Jnur, Timo Dakin, John Cromwell, John Hoag, Mercht John Hoag, the 2d John Wing, Reed Ferriss, Zeb Ferriss, Wing Kelly, Neheah Merritt, Abrm Thomas, Anthy Tripp, Elias Palmer, David Palmer, Saml Coe, George Soule, Elijah Doty, Peter Palmer, Josiah Bull, Josiah Bull Junr, John Hitchcock, John Brownson, Jona Dow, Jedediah Dow, Enoch Hoag, Steward Southgate, Nathl Potter Junr, Robt Southgate, John Southgate, Daniel Merritt, Neheah Merritt Jr, Stephn Noble, Dobson Wheeler, Saml Browne, Joshua Delaplace, Willm Field, Isaac Martin, John Laurence, John Burling, John Franklin, Walter Franklin, Thos Franklin Junr, Saml Franklin, James Franklin, Isaac Corsa, Elija West, Robt Caswell, Joseph Ferriss, Joseph Ferriss Junr, David Ferriss, Danl Chase, Patrick Thacher, Thos Darling, Hon. John Temple Esq, L. G. Theodore Atkinson Esq, Mark Hg Wentworth Esq, John Nelson Esq, George Frost, His Excellency Benning Wentworth Esq a Tract of Land to Contain Five Hundred Acres as marked B--W-- in the Plan which is to be Accounted two of the within shares, One whole share for the Incorporated Society for the Propagation of the Gospel in Foreign Parts, One Share for a Glebe for The Church of England as by Law Establish'd, One Share for the first Settled Minister of the Gospel & one Share for the benefitt of a School in sd Town--

Province of New Hampsr June 24, 1762

Recorded from the back of the Original Charter of Charlotte, under the Prov : Seal--

T Atkinson Junr Secry.

Editor's Note: The above is the text of the Grant of The Town of Charlotta. The grant and the original lotting out is in the town clerk's office. This text is from *The New Hampshire Grants, Being Transcripts of The Charters of Townships and Minor Grants of Lands Made by the Provincial Government of New Hampshire, Within the Present Boundaries of the State of Vermont.* Vol XXIV. Town Charters Vol. III. Edward N. Pearson, Public Printer. Concord 1895. Spelling is as in the grant.

The original name, Charlotta, after Queen Charlotta wife of George III, explains the pronunciation of the name of the town even though the spelling has changed.

Appendix II

A Commentary from a Reader

Editor's Note: The following article was found in the Daisy Williams scrapbook. The author, D. C. Barto, is answering comments made by W. W. Higbee in Chapter III. There is no date on this clipping but the type is that of the *Vergennes Vermonter and Citizen*. In another undated clipping from the Wheeler/Kingsland Collection, is this notice: "The town loses one of its best citizens in the death on Monday of David C. Barto." His secessionist feelings of an earlier year must have been forgiven.

An Echo From "Over The Creek"

We have wandered "Around the Mountain" with W. W. Higbee for a long time with interest and pleasure. He tells us what an enchanting picture we present to his sportsman on Fuller mountain and comments on our patriotic impulses, and our political importance when it's a close shave between the "Center" and "North Burg."

That's correct! We are greeted most cordially with a smile half mean, half meaningless; our hands pressed out of shape and our shoulder almost dislocated by a most enthusiastic hand shake, and our backs have been thumped with a force and companionable familiarity that would have dislodged a quarter of beef, had we attempted to swallow it whole and our lives been endangered.

The philosophy of life is to take things as they come and part with them as they go. Most of us are glad when election is over. Mr. Higbee remarks that "the adjoining town of Panton has sought on various occasions to engraft this territory onto their own." (That's news to us). But the people are loyal to their old town and old traditions, etc. That's the point.

On February 6th, 1847, the inhabitants of the west side of Otter Creek met and "Resolved, 1st, That we will use all lawful means to be set apart in a town by ourselves. 2d, To survey and petition the Legislature at the next session for the same." These resolutions were signed by fifty-five voters, whose names we append, and let the readers of fifteen or even twenty years, who were born and have been brought up in this territory, see how many of them they knew:

Alanson Hayes, William R. Barto, E. G. Warner, John S. Hobart, William Allen, Seth Warner, Jr., B. W. Ferris, Joseph Newton, Reuben Kellogg, John Conant, Putnam Allen, Obidiah Allen, Joseph Newton, Jr., Isbon Allen, Ephron Allen, Jehial C. Hayes, William R. Hayes, B. B. Warner, R. B. Brydia, Levi Beach, John Sibley, Isaac Demask, Seth Warner, Castle Warner, Charles Hatch, Henry Allen, Francis Welet, Joseph Longway, Norman Allen, Norman G. Needham, Horace Gage, Ebenezer Hatch, William Newton, William Allen, Jr., Wm. Maher, Josiah Baldwin, William Kingman, George Kingman, Allen Beach, John Montle, Stephen Beach, Oren Cram, M. W. Winans, J. B. Winans, Henry Cronk, I. Bisbee, Seymour Hayes, David Brydia, Seymour Hayes, Jr., Enoch Gregory, Simeon Millord, Isaac Hatch, Hiram Curler, John Gregory, David Curler.

This list does not seem to _____ [illegible: may be "include all" --Ed.] the voters because the "Subscriber" list to pay Mr. T. Grandey for surveying and mapping the said territory, includes the names of Jacob Curler and C. C. Curtis.

The map made from this survey can be seen framed and adorning the sitting-room in the residence of Mrs. J. N. Stag in Panton.

The next record is Feb. 16, 1847:

Met agreeable to adjournment and chose E. G. Warner, moderator, and William R. Barto, clerk.

Voted, That we survey and plot the West part of Ferrisburgh.

Voted, That a committee of three be appointed to hire a surveyor.

Committee--William Allen, Benjamin B. Warner, John Gregory.

This committee procured the services of Truman Grandey of Panton, previously mentioned.

The next record is a "Notice":

Agreeable to the 3d sec. of an act entitled an act to annex a part of the town of Ferrisburgh to the town of Panton, passed and approved Nov. 3d, 1847. The undersigned appointed by the General Assembly for that purpose hereby give notice...to meet at the public house of Ida Winans, in said district, on the 19th day of Nov. 1847, at 10 o'clock in the forenoon, for the following purposes, to wit:

1st, ...

2d. to see if a majority of said voters will give their assent to the act of the General Assembly above described.

3d. ...

Ferrisburgh, Basin Harbor District, Nov. 9th 1847.

William Allen
John Gregory,
Committee
Reuben B. Brydia

On November 19, 1847 the records show that:

Met agreeable to notice and made choice of William Allen, moderator, and W. R. Barto, clerk.

Voted, That the act be read by P. C. Tucker and explained.

Motion to adjourn three weeks from to-day at 10 o'clock a. m. at this place.

House divided twenty one yea; fifteen nay.

On Dec. 10, 1847 the adjourned meeting continued:

Met agreeable to adjournment. Voted to hear the report of Ferrisburgh. R. T. Robinson read the same. Voted to lay the report on the table--Voted that we try the question whether we go to Panton, by ballot. Ferrisburgh, 26; Panton 16, the act was lost.

Voted that we accept Ferrisburgh's report, and it was carried.

Adjourned without date.

William R. Barto, Clerk.

According to the best information that we can gather, the proposition of the town of Ferrisburgh, made through Mr. Robinson was to raise the road and bridge between Needham's and Donovan's and improve the road to the turnpike at the Smith place. This smothered the secession flames for twenty years, when they again broke out, fanned by an almost unanimous sentiment in favor of being set to Panton, which was again smothered by Representative David Smith, who summoned a couple of obstinate, pig-headed oppositionists to Montpelier, who worked with such zeal that the result was disastrous to the petitioners.

Any man who travels over this territory or will take a map and trace the boundaries, will admit, unless insane, that geographically we belong to Panton. There's where we go for our mail, our blacksmithing, our doctoring and our preaching--when any West Ferrisburghers feel the need of preaching.

And sooner or later another effort WILL BE MADE to be transferred there corporatively [sic]. It's already brewing, and we hope it will be a successful three-times-and-out.

D. C. Barto

Appendix III

Notes of Interest about Monkton
Rev. Benjamin Cox Recalls Many Interesting Occurrences in that Town.

Editor's note: This article was found in the Daisy Williams scrapbook and shows a reader's reaction to Higbee's writings. The date, January, 1898, was clipped from the *Vergennes Vermonter and Citizen* and pasted on the margin of the clipping.

Mr. Editor: As my friend Mr. Higbee has left the town of Monkton and is wandering "Around the Mountains," where he is gathering up fragments and items of information profitable and interesting for the numerous readers of the *Vermonter and Citizen*, and not knowing when he will return again to my native town, I thought I would note down a few items peculiar to the town of Monkton that might interest some of your readers.

The first thing I will mention is the great number of Smiths residing in this town in the days of my youth. Some of those whom I will name had large families of sons and daughters. There was Sylvanus, Thomas, Epophroditus, usually called Uncle Epp, Frederick, Joseph, John, Adoniram, Ira, Luman B., Burrill, Nathan, Harrison, Timothy C., Consul at Odessa, Russia, where he married a Russian lady, and reared a family, and Ethan Smith, who was at one time high sheriff of Addison county. It is said that there were more than forty voters by that name, at one time; all have passed away, and now only two are left by that name in the town.

I wish now to call attention to the size and some other things pertaining to the district school in East Monkton, where I spent my youthful years. The school was made up of Clapps, Smiths, Chamberlains, Haights, Cox's, Datons, Williams's and four or five families of Rutherfords, Eatons, Hoyts, Thomas's, Creeds, James; two large families of Barnums, and three of Spooners making in all between eighty and ninety scholars. It required a man of more than common ability to manage a school of such dimensions. In those early times we had no town or county superintendents; no school boards or teachers' institutes, but two or three men of good judgment were chosen as committee to hire a teacher. It was necessary that he be cultured, scholarly, apt to teach, able to classify and skilled in government. The scholars were not all in the primary department. There were young ladies and gentlemen, well advanced in the studies of those times. Quite a number of such teachers were found in the town. The first I remember was Charles Stone. I was about six years of age and the one event that made the deepest impression on my mind was being tied up under the table; while there I resolved, if I ever was large enough to teach school, his children would have to suffer as I did.

Our next teacher was Buell W. Smith. It seemed to me that he was a very superior teacher. He was a student from Middlebury college and introduced some Latin phrases into the school, which gave a fine stimulus to the scholars. I will name some: Unus, first class; age ad locum, take your places; subjice caput, bow your heads; tace, be still. Honorable mention might be made of other teachers, among whom were Ethan Smith, Warren Williams, Lyman Williams, Eben Spooner, Jackson Rutherford and Lewis L. Beers, all reared in Monkton.

These families named resided in the beautiful valley lying between the Hogback

304

on the east and Huckleberry Hill on the west, watered by a creek, the outlet of Bristol Pond which empties into Lewis creek in the edge of Hinesburgh, thence to the Lake. In winter it overflowed its banks, making acres of ice, affording a fine place for skating and sliding for the scholars. The spelling schools, which were frequent, were seasons of social enjoyment and intellectual improvement as well. The Lyceums, usually held weekly during winter, called out large audiences of old and young, developing the gifts of the young men for debates. Questions of interest were discussed pro and con.

I ought not to forget to mention the apple bees that were very common, where there was plenty of good cheer--pumpkin pies, doughnuts and home-made cheese.

Monkton was noted for the number of physicians it produced, among them were Dr. Ira Smith, who practiced for many years with success. Dr. Dan Stone, although not a native of the town, was a very popular physician and surgeon for many years. His two sons, George E. and Carter D. took up their father's profession. The former had a large practice for years; he then moved to Wisconsin, where he died. The latter was a successful physician in Vergennes for years. Nobel Finny after a few years of successful work in his native town moved to Michigan. Dr. Horatio Smith of Monkton Borough became a very successful practitioner in New Haven for many years. Dr. William Hutchison studied with Dr. George E. Stone, and after receiving his degree married a daughter of Burrill Smith and settled in Enosburgh, purchasing the home and practice of ex-Gov. Eaton. He soon became popular in the county and was chosen senator for the state legislature. He still lives, with many years and honors

on his head. Dr. Whitefield Day of Monkton Borough practiced mostly in Middlebury, where he died when he was quite young. Dr. George Rollin Thomas, still living, after his graduation at the Medical college at Burlington, practiced in Starksboro and Salisbury and then retired to his farm. Dr. O. L. Nimblet was a learned scholar, said to be one of the best read physicians in the county. He was an able speaker on public questions and was chosen to write a history of his native town for the *Vermont Historical Magazine*. He lived and practiced in his native town until he died a few years ago in the Mary Fletcher hospital.

The town was not as prolific of ministers as doctors. Buell W. Smith was a prominent minister of the Congregational church for years; at last -----[lines missing at end of column]----- in connection with Rev. J. H. Converse he instituted a Ladies Seminary in Burlington, which had a career of great prosperity for years. Myron Dean, son of Charles Dean of Monkton Borough, was a very popular minister of the Baptist church. He settled in Providence, R.I., where he had a very successful pastorate for many years.

There were two or three Baptist ministers by the name of Sawyer. I am unable to call their names. Franklin, son of Myron Day of Monkton Borough, an acceptable minister of the Methodist-Episcopal church, preached for a time in the Vermont Conference and then went West. Henry Chamberlain, now a retired member of the Erie Conference, was also reared in the same town. Monkton did not produce any lawyers, unless we accept Luman B. Smith. He was not educated for the bar, but it was said of him that in pleading cases he would whip out all the regular bred lawyers in the county.

Benjamin Cox

Appendix IV
Representatives of Ferrisburgh, Monkton and Charlotte.

Editor's note. Higbee published these lists in the *Vergennes Vermonter and Citizen* at various times: The Ferrisburgh list on 26 November 1897; Monkton and more on Ferrisburgh on 3 December 1897; Charlotte on 14 January 1898. He prefaced the 3 December 1897 column with comments as follows:

There is nothing particularly exciting in these enumerations of names and figures, and you, the reader, are at liberty to skip them if you choose, but in so doing you miss some of your own local history, and if the writer takes the trouble of looking them up, perhaps a few minutes expended in their perusal may not be altogether squandered.

As 1850 is comparatively a modern date, perhaps we will stop there in these statistics, unless the town clerks of Ferrisburgh and Monkton are kind enough to furnish me with a list of representatives up to date.

Ferrisburgh's representative from 1788 to 1798 was Abel Thompson.[118] In 1799, Theophilus Middlebrook; 1800, Amos Thompson; 1801 to 1804 Theophilus Middlebrook; 1805, John Frazier; Mr. Middlebrook again in 1806; 1807 to 1810, Obadiah Walker; 1811, G. Middlebrook; 1812, Obadiah Walker; 1813 to 1815, Mr. Middlebrook; 1816 to 1818, Benjamin Field; 1819, Thomas Marsh; 1820 to 1821, Robert P. Hazard; 1822 to 1823, Josiah Taft; 1824 to 1825, Stoddard Martin; 1826 to 1827, Daniel Marsh; 1828, David Hazard; 1829, Heman Barnum; 1830, David Hazard again; 1831, Harman Barnum; 1832, David Hazard; 1833 to 1835, Zuriel Walker; 1836 to 1837, Luther Carpenter; 1838 to 1839,

William Hazard; 1840 to 1841, Benjamin Ferris; 1842 to 1843, Nathan L. Keese; 1844, Noah P. Preston; 1845 to 1846, D. Middlebrook; 1847 to 1848, Hartwell Powers; 1849 to 1850, Ira Tupper. It seems Jonathan Saxton was the first town clerk.

Monkton commences in 1788-90, with Samuel Barnum; 1791, Joseph Willoughby; 1792, John Ferguson; 1793-94, Joseph Willoughby; 1795-96, John Ferguson; 1797, Joseph Willoughby. In 1798 it seems to have been Josiah Willoughby; 1799, Samuel Barnum; 1800, Daniel Smith; 1801, Samuel Barnum. In 1802 Daniel Smith was in the saddle again, remaining there until 1807, when Frederick Smith served one term, and Daniel Smith concluded to run things for another two years. In 1810 Jos. Willoughby, Jr., and in 1811 Daniel Smith again visited the State House officially.

In 1812 a new element was evidently injected into town politics, and Stephen Haight, Jr., was representative until 1823, when John Smith was elected, evidently much to the distaste of Stephen Haight, who served again in 1824. In the meantime, the Smith element had evidently been sufficiently active and thoughtful, for it seems John Smith carried the day in 1825-27. In 1828 Johnson Finney; 1829, Daniel Collins. About those days things were evidently bubbling again, for John Smith is on deck in 1830 and Stephen Haight runs up the flag in 1831; 1832-33, George E. Stone; 1834-35, Milo W. Kinsley; 1836-37, Luman B. Smith; 1838-39, it appears as Lyman Smith; 1840-41 Samuel Swift; 1842-44, Nathan Smith; 1845-46, John A. Beers; 1847-48, Gilbert D. Eastman; 1849-50, Lewis L. Beers.

It is, perhaps, safe to say that the

earnestness not infrequently manifested in Monkton on election days has come down to them as an inheritance, for tradition has it that politics had the middle of the road there and nobody was whipped until he was compelled to be. In Ferrisburgh, Abel Thompson served ten consecutive years, with Theophilus Middlebrook next to him in length of service. Zuriel Walker served three years; Obadiah Walker, five years.

The constitutional conventions of this state were represented from Ferrisburgh up to 1850 by Abel Thompson, 1791-93; 1814, Theophilus Middlebrook; 1822, Robert B. Hazard; 1828, Theophilus Middlebrook; 1836, Daniel Marsh; 1843, Noah W. Porter; 1850, Nicholas Guindon.

Monkton was represented in the same conventions by John Ferguson, Joseph Willoughby, Thomas Smith, Stephen Haight, Jr., Daniel Collins, Luman B. Smith, Roswell Atwood, Alson Collins.

Experience seems to have counted in an early day in Ferrisburgh and Monkton. In the latter town, Samuel Barnum led off well, followed by Daniel Smith, who received ten elections up to 1812, when Stephen Haight, Jr., served consecutively until 1823 and several times after that at intervals.

Ed. note: Higbee later published a note about this article. It appeared in the *Vermonter and Citizen* as "A Communication" and was dated 20 December 1897. This is what he wrote:

The suggestion of Mr. Cox in your last issue in reference to the representatives of Monkton is entirely correct and I thank him for calling my attention to the fact. In working from the original minutes, the name of Samuel Swift was inserted in place of Russel Eastman as the Monkton representative in 1840-41. Mr. Swift was the representative from Middlebury those years.

From correspondence and information otherwise obtained, I am sure Mr. Cox is quite right in conceding distinguished abilities to Stephen Haight, Jr., so long connected with the politics of Monkton.

In addition to his services as member of the legislature, he was four years Judge of the County Court, and four years Sheriff, ending the latter office in 1832. Right or wrong Mr. Haight was credited with large responsibility in the election of Martin Chittenden as Governor in 1813 over Jonas Galusha--when legislation stood still for over a week on a tie vote of 112 each for Chittenden and Galusha--Mr. Chittenden finally winning by 112 to 111.

I should fail in effecting anything desirable if my articles "Around the Mountains" were not substantially correct. Information is often obtained under difficulties and it will be taken as a kindness if readers will call attention to errors in names and places--at least it will show that some one takes the trouble to read them.

Several have kindly asked if the papers were likely to appear in any other form than through the columns of the *Vermonter*. Probably this is about the limit of their career and the writer thanks the public right heartily for its patience in this much of an affliction.

Perhaps it may not be uninteresting to know who have been representatives to the legislature from Charlotte, commencing with 1788.

1788 to 1794	John McNeil (six terms)[119]
1794 to 1795	David Hubbell
1796	John McNeil
1797	John Thorp
1798 to 1799	Hezekiah Barnes
1800 to 1802	Nathaniel Newell
1803	Samuel Rich
1804	Nathaniel Newell
1805	Ezra Meech

1806	Nathaniel Newell	1851 to 1852	Midas Prindle
1807	Ezra Meech	1853 to 1854	Charles B. Cook
1808	Nathaniel Newell	1855 to 1856	Benjamin Beers
1809 to 1810	Hezekiah Barnes	1857 to 1858	Joel Stone
1811 to 1812	Nathaniel Newell	1859 to 1860	Daniel C. Lake
1813 to 1815	Zadock Wheeler	1861 to 1862	Peter E. Pease
1816 to 1817	Hezekiah Barnes	1863 to 1864	Herman H. Newell
1818	Nathaniel Newell	1865 to 1866	Peter E. Pease
1819	Johiel Stone	1867 to 1868	James Squier
1820 to 1821	Nathaniel Newell	1869 to 1870	Alanson Edgerton
1822 to 1824	Jeremiah Barton	1871 to 1872	Lewis Nelson
1825	Nathaniel Newell	1873 to 1874	Joseph S. Shaw
1826 to 1827	William Noble	1876	Henry W. Prindle
1828	Nathaniel Newell	(biennial sessions instituted)	
1829 to 1831	William Rose	1878	Henry Thorp
1832 to 1833	Myron Powell	1880	Charles D. Prindle
1834 to 1835	Noble Lovely	1882	John H. Thorp
1836 to 1837	Pitt E. Hewett	1884	John Quinlan
1838 to 1839	Samuel H. Barnes	1886	W. W. Higbee
1840 to 1841	Aaron L. Beach	1888	W. H. Varney
1842 to 1843	Burke Leavenworth	1890	Alfred A. Byington
1844 to 1845	William R. Pease	1892	Brayton J. Clark
1846 to 1847	Abner Squier	1894	Myron N. Williams
1848	Elanson H. Wheeler	1896	Orrin Powell Read[120]
1849 to 1850	John Sherman		

Appendix V

Roster of Civil War Soldiers and a Sailor from Charlotte

Compiled by Fred Anderson in June, 1990 from the *Revised Roster of Vermonters in the War of The Great Rebellion 1861-1865* and the Charlotte Roster of *Enlisted Militia.*

Editor's note: Many Vermont towns and cities have civil war monuments prominently displayed in town centers, parks or squares. Higbee wrote his essays during the time when many other places were building and dedicating such memorials. Charlotte never had a memorial, but it has memorials for World War I and II, the Korean War and a recreational area dedicated to the town's only fatality in the Vietnam War. While doing this book we found that there was no list of townsmen who served in the Civil War. Since Higbee's data and this list include different information, we have included this roster to supplement the story of *Charlotte in the Civil War,* Chapter XLII of this book.

Name	Rank/Co.	Regiment
Abel, James H.	Pvt. Co. B	1st Vt Cav.
Archambault, Oliver T.	" " A	7th Vt Inf.
Ball, Daniel S.	" " F	9th Vt Inf.
Ball, James M.	" " F	1st US Sharpshooters
Baraur, Peter	" 3rd Batt.	Vt. Light Artillery.
Barton, Gilbert J.	" Co I	14th Vt. Inf.
Barton, Rollin W.	" " G	2nd Vt. Inf.
Barton, William P.	" " I	14th Vt. Inf.
Baslow, Frank	" " H	17th Vt. Inf.
Besette, Joseph	" " I	14th Vt. Inf.
Bessett, Alexander	" " F	11th Vt. Inf.
Bishop, Hiram	Musician Co. H	14th Vt. Inf.
Bissett, John	Pvt. Co. D	10th Vt. Inf.
Bissette, Joseph	Wagoner Co. B	17th Vt. Inf.
Bourbo, Joseph	Pvt. Co. B	17th Vt. Inf.
Burnham, Alfred S.	" " F	1st US Sharpshooters
Clark, George A.	" " I	14th Vt. Inf.
Clark, Lucius L.	" " H	9th Vt. Inf.
Coleman, John	" " I	5th Vt. Inf.
Corbett, Edward	" " A	17th Vt. Inf.
Cross, Peter	Unassigned	
Culver, Eliphalet	Pvt. Co. B	17th Vt. Inf.
Danforth, Alonzo	H.1st Lt. Co. B	17th Vt. Inf.
Daniel, John	Pvt. Co. G	2nd Vt. Inf.
Daniels, Charles	" " A	1st Vt. Cav.
Davis, James A.	Wagoner Co. B	1st Vt. Cav
Delmeater, Horace N.	Pvt. Co. I	14th Vt. Inf.
Deraur, Peter		
Drum, Henry	" " I	14th Vt. Inf.
Dunn, William	" " B	17th Vt. Inf.
Esser, William	" " A	5th Vt. Inf.
Fonda, Abner S.	Qm Sgt.-Staff	7th Vt. Inf.
Fonda, Joseph	Pvt. Co. A	7th Vt. Inf.
Franklin, John		
George, Alpheus	Pvt. Co. C	1st Vt. Cav.
German, James	Pvt. Co. D.	13th Vt. Inf.
Gorman, James		12th US Inf.
Gravel, Joseph	Pvt. Co. F	6th Vt. Inf.
Griffin, Joshua M.	" " " G	8th Vt. Inf.
Guillett, Joseph	Pvt. " I	14th Vt. Inf.
Guyett, Frank	Cpl. Co. K	1st Vt. Cav.
Haskell, Moody L.	" " B	17th Vt. Inf.
Hewitt, George W,	Cpl. Co. H	17th Vt. Inf.
Hibbard, Edward L.	Capt. Co. B.	17th Vt. Inf.
Hill, Frank R.	Cpl. Co. I	14th Vt. Inf.

Hoyt, George H.	Sgt. Co. B	17th Vt. Inf.
Huff, Henry H.	Pvt. Co. F	1st US Sharpshooters
Hyde, Heman	" " I	14th Vt. Inf.
Kehoe, Joseph	" " G	2nd Vt. Inf.
Kehoe, Michael	1st Sgt. Co. D	10th Vt. Inf.
Kinsley, William W.	Pvt. Co. G	Veteran Res. Corp.
Lacoy, Jacob	" " F.	1st US Sharpshooters
Laflam, John		
Larama, John	Pvt. Co. D	8th Vt. Inf.
Lincoln, William	Cpl. Co. I	14th Vt. Inf.
Little, James	" " L	1st Vt. Cav.
Macumber, J. M.		
Macy, Mitchael		
Mason, Freeman	Pvt Co. K	17th Vt. Inf.
McCandlish, Benjamin	Cpl.Co. G	6th Vt. Inf.
Melvin, Delinus L.	Pvt. Co. B	17th Vt. Inf.
Naramore, Truman C.	Cpl. Co. A	1st Vt. Cav.
Newell, Cassius	Pvt. Co. A	6th Vt. Inf.
Page, Samuel	Pvt. Co. I	14th Vt. Inf.
Parkhurst, Alfred S.		US Navy
Parks, Clark L.	1st Sgt. Co. F	9th Vt. Inf.
Patterson, David	Pvt. Co. K	17th Vt. Inf.
Poole, Archibald S.	" " D	10th Vt. Inf.
Potter, Job		
Powell, William C.	Pvt. 2nd Batt.	Vt. Light Artillery
Preston, Horace H.	" Co. J	9th Vt. Inf.
Prince, Isaac	Pvt.	54th Mass. Inf.
*Prindle, Cyrus C.	Pvt. Co. C	4th Vt. Inf.
Prindle, Gideon D.	1st Sgt. Co I	14th Vt. Inf.
Prindle, Lewis C.	Pvt. 3rd Batt.	Vt. Light Artillery
Pulsifier, Abel N.	" Co. H	9th Vt. Inf.
Quinlan, John	" " F	1st US Sharpshooters
Quinlan, Michael	Cpl. Co. A	1st Vt. Cav.
Read, James A.	Pvt. " F	1st US Sharpshooters
Robertson, David	" " A	7th Vt. Inf.
Root, Alonzo E.	Cpl. Co I	14th Vt. Inf.
St Martin, Joseph	Pvt. Co. I	7th Vt. Inf.
Schofield, Daniel		
Scott, Edward C.	Pvt. Co. K	17th Vt. Inf.
Seaton, Charles W.	Capt. Co. F	1st US Sharpshooters
Sherman, George D.	Pvt. Co. A	1st Vt. Cav.
Smith, Adam	" " K	17th Vt. Inf.
Smith, Gaylord B.	" 3rd Batt.	Vt Light Artillery
Spear, George W.	" Co. F	1st US Sharpshooters

*This is the listing in the source, but the name was Cyrus Guernsey Pringle.

Stearns, Alonzo B.	Cpl. Co. F	9th Vt. Inf.
Stone, James	Pvt. Co. B	17th Vt.Inf.
Taggert, Benjamin H.	" " I	14th Vt. Inf.
Tatro, Alfred	" " F	9th Vt. Inf.
Townson, Joseph W.	1st Lt. Co. A	17th Vt. Inf.
Washburn, James	Pvt. Co. I	14th Vt. Inf.
Whitney, John	" " B	17th Vt. Inf.
Wilder, Henry B.	" " F	1st US Sharpshooters
Williams, James B.	Cpl. Co. K	17th Vt. Inf.
Williams, Milo A.	1st Lt. Co. I	14th Vt. Inf.
Williams, Myron	Wagoner Co. I	14th Vt. Inf.
York, George W.	Sgt. Co. H	17th Vt. Inf.
Young, Thomas	Pvt. Co. F	4th Vt. Inf.

Totals: 102 Charlotte men in the roster, of whom six were officers. There were nine 1st US Sharpshooters in Company F including the captain. Company F, all told, had 100 men and was the Vermont company in the regiment.

Appendix VI

Letters from a Charlotte Officer in the War of 1812

Editor's Note: These two letters are owned by a descendant of the McNeil family of Charlotte. Charles McNeil, Lieutenant, sent them from his post in upstate New York on the Canadian border to his mother Thankful McNeil, widow of Captain Charles McNeil who had operated the ferry in Charlotte. They were deciphered and transcribed by Kathleen McKinley Harris and Hazel Prindle. They have not been edited. Though not directly related to the Higbee writings, they show another episode in Charlotte history, have not been widely circulated and now exist only in photocopies. We put them here with the same spirit that Higbee showed when he wrote about his papers being found at some future date in some old scrapbook.

Chatageuy july 14 1812
honored Mother - I arrived at this place the 14 day with much trouble and pain -

after traveling through mud & rain to get to plattsburgh - the major jeneral Moor gave us express orders to leave Capt Sanfords company - & go with our own company alone directly into the wilderness forty five miles northwest from platsburgh - to fite savages - it was said to be very dangerous - we heard frightfull storys every day on the road - the last knight we lay out in the woods before we came here - we was allarmed at the dawn of day with dreadful news of savage depravations - fires murders etc., etc., in three miles of us said to be hundreds of indians we all joined together determined to go on and conquer or dy - when we came here we found a fine small village plesantly situated - and found all the indian storys to be totaly fals & groundless - we lay ourselves down contented at knight - but are sure to keep a good gard of soldiers - we live in an eligant house - and as the old say is on the fat of the land - we apprehend no danger - but are careful - I would not be understood that my trouble & pain on the rode was fear -- I was taken violently with the disentary which reduced me verry low - in addition to that my horse fell with me and bruised me extremely bad - but I am now verry well as to helth & my bruises are almost well - the traveler will wait no more for me to write I wish you to inform office - thankful McNeil

yours etc. Charles McNeil

French Hills Head Quarters October 12, 1812

Honored Mother

I have one moment to write you - I am now stationed at this place within threee quarters of mile of Canada line - we have strength sufficient to repell any invasion which may take place from our enemies - the troy invinsibles and the troy fusaliers - two companies of the best infantry in this state. Captains Miller from Washington county and tilden from this county - and the company that I command which is well known to be the flower of the united states - the whole is five company. we are on command by Maj. Young - he is extremely kind and friendly to me - he has made me [torn] standard as A disciplinarian by which his battalian is governed - my men respect me - but think hard of government [torn] want their pay to cover their naked boddys - we live in Cold Cloth tents - only 23 blankets to 55 men - the snow is four inches deep in this northern country - the cold wind strikes them to the verry hart as they stand on perade [torn] -- poor boys my blood boyls for them - when the snow fell there was some barefooted - I bought them shoes - If I never [torn] get my pay of them I shall think myself justifyable [torn] I would not beare to order the drummer to call them from their tents with beare feet in the snow - I have been so long with them that they appear like my own family - poor fellows will follow me until their legs and arms are num as sticks without murmering a single word - I often think of my being uneasy at home when I was there for want of better liveing - O my god how ignorant was I - I get my vituals in a good house for $2.25 cents per week and only stay in the house while I eat - I have only received $28 - and have about $100 due me - my pay will now be the same as Captain - which pay and rations is $60 per month - if I ever get it - Mr Pankel is well - you have undoubtedly heard that Capt Richardson has gone home not to return again - my business calls I must go - write soon and often remember me to all - I received your letters by mr pankel - and these only - your obedient --- unfortunate son

Mrs. Thankful McNeil Lieut. Charles McNeil

Constable in Franklin County -NY

Notes

1. Election Day. Until January 1, 1752, New England observed March 25 as the first day of the new year in connection with the vernal equinox. The custom of having town elections in the first part of March continued even after England and her colonies adopted the Gregorian Calendar in 1752. Charlotte now has its annual town meeting on the first Tuesday in March.

2. York money is perhaps a reference to the York shilling or New York shilling, 12.5 pence to the shilling, so four shillings York money would equal fifty cents.

3. Town meetings from 1762 to 1785 were held mainly in Dutchess County, New York. The first town meeting held in Charlotta was on July 6, 1785.

4. The Ferris survey is now bound in a leather folder and has been deacidified and preserved by the best methods available. It is in the vault of the town clerk's office. See Appendix I for the full text of this charter.

5. The map in *The Beers Atlas of Chittenden County*, 1869, lists a J. Stapleton as being north of the Quinlan (Sherman) Bridge on Spear St. Extension, east side. The deed was signed on 30 September 1854. Mehitable Peck was Walter M. Ferris' sister who had received the land from Elijah Peck, who in turn received it from George S. Ferris. The will of Walter M. Ferris was recorded shortly before he died in 1879. It made Mehitable Peck his sole heir, so then she apparently reacquired the land, thus ending ownership of land in Charlotte by anyone named Ferris.

6. Higbee later corrected this number, but the elevation given on present day maps is 980 feet.

7. Shellhouse Mountain, 680 feet high, was used as a storage place for ammunition for MacDonough's little fleet in the war of 1812. See Esther Monroe Swift *Vermont Place Names*, p. 168, Stephen Greene Press, Brattleboro, Vt. 1977. The name "Shellhaus" appears in an early census record in Ferrisburgh.

8. Vergennes is the third oldest city in New England, chartered in 1788, four years after Hartford and New Haven.

9. A "cross the creek" resident wrote more about past political affairs of this area. His letter from the *Vermonter and Citizen* appears as Appendix II.

10. Abby Hemenway on page 735 of her *Vermont Gazetteer* writes, "Stoddard Martin, Esq. of North Ferrisburg ... came to Charlotte with his parents in March 1787, and ... is the best living authority with reference to the early settlement of the town... ."

11. During the nineteenth century Mt. Philo had been known at Sugar Bush Hill. Mt. Philo may have been named during one of the bursts of enthusiasm for classical names. See Swift, p. 168.

12. Henry Miles married George Hagen's sister, Mary, before both families migrated from England. He was an accomplished amateur naturalist as reported by Kevin Dann in the *Chittenden County Historical Society Bulletin*, Vol. 20, No. 2, pp. 6-8, 1985.

13. According to Norman J. Allen's obituary found in the Wheeler/Kingsland collection he ran the store until 1838.

14. Traditionally from the beginnings of New England people observed fast days, days of prayer and fasting. New Hampshire still carries the fourth Monday in April as a legal holiday. Gradually the fast days became secularized: holidays instead of holy days.

15. To fugle is to act like a fugleman, i.e. to give signals, lead or organize.

16. One of the thirteen was Miranda Harding who was William Wallace Higbee's mother, born in Shelburne Vt. 1814, daughter of Caleb and Judith (Bartlett) Harding. The Hardings settled in the county about 1790.

17. This William is the author's grandfather. His grandmother was Olive (Van Vliet) Higbee. They settled in Charlotte in 1816. "They had a family of eight children born to them, five of whom are now living...." (Rann, Wiiliam S., ed. *History of Chittenden County, Vermont* p 835. Syracuse: D. Mason & Co. 1886)

18. The Palmer family still lives on some of that land. Avery Palmer is a town lister and his son Danny is active in town affairs, most recently as a candidate for the Board of Selectmen.

19. Drummer: a traveling salesman, drumming up business.

20. "Ferris Creek" appears on neither the Beers nor Walling old maps nor on the new USGS maps. From the content it seems that Higbee means one of the small unnamed streams or Lewis Creek.

21. In 1841 the town selectmen leased lot #1 of the second division, the glebe lot, for 999 years to George Pease. In 1949 trustees for the Pease estate handed over the land to the University of Vermont.

22. Eugene Shortsleeves of North Ferrisburgh who celebrated his 95th birthday in 1990 tells of coming to Charlotte from "across the lake" to work for Edward Pease in the cider mill and to log off the west side of Pease Mountain not many years after Higbee wrote this.

23. The old road to the west of Jones Hill is now Route 7, or in local terms, the new Route 7. According to the Vermont Department of Libraries which is the authority on Vermont place names all the elevation north of the Congregational Church is named Mutton Hill. They have so advised the U.S. Board on Geographic Names and new editions of the U. S. Coast and Geodetic Survey maps of that quadrant will be changed from Jones Hill to Mutton Hill. Mutton Hill, on the east side of Old Route 7 will take back its old name of Spruce Ridge. The Church is on Church Hill Road, but there is no Church Hill.

24. The spot is east of the intersection of Routes 7, F5 and Church Hill Rd. A close look shows where Old Rt. 7 followed along the slope of Pease Mountain at the foot of Church Hill Rd., east of the present Spear's Garage and north of the former garage.

25. The East Charlotte post office, opened in 1875, was closed in 1912. See Swift, p. 167.

26. Hames are curved wooden or metal pieces of a harness which fit around the neck of a draft animal and to which the traces are attached.

27. "The Honorable John A. Kasson is one of the most distinguished men that Charlotte has produced. He graduated at the University of Vermont in 1842, practised law for a time in New Bedford, Mass., and subsequently settled in Iowa. He was a member of the Chicago Convention of 1860 by which President Lincoln was nominated. Under his administration Mr. Kasson was appointed First Assistant Paymaster General, which office he filled with great ability.... He resigned in 1862, and was elected a representative in Congress." Hemenway, p 745.

28. Higbee expanded on this theme in a later article appearing here as Chapter XLIV.

29. Chaise became "shay" and the reference is to "The Deacon's Masterpiece" by Oliver Wendell Holmes, a poem about a deacon's two-wheeled carriage built to last forever but which "went to pieces all at once" exactly one hundred years to the day after it was finished.

30. See note 23 above.

31. Both William and Peter V. Higbee owned the present Hebert house at the corner of Route 7 and Higbee Rd. They were our author's grandfather and father.

32. As clerk, Daniel Horsford signed many of the earliest town records. Searching through them only one instance was found where he signed not with the "r". Some present day Horsford family members say the early spelling changes in the name may be due to the so-called Boston "r", as for example in Hah'vahd, the school in Cambridge, Mass.

33. This location is the southwest corner of the intersection of Mt. Philo Rd. and the Hinesburgh road. It is east of the present Central School.

34. The round shot has been preserved and is now in the collection of the Charlotte Memorial Museum. On a similar note, the *Burlington Free Press* on 20 November, 1879 reports under the heading "Charlotte" that "W. W. Higbee has in his possession a grapeshot fired by the British from their gunboats at our militia on Thompson's Point in 1812."

35. Higbee may record these actions of the legislature from his own experience. He served in both the House and the Senate for a term each.

36. The Cove, as used by Higbee, refers to the deep portion of Town Farm Bay where Thorp Brook enters the Bay and Lake Champlain.

37. The Deerfield massacre was "the most famous assault on Deerfield, Massachusetts." It occurred on February 29, 1704, when French soldiers and Indians burned the village, killed 49 persons and took more than 100 residents captive to Canada. A personal account of this experience, *The Redeemed Captive Returning to Zion* (1707) by the Rev. John Williams, the village minister, is one of the best-known narratives of pioneer life." (David R. Proper. *Encyclopedia Americana*). Some descendants of the Reverend John Williams are residents of Charlotte.

38. For the benefit of treasure seekers, the Walling 1857 map has Mud Hollow Creek flowing north in the valley between Mt. Philo Rd. and Guinea Rd., crossing Hinesburgh Rd, crossing Spear St. Extension north of the Carpenter Rd. intersection and joining the LaPlatte river near the Shelburne/Charlotte town line. The 1869 Beers map has no such name. It has Bingham Brook flowing south and Beaver Brook flowing north in approximately the same area.

39. The "seal" refers to the "beech sealing" that the Green Mountian Boys inflicted on New Yorkers who tried to claim land based on New York grants. They flogged them with a beech stick and sent them off.

40. Blue beech, American Hornbeam (Carpinus caroliniana), is a hard wood good for making a gad instanter or club.

41. A recent search of the town records did not find such a signature. All records are written and attested by the town clerk.

42. In Chapter I, Higbee reports that Ferris was elected "proprietors' clerk and register" at the July 1762 meeting.

43. A glebe was land set aside, such as in a town division, for the benefit or the support of the Episcopal Church. The glebe house was the residence of the minister.

44. The incorporated society was The Society for the Propagation of the Gospel in Foreign Parts. This was the London based missionary society for the Church of England.

45. The grant for the town gives this as point three. (See Appendix I.) Higbee gives its location again in Chapter XLIV.

46. A list of all the town representatives from the first to Higbee's time was presented in a later paper and is in Appendix IV along with his lists of representatives from both Ferrisburgh and Monkton.

47. The name Breakenridge appears spelled thusly in town land records with one exception which can be read with either an "a" or a "c". The Chittenden County Historical Society used this spelling in their *Look Around* series. Some personal papers use the other version but without knowing who in the family used which spelling we have followed the official town records. In Chapter XLV Higbee wrote more of the history of the Methodist church. In 1950 the building was damaged by a hurricane and donated to the Shelburne Museum. It was moved, rebuilt and renamed to be the Charlotte Meeting House.

48. At Rokeby there is a Robinson family tradition that a crew was hurrying all that day to complete roofing the house, fearing that the "thunder" would mean rain and apparently not knowing of the battle going on. Since it was only three miles to Mount Philo from Rokeby, the lack of communication in those days seems unbelievable to us.

49. Whit is related to "whight" an obsolete adjective meaning strong or full of prowess.

50. Sweep power was a system using a horse to tread a circle pulling a "sweep" connected to a stone that rolled over the wheat plants beating out the grain.

51. Black Hawk was the grandson of Justin Morgan and according to records of the American Morgan Horse Association in Shelburne, Vermont, is now ancestor to perhaps eighty percent of all registered Morgans.

52. Corduroy roads were built in the early nineteenth century by laying logs side by side transversely to the road bed.

53. Higbee must have spent hours in the neighboring town clerks' offices to collect the information he used in his columns. His own entries are among the easiest to read and most accurate of Charlotte's handwritten records.

54. Noted herewith. Your townsmen have thanked you by supporting this publication of your work.

55. Higbee is always careful about going up and down the lake. Since the lake flows north, going north is going "down."

56. See Chapter VIII for this early town activity.

57. The site of one of these mills is north of the bridge on the Falls Rd. in Shelburne and can be seen from the bridge.

58. This part of the river can be seen from the bridge on Route 7 north of Shelburne village. A covered bridge used to cross the LaPlatte where there is now a turn-off for parking by the river.

59. The *Era* was an anti-slavery paper published in Washington, D.C. The alternate title for Mrs. Stowe's book was *Life Among the Lowly*.

60. A jag is a load for one horse, thus a small load.

61. The Underground Railroad of fact and folklore was active in the region and was enhanced by the strong abolitionist feelings of the large Quaker population. Stories like this one of Higbee's have given the Underground Railroad a much greater part in freeing runaway slaves than it perhaps had. It is known that Rokeby, the home of the Robinson family, was a safe refuge for blacks. Several other area houses are reputed to have had secret rooms for sheltering runaways.

62. Peter Dakin, Cyrus G. Pringle and Lindley Macomber of Grand Isle were Quakers who refused service in the Civil War, were imprisoned under unconscionable conditions, and eventually were released on an order from President Lincoln. Pringle had refused the offer of his uncle, Pitt Hewitt, to buy him a substitute. (See "Cyrus G. Pringle's Neighborhood: Baptist Four Corners and Prindle Corners, Charlotte Vt." by Kathleen McKinley Harris, *Chittenden County Historical Society Bulletin*, Vol. 21, No. 3, 1986.) Lydia Macomber was Peter Dakins's sister and wife of Lindley.

63. A liberal movement in the Society of Friends took its unofficial name, Hicksite, from Elias Hicks (1748-1830) whose preaching in 1827 caused a separation from the so-called Orthodox group. This had far reaching effects in the strong Quaker community in this area.

64. The Robinson farm remained in the family until 1962. Rokeby is a museum and a treasure-trove of farming artifacts and lore, Robinson family memorabilia, publications and art works. Various members of the family were Ferrisburgh town clerks with service totaling over one hundred years. Several of the illustrations herein were generously furnished by the staff at Rokeby.

65. Calvin Pease was born in Canaan, Connecticut in 1813, moved to Charlotte in 1826, graduated first in his class from UVM in 1838, received an A. M. three years later and in 1843 was elected professor of Greek and Latin. He became president in 1855 but resigned for reasons of health in 1861 and died in Burlington in 1863.

66. Kersye was a coarse woolen material.

67. Kevin Dann in his manuscript *Lewis Creek Log* writes of the extinction of the Lewis Creek salmon: "As chronicler of the creek it was [Rowland E.] Robinson's role to discover this dismal date. His 1880 notebook records the information: 'Stephen Hazard tells me again of the "last salmon" of Lewis Creek. It must have been in the later part of June or first part of July, for they were going to haying when they found him--it was in the straight reach between the lower road bridge toward the lower end of it. This was the only one he ever knew of being caught. Thinks his weight 10 lbs.'" Robinson identified the fishermen as three brothers, Rowland, David and Stephen Hazard. They had speared the fish with a pitchfork.

68. See Chapter XLIII, 20 July 1903 where Higbee reports about the new road up Mt. Philo. Pease Mountain never got its road but in recent years has been laced with cross-country ski trails.

69. Joseph Hoag had many visions during his lifetime, but the one referred to here occurred in 1803 in a field on his farm, but he only recorded it three years before he died in 1846. The vision foresaw the civil war and the abolition of slavery. See *Look Around Hinesburg and Charlotte, Vermont*, Chittenden County Historical Society, Lillian Baker Carlisle, Editor, p. 42. 1973.

70. For more on these mills and Mr. Scott see Chapter XXIII.

71. This road was recorded in the town records Vol. 2, p. 2, the earliest such record. With some changes in location it has become our Route 7. Museum Road is a section of the stage road which remains very much as it was originally, except in mud time when help like Hezekiah Barnes' oxen is no longer needed for the uphill trip. (See "Charlotte Road Statistics, Their Locations and Widths As Recorded In The Charlotte Town Records." by Francis J. Thornton. 1986. Copies in the town clerk's office, the Charlotte Memorial Museum and Special Collections of the University of Vermont Libraries.)

72. The Dr. Cram place was south of Greenbush Road and west of Route 7 where they interesect just north of Rokeby and opposite Robinson Rd. in Ferrisburgh.

73. Charlotte roads were catalogued in the unique and extensive study by Francis J. Thornton referred to above. He collected the information on roads in the town records, mapped them, and found evidence in the landscape for several of the changes. Few other Vermont towns have such a thorough study of their road systems.

74. "Ezra Alexander did business alone from 1848 to 1872. For years Alexander did a very large business, buying country produce in connection with a Boston commission house. Trade came here from a number of Eastern towns, and goods were sold by the wagonload." So Higbee wrote on 8 January 1897 (Chapter VI). We assume his business failed in 1872.

75. In 1989 Lewis Creek Road was designated a Scenic Road by the town of Charlotte with the goal of preserving it. Higbee's description is accurate at this time.

76. A tympan is a sheet of paper, cloth or other material, placed between the impression surface and the paper which is being printed.

77. Modern maps show that it is three miles from Mt. Philo to Fuller Mountain. As for the rest of this paragraph, Higbee is referring to Chapter III were his data on Fuller Mountain were not too accurate as originally printed in the newspaper, but have been corrected in this edition.

78. A small tributary of the Little Otter comes through the intervale between Fuller and Shellhouse mountains. Two main branches come out of Bristol, according to USGS maps.

79. Higbee's description of a pioneer house resembles the Sawyer's Cabin on display in the Shelburne Museum. This cabin was on the late Thomas Schemerhorn's property on Mt. Philo Rd. and was given by him to the museum around 1957.

80. Cronkhite, Cronk and Cronkite all appear in the Ferrisburgh area around a hill of the same--Cronkhite--name. According to some local historians the names are used by different branches of the same family.

81. A popular view of Stowe, Vermont shows Alanson Edgerton's work, the spire of the United Church there, and enhanced his reputation with its outstanding design.

82. Hinesburgh and Monkton were also chartered on that day.

83. For comparison, populations in 1980 were: Charlotte, 2561; Monkton, 1201; Vergennes, 2273; Bristol, 3293; Hinesburgh, 2690; Ferrisburgh, 2117.

84. In 1990 voters in Granville decided to keep their one-room school, one of the last remaining in the state.

85. The "Canadas" refers to the two divisions of Canada used at that time: Upper and Lower Canada or what are now Ontario and Quebec.

86.. President McKinley was the guest of the Vermont Fish and Game League at a banquet on Isle LaMotte on August 6, 1897. In his speech as reported by Charles Spooner Forbes, in *The Vermonter*, Vol. 2, p. 65. 1897, he said:

> I am glad to meet and greet you all here today. As Americans we have a right to rejoice in our glorious civilization. I say to Vermonters and say to all New England that to them this country owes much--more than it can ever repay for the splendid civilization it has sent through all the States of the Union. Cling to your Puritan heritage, and let the free light of the age "Its light and hope and sweetness add / To the sterner faith our fathers had."

87. The Washingtonians were members of the Washington Temperance Society, started in 1840 in Baltimore, Maryland. They believed in total abstinence from alcohol. At one time the society had 600,000 members.

88. No, they weren't escaping from their children by hiring a babysitter. "Kids" was a slang term for kid gloves and without them neighborhood bees were informal gatherings.

89. The ALABAMA was the most famous Confederate cruiser. It was built in Liverpool and captured 70 ships in privateering activities before it was sunk by the USS KEARSARGE off Cherbourg, France.

90. The Charlotte Memorial Museum now occupies the building, using it for exhibits and meetings of the Charlotte Historical Society. In recent years it has been open on Sunday afternoons in summer and for a town Christmas party in December.

91. Higbee is quoting "Break, Break, Break" by Alfred, Lord Tennyson.
"...But oh, for the touch of a vanished hand / And the sound of a voice that is still! / Break, break break / At the foot of thy crags, Oh sea! / But the tender grace of a day that is dead / Will never come back to me."

92. King Philip was an American Indian chief who made war on the New England colonists, hence King Philip's War (1675-76).

93. The dates of the charters for these towns were: Shelburne, 1763; Charlotte, Ferrisburgh and Monkton, 1762, and all on 24 June; Panton, 1764; Addison, 1761. (All data are from the Whitelaw map of 1796.)

94. To clear up the confusion between the names Tandaw and Guindon in this paragraph, Ferrisburgh historians, Karl Devine and Charlotte Tatro, have searched the town records. There are many deeds in the names of both Frank and Nicholas Guindon, but no reference to Tandaw. Where or what Higbee meant using both names is not known. Nicolas Guindon, his wife and three infant children are buried in the family lot in Barber cemetery. "Uncle Nick" died in 1868.

95. Cassimere was a woolen cloth for men's wear also called kerseymere. Satinet was a strong fabric with cotton warp and woolen filling or a thin satin.

96. A tenter was a frame or a machine for stretching cloth to prevent shrinkage while drying. Fulling was a process to make cloth thicker and more compact by shrinking. Knapping was a process to raise the fibers of the wool, which were then sheared off to give a smoother fabric.

97. "Burning coal" was making charcoal from hard wood.

98. Blue Earth County is west of Steele County. Higbee lived in Owatonna, the county seat of Steele County after he finished law school in 1865. The Champlin connection may have had an influence on his migration.

99. Higbee had foresight as well as hindsight. Many of these columns were found in a scrapbook made by Daisy Williams who lived across from the Higbee house on Route 7. The scrapbook was crucial in researching and editing this book. No domestic helps and hints were included, however.

100. The Indian origin and early use of part of this route is reported in *Vermont, Wilderness to Statehood, 1748-1791,* by Warren W. Dexter and Barbara C. Hanson. Academy Books, Rutland, Vt. 1989.

101. "Beech sealing was a favorite mode of punishment awarded the obnoxious New York official. This consisted of tying the victim to a tree and administering a certain number of lashes with a beech gad." *Gazetteer and Business Directory of Chittenden County, Vt. for 1882-83*, Hamilton Child, publisher. Syracuse N.Y., p. 66.

102. Modern practice in counting generations from Champlain's trip in 1609 to the writing of this article in 1899 would give an average of thirteen generations.

103. Charlotte, like many other Vermont towns, had a "poor farm" where the indigent, old and infirm were supported by the town under the care of an Overseer of the Poor. In Charlotte it was located on Thompson's

Point Road. The system was finally changed by the Social Welfare Act of 1967 which made the state the purveyor of social welfare. Presently the Charlotte Pony Club leases one of the fields from the town for its activities. The name, Town Farm Bay, might remind one of the older system.

104. Claude Joseph Sauthier published a "chronological map of the Province of New York showing all private grants of land, manors, patents, townships by order of General William Tryon" in London, 1779.

105. The diligent searches of Higbee's descendants and various local historians have found no manuscript or other evidence of this paper or any other writings by Higbee.

106. Buffaloes are robes or blankets made of buffalo skins. At this time in Charlotte you can see them on the hoof in two of Tony Perry's pastures, one on the old (Beers Map) C. Stebbins place and the other near a T. C. Hill house on Lake Rd. west of Orchard Rd.

107. The Club originally meeting at Camp Pleasant on the south shore continued. The present Thompson's Point Country Club built a clubhouse in 1921.

108. For a nostalgic history see the booklet, *Thompson's Point--A Few Facts and Fancies About A Favorite Summer Resort,* by Jessie S. Gibbs.

109. The station was on the northeast corner of the intersection of the railroad and Thompson's Point Rd. See photo on page 142.

110. This article from the *Vergennes Vermonter* was the most extensive and the only illustrated article published by Higbee. The chapter heading used here is the one used in the newspaper. The article took up nearly two full pages and had photographs of many of these cottages. As in some of the shorter pieces he reused information from previous columns. Since it was published late in his career as a writer and is the last that appeared in the *Vermonter*, it appears to be the peak of his creative work. (The last three articles here with their original headlines appeared in the *Burlington Free Press.*) An original copy of this report that belonged to the late Allen C. "Pat" Moore of Charlotte and Thompson's Point was donated to the Charlotte Memorial Museum in 1990 by Mrs. Moore.

111. This report on Charlotte's part in the Civil war was published in the *Burlington Free Press and Times.* A photocopy of part of the article was in the Charlotte Memorial Museum Collection. A complete copy was made from the files in the UVM Libraries. No other copy has been found, it is not in the Williams scrapbook nor in the manuscript copy of the Higbee essays at the Bixby Library.

112. John H. Thorp's substitute was Lewis Pecor, Pvt. Co. F, 17th Vt. Inf.

113. James H. Humphreys died in 1914. In 1924, his widow, Frances, deeded what became Mt. Philo State Park to the State of Vermont. The Humphreys had carefully pieced together this park by several land purchases. In its present splendor, it is a testimonial to the Humphreys' love affair with the Town of Charlotte. Their home was the next house north of the Mt. Philo Inn and is still a private home. The original newspaper clipping of this article was in the Daisy Williams scrapbook, with no other copy found.

114. It may be a bit late to supply the name. The *National Geographic* had an article about such boats in the October 1989 issue. They show the boat as the ECLIPSE as does the illustration from a broadside owned by the Lake Champlain Transportation Co.

115. Robert Fulton has been credited with the invention of the steamboat by running his CLERMONT on the Hudson in 1807, but Samuel Morey of Fairlee, Vermont ran a steam-driven boat on the Connecticut River in 1790, and John Fitch of Connecticut made his first trial run with a steamboat in 1787. It is surprising that Higbee did not take this the opportunity to promote Morey's Vermont-based enterprise.

116. The first named woman was probably Mary Cook who in 1902 became Mrs. W. W. Higbee, the author's third wife. Miss Pearl Cook married John Spear. In 1943 the Spears along with May (Mrs. Charles) Foote and Daisy (Mrs. John) Williams founded the Charlotte War Memorial Museum in the Town Meeting House. Miss Mabel Higbee was W. W. Higbee's younger daughter, who married Henry Chittenden Hill in 1902 and lived in Matteawan (Beacon), New York at the time of Higbee's death in 1911.

117. The Troy Conference Academy that moved from Charlotte to Poultney finally became Green Mountain College.

118. Abel Thompson's terms span the last years of the Republic of Vermont and the first of the State of Vermont. His name appears on the list of those who voted in favor of joining the union at the Bennington Convention on January 10th, 1791 in *Records of the Governors and Council*, Vol. 3, page 480-1.

119. John McNeil's terms as representative from 1788 to 1794 indicate that he voted in favor of joining the union at the Bennington Convention on January 10th, 1791. See note 118 above.

120. This list of representatives in the state legislature has many differences from the list given by Hemenway in her *Vermont Historical Gazetteer.* Higbee probably combed the town meeting reports for his more complete information. Hemenway does not list representatives from the other towns listed here.

Editor's Afterword

Every unpublished author dreams of being discovered, appreciated and finally published. In one of his columns, Higbee mentions in a tone of regret that his works will end with newspaper publication.

When a group of interested residents started the Charlotte Historical Society in 1979, Russell Williams encouraged "doing something" with Higbee's writings. Harold Carr began work on this project after he retired to Charlotte. He, like a few before him, found the Higbee typescripts--one in the Bixby library in Vergennes, the other at UVM. These had been made by Mary Waller while she was town clerk and William Wicker who wanted copies made. Now the original borrowed from Higbee's granddaughter cannot be located. After the Daisy Williams scrapbook was found Harold Carr ferreted out additional newspaper columns, photocopied and typed them. A disabling auto accident stopped his work and the committee members were unable to carry on due to other full-time commitments.

In the years after Harold's strong beginning, computer technology became available and affordable. It was crucial and at times a hazard to the production of this book. For the technically minded, the word processing and indexing was done with XY-Write III Plus (XYQUEST, Inc., Billerica, MA 01821) using a Smart Micro 286 computer (Microsmart, Inc., Ashland MA, 01721) and a LaserJet IIP printer (Hewlett Packard Company, Mountain View CA 94043). The typeface, Century Schoolbook from Bitstream Inc., Cambridge, MA 02142, was chosen for its clarity and legibility. Names are registered trademarks. The equipment was owned by the editor, and that is why I got the job.

Bob Sharp and Rejane Danforth of Academy Books, Rutland, bookmakers par excellence, gave us unstinting help in using the computer out-put to produce this book.

At first it seemed a great asset to have a local history already written; it only needed editing and publication would be the society's celebration of the Vermont bicentennial. Hindsight shows a more traditional town history would have been easier. Instead we have gone round and round on facts and figures as well as mountains, and been aware of omissions.

This is not a comprehensive history of the town nor the area. Higbee could write as he pleased. We have tried to fill in with illustrations, endnotes and the appendixes.

Higbee published his columns over a period of thirty years. He did repeat and go back. We have removed the repeats and, truth must be told, cut out some of the less readable preachings and prose. To erase our guilt for this we have produced nine copies of the unedited, intact, original columns, "The Writings of William Wallace Higbee," for archives and future researchers. These books have been donated by the historical society to: Charlotte's town offices, school library and Memorial Museum; the Ferrisburgh Historical Society, Rokeby, Bixby library, Sheldon museum, Special collections of UVM libraries and the Vermont Historical Society library.

After my intensive work on his essays I still enjoy this 19th-century Charlotter--his stories about "The Boy", his love for the "fathers and mothers" and all the past, his sly humor, his kindliness to contemporaries. If my contemporaries discover these traits and lots of local lore from his book, the work has paid off. And a lot of that work was done by the committee. Their names listed herein in no way give them enough credit for their major part in this book.

Mary G. Lighthall

Corrections and Additions

The following errors have been found in the first printing of this book:

p. ix, paragraph 2, name should be Elinor Prindle Benning. The list in the last paragraph should include David Blow and Eugene and Ruth Williams Bishop.

p. xi, col. 1, paragraph 1, should be *manuscript*.

p. xii, col. 2, 2nd paragraph, should be *Ayrshire*.

p. 13, caption should read *Rachel Robinson Elmer* and the picture is courtesy of Karl and Beatrice Devine.

p. 36, caption should read *Green Meadows Bed and Breakfast*.

p. 37, caption should read *now abandoned*.

p. 113, photograph is courtesy of Karl and Beatrice Devine.

p. 163, the illustration owned by Karl and Beatrice Devine was inadvertently printed backwards; the location is Ferrisburgh.

p. 170, caption of top photo should be *...of the Chapman flock with J. B. Chapman on the left. Courtesy of Karl and Beatrice Devine*.

p. 191, caption has been corrected by a descendant of the Holmes family: in the front row second from right is *Rena Johns*. The identity of the man on her left is not known. The dog was "Queenie." The data written on the back of the original photograph was incorrect.

p. 198, lower caption should read *Whatever the use of the apples, ...*

p. 206, the caption should read as the text of the illustration: *barn yard*.

p. 243, caption of top photograph should read *Albert B. Hawley*.

p. 262, col. 1, 1st paragraph, *Sumpter* is as spelled in the original newspaper, but should be *Sumter*.

p. 268, col. 2, 2nd paragraph, *minnie* appears in the original newspaper, but it should be *Minié*.

p. 283, caption of the top left photograph should not indentify the dock as at Thompson's Point. The location is not known.

In the index some of the page references are wrong. The correct page reference in the erroneous listings is one page number lower, that is p. 301 should be 300; some of p. 303 should be 302; p. 304 through 310 should be one page lower, namely all references to p. 305 are p. 304 and so on. The one reference to page 312 should be to 311.

The following additions contain information gathered since the first printing:

The photograph of Harold Carr on the jacket was taken by Marleen Mansfield.

Ruth Williams has given more information about W. W. Higbee's funeral. She remembers hearing the church bell tolling while the funeral cortege moved from the Higbee house on Greenbush Road to the Congregational Church. She had never heard such tolling before and has never heard it since.

William Chittenden Hill of San Diego, California, a grandson of W. W. Higbee has written to the editor about Higbee, agreeing with details given in the biography. His father Henry Prindle Hill married Mabel Ada Higbee, W. W.'s second daughter. He reports that he knew little of his grandfather Higbee. His grandmother Ada Booth financed the building of the house on Greenbush Road from her considerable inheritance. The Hill family lived for a while in Beacon, New York, and in New York City.

Henry Hill died in 1921 and his widow, Mabel Ada, brought the family back to Charlotte. She and William lived in the house north of the Old Brick Store. They went to San Diego in 1934, followed later by William's uncles, Monroe and Martin Hill. William is the only surviving member of that branch of the Hill family. This is the family for whom Hill's Point is named.

In making these corrections we are reminded of a recent complete edition of Shakespeare which was printed with his most famous line as: "To be or to be, that is the question."

Index

D

Ferrisburgh
Business Notices

Adams J. Q.. Farmer, Dairyman and Stock Raiser, District No. 15
Allen N. J.. Res. North Ferrisburgh
Allen Putnam.. Farmer, Dairyman and Stock Grower, District No. 11
Bell John.. Postmaster and Dealer in Staple and Fancy Dry Goods, Hats, Caps, Boots and Shoes, Groceries, Hardware, Drugs and Medicines, &c., Ferrisburgh Centre
Boore R.. Res. Dist No. 16
Barnoin J. R.. Manufr and Dealer in Lumber and Shingles, Ferrisburgh Centre
Ball S.. Manufr of choice Cider, Cider Vinegar, and Farmer, Dairyman and Stock Raiser. Also dealer in Graft Apples, North Ferrisburgh
Ball Michael.. Farmer, Dairyman and Stock Raiser, District No. 14
Ball A. O.. Farmer, Dairyman and Stock Raiser, Dist. No. 14
Ball A.. " " " " Dist. No. 3
Ball H. R.. Farmer and Dairyman, Dist. No. 4
Beach H. H.. R. R. Station Agent, North Ferrisburgh
Birkett John.. Farmer, Dairyman, Stock Dealer and Breeder of thorough-bred Merino Sheep, Dist. No. 7
Birkett Joseph.. Farmer and Breeder of thorough-bred Hound Dogs, Dist. No. 17
Burroughs Joseph.. Farmer and Dairyman and Stock Raiser, Dist. No. 6

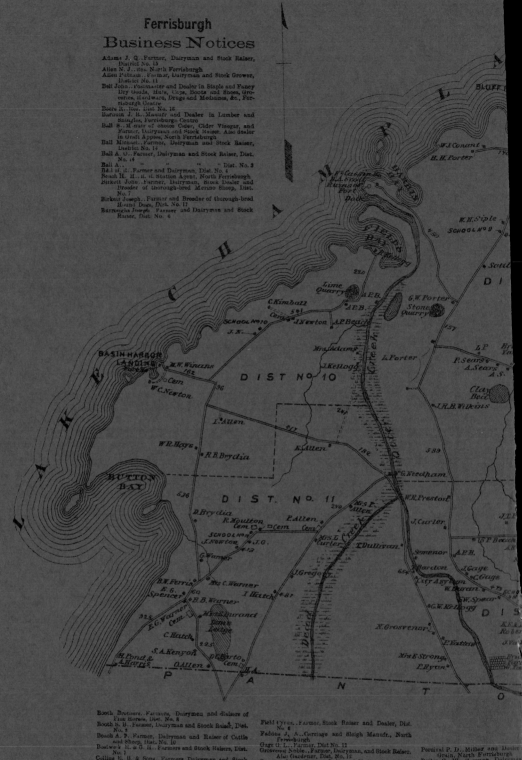

Booth Brothers.. Farmers, Dairymen and Raisers of Fine Horses, Dist. No. 8
Booth S. B.. Farmer, Dairyman and Stock Raiser, Dist. No. 8
Beach A. P.. Farmer, Dairyman and Raiser of Cattle and Sheep, Dist. No. 10
Bostwick R. & R. H.. Farmers and Stock Raisers, Dist. No. 7
Collins E. B. & Sons.. Farmers, Dairymen and Stock Raisers. Dist. No. 4
Crookate P. & H. W.. Farmers, Dairymen and Stock Raisers, Dist. No. 3
Cram H. F.. Physician and Surgeon, Dist. No. 13
Daniels E.. Propr North Ferrisburgh Woolen Mills and Manufr of plain and fancy Cassimeres, Full Cloths and Flannel, North Ferrisburgh
Dean Wm.. Res. Dist No. 1
De Courcy E.. Farmer and Stock Raiser, Dist. No. 16
Field George E.. Dealer in Dry Goods, Groceries, Flour, Crockery and Glass-ware, Boots and Shoes, Hats, Caps, &c., Ferrisburgh Centre
Fuller L. B.. Farmer, Stock Raiser and Dealer, Dist. No. 1
Field Thomas.. Farmer and Dealer in Stock and Fat Cattle, Dist. No. 6
Field Stephen 2d & Son.. Farmers and Dairymen, Stock Raisers and Dealers, Dist. No. 15
Field Walker.. Farmer and Dairyman, Ferrisburgh Centre
Field William.. Farmer, Dairyman and Lumber Dealer, Dist. No. 1
Field James.. Farmer, Dairyman and Stock Raiser, Dist. No. 4

Field Cyrus.. Farmer, Stock Raiser and Dealer, Dist. No. 4
Fadden J. A.. Carriage and Sleigh Manufr., North Ferrisburgh
Gage O. L.. Farmer, Dist No. 12
Grosvenor Noble.. Farmer, Dairyman, and Stock Raiser. Also Gardener, Dist. No. 12
Gregory John.. Farmer, Raiser of Horses, Cattle and Cotswell Sheep, Dist No. 11
Hand O. H.. Farmer, Dairyman and Breeder of shorthorns, and fine Sheep. Dist. No. 4
Hallock H.. Farmer, Dairyman, and Stock Raiser, Dist. No. 13
Hazard E. A.. Farmer and Dairyman, Dist. No. 1
Kimball George B.. Farmer, Dairyman and Stock Raiser, and Manufr of Cider and Vinegar, Dist. No. 14
Kellogg Jacob.. Farmer, Produce and Butter Dealer, P. O. Vergennes, Dist. No. 10
Martin C. C.. Farmer, Dairyman and Banker, North Ferrisburgh
Martin S B.. Farmer and Propr "Martin House," North Ferrisburgh
Meade A. W.. Farmer, Dairyman and Stock Raiser, Dist. No. 3
Middlebrook, D. D.. Farmer, Stock Raiser and Horse Dealer, Dist. No. 6
Middlebrook T. C.. Farmer, Horse Raiser and Dealer, Dist. No. 6
Newell B.. Res., North Ferrisburgh
Newton T. J.. Farmer and Stock Raiser, Dist. No. 8

Percival P. D.. Miller and Dealer in Grain, North Ferrisburgh
Porter G. W.. Farmer, Dairyman, Dist. No. 9
Preston J. T.. Farmer and Stock Raiser, Dist. No. 15
Robinson H. T. & Sons.. Farmers and Dealers, Dist. No. 13
Robinson G. G.. Town Clerk, Dist. No. 13
Roberts E. E. & E. D.. Farmers and Dealers, Dist. No. 13
Rogers H.. Farmer, Dist. No. 17
Rogers J. W.. Mason, Farmer and Dealer, Dist. No. 10
Sattley R. M.. Farmer, Dairyman and Dealer in Fine Horses, Dist. No. 7
Sattley R. P.. Farmer, Stock Raiser. Also dealer in Hay, Dist. No. 7
Stone O. E.. Farmer, Dairyman and Dealer, Dist. No. 1
Tupper J. & A.. Farmers, Dairymen and Dealers, Dist. No. 1
Tappan D. M.. Farmer, Dairyman and Dealer, Dist. No. 7
Wilkins J. R. B.. Farmer and Stock Raiser, Dist. No. 10
Wheeler & Allen.. Dealers in Dry Goods, Groceries, Boots and Shoes, Clothing, Hats, Caps, &c., North Ferrisburgh